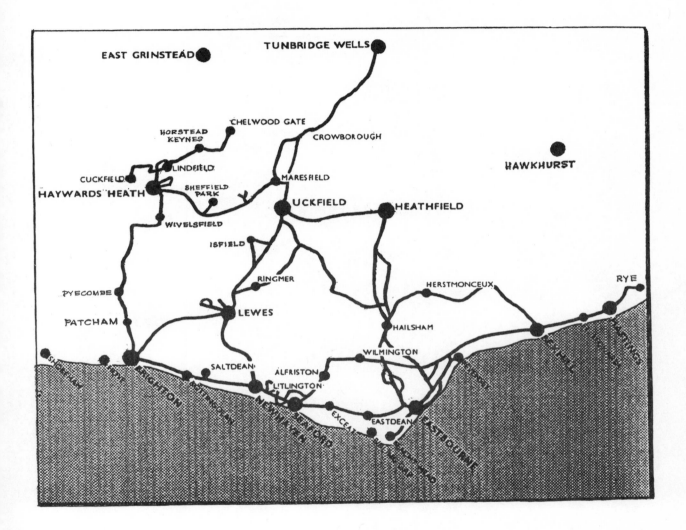

Services contributed by Southdown's East Sussex Division to South Coast Buses Ltd, 2nd April 1992.

SOUTHDOWN

Volume Two

The Details

ISBN 1 898432 10 4

DEDICATION

To the memory of
Joe Carr
Publicity Officer
Southdown Motor Services Ltd
1971-1974

Front Cover Illustration

Towards the end of World War II, the British public at large became aware of two stop-gap innovations – the pre-fabricated house and the utility bus. Both were meant to be temporary, but succeeded in being around much longer than envisaged. The Guy Arab utility double-decker was a case in point. Southdown received 100 of them, the first delivered in 1943. Thirty-six were still in service 20 years later. Still largely unaltered No. 418 (GUF 118) provides the residents of Ringmer Road, Worthing with a local town service on 5th October 1962.

Typeset and produced electronically for the Publishers by
Mopok Graphics, 128, Pikes Lane, Glossop, Derbyshire
Printed and bound in Great Britain

The British Bus Heritage

SOUTHDOWN

Volume Two

The Details

by

Colin Morris

Principal Photographer

Alan Lambert

Venture *publications*

CONTENTS

PHOTOCREDITS

All black and white photographs in this volume are the work of Alan Lambert or are from his collection, with the exception of those supplied by Stagecoach or the photographers listed below to whom we extend our grateful thanks:

Philip Ayers, Alan Bell, F. Case, E. C. Churchill, Paul Gainsbury, M. J. Hart, W. J. Haynes, Gordon Gangloff, Charles F. Klapper, Paul Llewellyn, Roy Marshall, Colin Morris, Michael Plunkett, Southdown Enthusiasts Club, Eric Surfleet, Chris Warren, F. W. York.

Coloured illustrations were supplied by PR Gainsbury and the Southdown Enthusiasts Club.

INTRODUCTION

This the second part of the two-volume history of Southdown Motor Services Ltd is, as the sub-title suggests, concerned with those aspects too detailed for inclusion within a narrative text. It speaks volumes for the growth of interest in the history of the road passenger transport industry generally and of Southdown in particular that a two-part story has become a feasible project. In 1950, the first publication devoted solely to Southdown was a 41-page booklet in the pioneering ABC series published by Ian Allan Ltd. Eighteen pages were devoted to a general history and all the rest of the material was concerned with an outline of the kind of matters dealt with in this volume. That booklet appeared before the founding of the Southdown Enthusiasts Club and acted as the spur to an organised interest in the company – just as it did with other operators when they too were the subject of similar little publications.

It is worth noting that the booklet was 'produced in collaboration with Southdown Motor Services Ltd' all those years ago. I'm not sure why it came as a surprise to me, but I had been for some while researching into the history of omnibus operators in the south of England, when it dawned upon me that many of the top officers of the companies and municipalities were themselves enthusiasts. They actually loved buses, in addition to steering their respective companies to financial success. There had never been any doubt about a character like Douglas Mackenzie, but to discover that figures like George French of Maidstone & District who used to visit the depots just to look at them was one; and that David Deacon who was chairman of more companies than can be named here (except Southdown 1971-72) had been an avid photographer of them since his schooldays – and very good pictures they were too – was a revelation.

When I first set foot in Southdown headquarters, notebook in hand, Len Higgins was general manager. Six gentlemen have occupied that post since then and I owe each of them a debt of gratitude for their unfailing courtesy and access to necessary information over the years. Much of that information has now found its way in abbreviated form into this volume. The latter is rather too large to be considered a genuine 'hand-book', but that 'ready source of information' format is what this book sets out to provide. Needless to say, constraints imposed by space mean that there is still much which remains unpublished. In the meantime if you would wish to read more, do keep an eye upon the publications of the Southdown Enthusiasts Club.

Colin Morris
Roscote Mews
Heswall,
1994.

Below and facing: Forty years of design evolution: coaches by Harrington of Hove in 1926 and 1965 – the latter a short-tailed Grenadier.

ACKNOWLEDGEMENTS

Not surprisingly, many of those who granted invaluable help with the production of Volume I must be thanked again in relation to this one. First, Brian Souter – on behalf of Stagecoach Holdings PLC – gave his permission for me to delve within that group's Stagecoach South subsidiary for information relating to Southdown. Brian Cox, of course, was the prime mover in Sussex and, upon this occasion, I am most grateful to his personal assistant Janet Campbell for dealing good-humouredly with numerous questions fired at intervals; and to David White at Chichester for taking the trouble to outline some maps for me.

Once again Michael Sedgley and Philip Ayers got out their respective files and, upon this occasion, my enlisting the help of John Birks, ex-general manager of Southdown, and author of that major tome on the history of the National Bus Company, yielded information at last as to the whereabouts of the Southdown minute books. So, thanks to John Birks and the work of Roger Davey, County Archivist of East Sussex and members of his staff, this volume incorporates the kind of detail which otherwise would not have been available. In time for publication we have now the prices paid for most of those rival firms acquired over the years and details of numerous other transactions, leaseholds, freeholds and the like.

'Details', of course, mean detailed questioning – and there at the end of the telephone have been, at odd hours, Alan Lambert, Paul Gainsbury and John Allpress. The development of Southdown services in the 'twenties in the form of maps has been based upon initial research by the latter, together with much groundwork upon the location of premises, and his extensive knowledge of Southdown route history. The title of the third colour section of this volume has been 'lifted' from that of an SEC publication, plus supplements, by Paul Gainsbury which are recommended for further reading in that area. For the loan of additional SEC material I am grateful to marketing officer David Start.

Finally, I wish to pay tribute to the work of two local photographers whose pictures I have also admired greatly over the years. First, Fred York of Fareham whose work has been largely concerned with central southern operators, but who demonstrates the knack of catching the fleeting moment time and again with apparent consummate ease. Secondly, the late Eric Surfleet, Worthing Art School student, graphic artist of great skill, Southdown bus conductor and bookseller of Lancing, whose premises were always a delight to visit, not least for his excellent studies of Southdown vehicles.

FRONTISPIECE

In a delightful cleft of the Southdown Hills at Amberley lie the well-tended acres of an open-air industrial museum. A major working exhibit there is a replica Southdown country bus depot. The actual buses, however, are the real thing, dating from 1914-30 and lovingly, painstakingly restored and maintained by dedicated enthusiast craftsmen like Bill Thornycroft, Michael Plunkett, Fred King, Tim Nicholson, Vincent Peters and Gerald Sweatman; and, to the delight of the many visitors who take lengthy rides belonging to another age, crewed in-season by experienced volunteers like Alan Lambert and Alan Regan. Quite recently, nevertheless, the stalwart re-creators of 'the good old days' were rendered momentarily speechless. Asked an earnest young visitor – 'Haven't you got a Leyland National, then?' Well, that's quite a thought-provoking question. 'No' they hadn't, of course (although they've been known to visit on special days), but 'yes': an interest in local history usually begins from a personal reference point. The rest should fall into place later; so just for him – whoever he was – here's a Southdown Leyland National, one of the first received – long ago in 1973.

BEATING THE BOUNDS

The traditional concept of Southdown Motor Services Ltd is of a company whose territory was a broad swathe of coastal countryside its backbone that eponymous range of hills, from the Hampshire boundary in the west to their final gigantic step into the sea at Beachy Head. By and large that is correct. Yet there's a tale of frustrated ambition hidden by such a geographical limitation. And it goes something like this:

Although the name South Coast Motor Services Ltd was initially chosen as the company title in 1915 and was inspired by Walter Flexman French's contribution – the London & South Coast Haulage Company – it would have come as something of a disappointment in one quarter when he and Clark were obliged by Companies House to come up with the more constrained alternative 'Southdown'. It is clear, both from correspondence and documentation, that some at least of the founding fathers had their rights set much farther west in those early days – and a wee bit north and east also. Ironically, it would be French who effectively scotched expansion in the west, by virtue of his interest in another company.

Who were the more frustrated members of the board? There can be little doubt that Mackenzie and Cannon were among them. They had taken over Wilts & Dorset on 4th January 1915 (see Vol 1, p47), before the launch of 'Southdown' and, at the very least, intended to make the two territories contiguous. How so?

Although the Provincial Omnibus Owner's Association had been set up in 1913 and had already considered the business of where boundaries should be drawn, it was not until much later that the first such arrangements were agreed. A 'Competition Agreement' of 28th November 1916 made between Southdown and Thomas Tilling Ltd is an example. Tillings had

What all that fighting was for? Beautiful Sussex downland between Brighton and Eastbourne – the rolling Southdown Hills. Needless to say, much of the competitive effort of Southdown Motor Services Ltd had to do with consolidating its position within such territory. Yet some fascinating efforts were made around the edges of the company area, particularly in the early days, and this section looks briefly at some of them. Although delivered in that first year of peace, 1946, the bus has still been painted with the dark green roof adopted to make the company's vehicles less conspicuous to German aircraft. It is No. 280, (GUF 680) a Leyland Titan PD1 with Park Royal wooden-framed construction, and is on its way to Eastbourne from Brighton. Despite the apparent lack of blue sky, Alfred Cannon liked this picture and for several years it graced the cover of Southdown's time-table booklets.

recently acquired the (larger) remainder of the Brighton, Hove & Preston United company and laid claim to Brighton, Hove, Portslade, Southwick, the parish of Preston, Patcham and Rottingdean. Excepting that enclave, the 'Southdown Area' referred to in that agreement was considered to be:

'a line drawn from and including **Weymouth** (Dorset) to **Salisbury** (Wilts) to **Winchester** then, (less surprisingly) to Horsham-Handcross-Uckfield and Eastbourne'.

Clearly Southdown had intended to cast the net much farther west and, in so doing perhaps, incorporate the then territory of the developing Wilts & Dorset. How could that be, with William Wreathall representing the interests of BET upon the board (from October 1915) or, indeed, W. F. French the chairman himself? French had already been the prime mover in the setting up of Bournemouth & District Motor Services Ltd (on 17th March 1916). Sidney Garke of BET was also a founding director of that firm (which became Hants & Dorset in 1920) and the territory earmarked for it would eventually reach out from the centres of Bournemouth and Southampton to **Weymouth**, **Salisbury**, north of **Winchester** to Andover and east to Fareham and Gosport on the western shore of Portsmouth Harbour effectively a whole **half** of the 'Southdown Area' named in the November 1916 agreement. Probably, the memory of their Sussex Motor Road Car sortie from Southampton to Lyndhurst in 1908 (see Vol 1, p23), and their contemporary attempt to set up in Southampton itself with help from an office opened in that town, had convinced Mackenzie and Cannon that such exploration could still lead to colonisation.

The Thomas Tilling organisation was represented on the board of Southdown from the date of the 1916 agreement and on Hants & Dorset's from 1920. That, however, did not stop Southdown from continuing to cast covetous eyes westward, even though the claimed 'Southdown Area' western boundary had, from 5th July 1917, been drawn inward 'east of a line from Southampton to Winchester'.

Hants & Dorset reached Fareham from Southampton in May 1921; Southdown the following September. Yet Southdown took its Portsmouth-Fareham route 33 (35 after December 1922) on to Sussex Place, Southampton in June 1922 – and it was not until the following November that the service became a joint one with Hants & Dorset going on a reciprocal course to the Victoria Hall, Portsmouth. Similarly, Southdown went to the Broadway, Winchester (service 36) from 1st January 1923 (where it rented a waiting room from H&D for £2.12s. 6d a quarter). Hants & Dorset's joint contribution started in April of that year. It was service 41 started in October

1923, however, which disclosed that Southdown was still probing westward. This ran from Fareham West Street to the Clock Tower, Warsash – and an interesting feature of the operation was a 'through-travel' arrangement with Gosport & Fareham Tramways – a 1/- (5p) return ticket from Warsash to Fareham by Southdown was transferable on a Provincial tram from there to Gosport and vice versa.

Hants & Dorset established a base at Gosport on 28th July 1924 – and Southdown withdrew its Warsash to Fareham service forthwith. That territory was now Hants & Dorset's. On 28th February 1926, Southdown drew back from Southampton and Winchester and both companies transferred their passengers at Fareham. This was confirmed by an agreement on 20th March 1926 which withdrew Southdown east of a line from Fareham to Wickham-Swanmore-Droxford-West and East Meon to Petersfield. In fact, both companies' retreat to Fareham benefitted few bar the Southern Railway. Droxford, Corhampton and Exton were declared Southdown territory should the company decide to operate services from Hambledon. Instead, this clause enabled Southdown (rather than Hants & Dorset) to provide a replacement bus service to Alton Station when British Railways' Meon Valley line was closed in February 1955.

But for the intrusion into Portsmouth of Charles Fuger in 1929 (see Vol 1, p43) that would have been that. So, Hants & Dorset withdrew from its Fareham-Warsash route, Southdown returned, rented a garage at Warsash (qv) and proceeded to swamp Fuger's

Left: A Southdown bus service from Fareham went westward to Warsash via Titchfield Square on 17th October 1923 with two crew members outstationed to run early and late journeys. A third colleague joined them that winter and an agreement was reached with Provincial Tramways for a 'through-facility' from Fareham to Gosport – the 'Improved Service' mentioned here. Hants & Dorset Motor Services arrived in Gosport from Southampton on 28th July 1924 and Southdown withdrew the service the following week.

Below: As a result of the small-print of a boundary agreement signed with Hants & Dorset on 28th February 1926, when British Railways' Meon Valley Line (Fareham-Alton) closed on 5th February 1955 a replacement service was provided not by Hants & Dorset but by extending Southdown's service 38 from Portsmouth to Meonstoke through to Alton. Titan No. 389 (JCD 89) was the first through vehicle. In 1968, however, it is a brand-new Bristol RE No. 236 (KUF 236F) which rests at Alton beside fellow-guest, Wilts & Dorset Bristol LS No. 572 (LWV 848) at the local Aldershot & District depot.

From 1st May 1930 until 1st November 1981, the Fareham to Warsash route was a joint operation between Southdown (service 45) and Hants & Dorset (77). Demonstrating his knack of being in the right place at the right time, Fred York catches No. 969 (969 CUF), a Leyland Titan PD3/4 of 1964 and Hants & Dorset Bristol KSW6G No. 1332 (LRU 61) of 1953 passing at Locksheath in 1968, some two miles north of Warsash. The Titan had run through from Southsea.

How long might one expect to wait for an unposed shot like this? Not beyond the patience of Fred York it seems, yet the picture encapsulates the history of Southdown west of Fareham. First Provincial AEC Regent V No. 66 (975 CWL) is a reminder of the transfer facility with Provincial Tramways in 1923-24; secondly Southdown Titan No. 310 (FCD 310D) is running through to Southsea from Warsash; and Hants & Dorset Bristol Lodekka No. 1368 (SRU 981) is arriving in Fareham from Southampton – a city served by Southdown also until 28th February 1926, after which Fareham became transfer-ticket territory. This remarkable procession is in West Street, Fareham on 7th September 1970, just a hundred yards east of Southdown's Fareham garage.

The hand-drawn list of time-table posters required at the various depots in relation to the relative routes in November 1923. Douglas Mackenzie got a copy of all of them and the relative importance of each route may be traced from the allocations. The core service 31 was divided into west and east sectors. Services 1-5 are Worthing-based; 6 Littlehampton-Chichester; 11-14 Brighton to Worthing, Eastbourne, Lewes and Lindfield respectively; 15 Eastbourne-Hastings; 17 Brighton-Horsham; 22 to Steyning, 25 to Eastbourne via Lewes; 32-33 Chichester to Selsey, to West Wittering; 34 Havant to Rowlands Castle; 35-36 Portsmouth to Southampton and to Winchester. There were ten other services operating at the time which are not listed.

Return of Posters required monthly. During last bus list

	1/5	6	11	12	13	14	15	17	22	25	31E	31W	32/33	34	35/36
Office															
Mr Mackenzie	1	1	1	1	1	1	1	1	1	1	1	1	1	1	1
Steine St.	9	9	40	20	45	43	10	46	23	28	10	5	5	5	5
B'ton Kirksons	-	-	5	5	4	4	1	3	4	1	4	-	-	-	-
Shoreham	-	-	15	2	10	-	-	-	10	-	10	2	-	-	-
Worthing	40	10	10	2	3	-	-	-	12	-	20	2	-	2	2
Littlehampton	-	10	5	-	3	-	-	-	-	-	20	6	-	2	-
Bognor	-	30	-	-	-	-	-	-	-	-	50	75	24	4	2
Portsmouth	-	-	-	-	-	-	-	-	-	-	10	34	20	30	36
Chichester	-	15	-	-	-	-	-	-	-	-	25	25	-	6	4
Lewes	-	-	-	2	20	2	-	-	-	-	-	-	-	-	-
Newhaven	-	-	-	54	6	-	3	-	-	-	-	-	-	-	-
Seaford	-	-	-	24	6	-	3	-	-	-	-	-	-	-	-
Eastbourne	-	-	-	15	2	-	32	-	-	45	-	-	-	-	-
TOTALS.	50	75	75	125	100	50	50	50	50	75	150	150	50	50	50

headways. The opposition defeated, Hants & Dorset returned to share the Fareham-Warsash route on a half-hourly headway, receiving the princely sum of £300 from Southdown by way of compensation. That one return westward represented the only breach of the boundary until March 1976 when the joint 'Solenteer' limited stop service Southsea-Portsmouth-Fareham-Southampton commenced (Vol 1, p96ff). A serious effort to establish joint working between Warsash and Southsea, and to re-establish through journeys beyond Fareham to Southsea and Southampton, and from Theatre Royal, Portsmouth to Winchester, had been made in November 1952, but difficulties with balancing mileage and relative speeds on service seem to have put paid to that.

Southdown also originally eyed the line Winchester-Petersfield-Hindhead-Haslemere-Horsham as the boundary with the Aldershot & District Traction Co Ltd. In the event, the line between Petersfield and Horsham was drawn much farther south through Petworth and

Midhurst – and the A&D latterly enjoyed an extended journey from Haslemere, beyond Midhurst to Chichester and Bognor Regis. A series of through-tickets to such places as Bordon, Aldershot, Hindhead and Guildford were made available from Portsmouth, Worthing and Brighton.

The company's first boundary agreement (and probably the first in the country) was with the East Surrey Traction Co Ltd. A line from Horsham-Handcross-East Grinstead and Crowborough was agreed as the territorial border in March 1916. East Surrey, however, won the right to serve the road south to Uckfield station where connections were provided by Southdown. In July 1925, rather than run a proposed joint service between East Grinstead and Haywards Heath, Southdown and East Surrey made connections at Turners Hill (The Crown Hotel). For four months in 1927, the company cheekily extended this route (28) to Copthorne, rolling stage-carriage wheels over the border into Surrey for the first time – only to retreat to Turners Hill.

With its operating area expanded to include services around the north of London, 'East Surrey' became London General County Services Ltd in January 1932. This was absorbed by the new London Passenger Transport Board on 1st July 1933 as London Country

Meanwhile, from the time that it first ran through from Portsmouth Town Hall to Brighton Aquarium on 1st April 1920, service 31, the core south coast route, was developed into the distinguished allocation which it became. For many years it was Southdown's longest stage-carriage route, an honour to serve upon it. Leyland Titan TD1 No. 902 (UF 7402) of 1931 safely negotiates the early 16th Century Chichester Cross with the aid of Sussex Constabulary.

Buses, which now became the company's neighbour. Southdown promptly advanced its service 23 from Handcross to the George Hotel, Crawley; but between September 1926 and December 1945 the company's presence in that town was instead represented by service 82 from Haywards Heath station.

Having tried to get its eastern boundary accepted as a line northward from Hastings to Tunbridge Wells, Southdown was obliged to come to an agreement with the East Kent Road Car Co Ltd and Maidstone & District Motor Services Ltd, made on 5th July 1917. Southdown's eastern boundary would be established

Below: Southdown's express coach routes, of course, went way beyond the confines of the company's stage-carriage area. One which started in May 1929, in conjunction with East Kent and Wilts & Dorset initially, was called the South Coast Express, and probably raised one or two rueful smiles at the time, for Bournemouth had been a hoped-for stage-carriage destination in 1915. So some Southdown coaches at least went there regularly, in conjunction with Royal Blue, instead of Wilts & Dorset, from 1932 onwards.

Above: In the inner regions of the company's territory the web of routes got thicker. Leyland Titan TD4 No. 100 (BUF 200) is operating on the 50A service from Elmer to Pagham Beach via Bognor Bus Station and the delightfully-named Gossamer Lane in the summer of 1939. That service had its origins in one acquired by Southdown from C. G. Shore's 'Royal Blue Services' of Bognor on 24th November 1923. That 'Royal Blue' was not, of course, the Bournemouth (and later Exeter) based express coach concern.

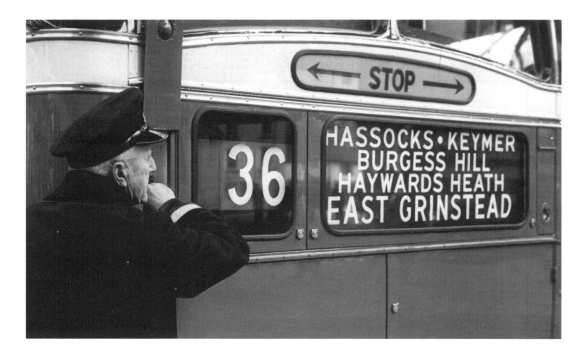

along a line northward to Tunbridge Wells from Eastbourne and Hailsham instead. Nevertheless, the company breached that line at Hailsham in 1919 with service 15 run jointly with M&D from Eastbourne to Bexhill and Hastings, and at Heathfield on 1st April 1920 with a through service from Brighton Aquarium to the Royal Oak, Hawkhurst.

Later developments in this region are described in Vol 1, p70. A note of whimsy enters the description of Southdown's 'restricted area' (from which operators selling their businesses to the company would be excluded in the 'twenties) – and bounded on the south by the sea'. True, until August 1962, of course, when Southdown breached that also – with a hovercraft service to the Isle of Wight.

A Southdown conductor in winter garb demonstrates the destination changing equipment of No. 1509 (LUF 509), a Leyland Royal Tiger of 1952. Route 36 to East Grinstead has been wound up. That town was part of the company's agreed demarcation line, in the north, with East Surrey from March 1916 – and with London Country Buses from July 1933. Route No. 36 had originally been used for Portsmouth-Winchester. It had lain dormant from February 1926 until November 1940.

All legal documentation relating to Southdown's territorial area referred to the company's area west, north and east and concluded '... and bounded on the south by the sea'. That was well and good until August 1962, when Southdown skimmed a hovercraft service across the Solent from Eastney to Ryde, Isle of Wight in cooperation with Westland and their SRN2. The service flattened new waves, pre-dating the Hovertravel and Seaspeed operations which were inspired to follow.

Southdown Engineering and Maintenance

One of the most important aspects of setting up an omnibus service is that it should, from the outset, be seen by its customers to be utterly reliable. There is nothing more likely to drive the public toward alternative means of transport than the repeated non-appearance of vehicles where and when they are expected. Indeed, in Alfred Cannon's view, 'accurate time-keeping is the essence of the business'. Accordingly, from horse bus days onward, proprietors have seen the need to employ specialised members of staff to minimise the risk of vehicular breakdown.

Southdown's garage built in 1916 at Freshfield Road, Kemp Town, Brighton provided covered space for 50 vehicles within its 75ft x 170ft dimensions. Buses and charabancs entered through one door and left by another, whilst at the north end of the building were repair and overhaul bays and a parts store. As each vehicle finished its day's work and entered it was refuelled immediately from a 5,000 gallon Bowser

underground petrol tank. Two members of staff acted as full-time oilers and greasers, keeping a record of work done in a special book marked on one side with the 'car number' of the vehicle and the other with spaces to tick off engine, gearbox, back axle, spring lubricants and other parts needing regular attention. Primarily as an inducement for the men to do their work properly the book was subject to a periodical inspection by the garage superintendent. He was aided in his supervisory task by a general foreman and the premises were kept almost impossibly spick, span and clean, the floor included. Running the whole length of one side of the garage was a trough filled with rain water for washing the vehicles and filling radiators.

A system of vehicle-marshalling was employed from the outset. Buses needed on early-morning shift had their numbers hung on a tag on an indicator board near the timekeeper's office and were given priority parking places near the exit. Drivers coming in each evening checked the board and parked as indicated. These routines were adopted on a smaller scale as depots were established elsewhere in the 'twenties commencing with the North Garage at Worthing (qv) in 1920.

Adjoining the Freshfield Road garage in the early 'twenties was a paintshop capable of dealing with three vehicles at a time, usually in winter. Extra space was provided and, as this too became inadequate, the Lord Roberts Memorial workshops were hired to repaint coaches. All painting requirements were then dealt with for some three years in the Park Street extension to Freshfield Road garage, from 1926.

Above left: Southdown's first major workshop was built as an integral part of Freshfield Road garage, Brighton in 1916. Located at the north end of this building were the repair and overhaul bays, a parts store, offices and a timekeeper's 'bridge' – the whole overseen by a garage superintendent; The van was Southdown's first maintenance vehicle which was not a retired bus. It was No. V1 (PA 6030), a Ford 10 cwt model. Behind it and to the right is the stores counter with attendant.

Left: The first depot to adopt the maintenance procedures developed at Freshfield Road was the new North Garage at Worthing in 1920. Number 61 (CD 4861) a Tilling-Stevens double-decker just one year old refuels at the Pratt's Perfection Spirit pump, the mechanic cranking it in by hand. Pratts became British Mexican, then Anglo-American, and finally Standard Oil of New Jersey (Esso) – and Southdown stayed with them.

Whilst Douglas Mackenzie concentrated upon the traffic side of the business, Alfred Cannon – following his 1919 release from the Royal Engineer's Railway Division and in addition to his duties as general manager – had acted also as chief engineer of the company. This arrangement lasted until 1926 when, as a result of an enlarged influx of vehicles, particularly following the acquisition of the Southsea Tourist Company at Portsmouth, it became clear that the engineering activities now needed the exclusive attention of a full-time appointee.

Thus R. G. Porte became chief engineer; a post he would hold for some seven years. Among his initial actions was to press for and help draw up the requisite specifications for a central maintenance and repair works. The existing procedure of carrying out detailed inspections of vehicles at the depots, largely because they could not all be accommodated at the now hard-pressed Freshfield Road complex, was seen as an unnecessary duplication of both staff and materials and occupied local garage space which could be better used for less rigorous 'dock overhauls'.

Accordingly, Southdown purchased land in Victoria Road, Portslade, to the west of Hove and had designed and constructed what would become its much-admired 'central overhaul workshops'. They opened for business in 1928 and permitted a clear distinction to be drawn between the maintenance work done at the then five principal depots (Bognor, Brighton, Eastbourne, Portsmouth and Worthing) together, to a lesser extent, with four subsidiary depots (Chichester, Haywards Heath, Horsham and Littlehampton), and that at the Central Works, Portslade. Since, as the 20th Century draws to its close, improved reliability and commercial expediency are among the reasons offered for a shift away from operator-owned facilities on such a scale, a record of maintenance procedures carried out by Southdown following the opening of Portslade Works provides a fascinating glimpse of times now relegated to passenger-transport history. The labour-intensive activities involved emphasise the large number of personnel necessary to provide such a facility.

Maintenance at the Depots

Whilst his conductor concerned himself with the details of the waybill and cashing-in, each driver coming off duty across the company area made out a report upon the condition of his vehicle. It was then the job of the depot's garage charge-hand to ensure that every defect listed received attention before the bus was re-allocated for service duty.

At the depots, sufficient fitters were on hand for each to be allotted a special role. One would examine the steering gear of every bus and see that it remained roadworthy. Another was responsible for carburettors, ensuring that each was checked at least once a week. An electrician and his assistant examined batteries, dynamos, lights and (from the later 'thirties) self-starters where fitted. Batteries were filled with acid and distilled water once a week and each light bulb,

inside and out, was tested every day; every vehicle was washed, inside and out, disinfected and the cushions cleaned each day, latterly by vacuum cleaner,

A careful record was kept of the number of miles each bus (or **car**, as Southdown parlance would have it) had travelled each day. The petrol and (from the mid 'thirties) diesel consumption would be checked daily from this mileage and if the figures had gone up, the cause was immediately to be established and remedied. The actual miles run were credited each week to tyre covers (these were the days of inner tubes) and to each unit of the vehicle's mechanism (see below).

The tyres were not purchased by Southdown but, in common with other bus operators, were the first items supplied on a contract basis – in this case by Dunlop, who provided their own staff to examine the tyres daily and ensure that pressures were at the correct level. This particularly contributed to reliable service performance; the early pneumatic tyres (fitted to larger vehicles from 1926 onwards) and their frequent punctures, having been replaced with improved examples tested daily to the point where a puncture became a positive rarity.

At each 12,000 mile interval, every vehicle was given a 'dock overhaul' at its depot garage, which involved its being placed over a pit and each detail

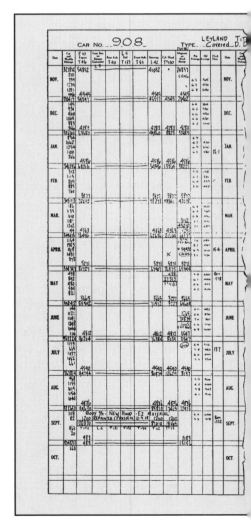

One half of a sheet from Chichester depot's mileage record book for 1938. The vehicle concerned was Leyland Titan TD1 No. 908 (UF 7408), a seven-year-old double-decker. The sheet gives the weekly mileage of the bus and of its engine, steering unit, cylinder head and magneto, together with petrol and oil consumption. In September the bodywork was overhauled, a new hood of 'E2 material' was fitted and the whole was repainted with Parasolac before re-entry into service with 374,833 miles on the clock.

examined and tested so far as could be done without taking the entire mechanism to pieces. Engine-heads were taken off and the pistons and valves examined, ground in or replaced as necessary during this procedure.

Unit System of Maintenance at Portslade

When each service bus had travelled 100,000 miles (and 75,000 miles for coaches), it was sent to the Central Works at Portslade where it underwent what was called a 'strip overhaul' – every nut and bold being separated and examined. Worn parts and anything which showed a crack or the slightest weakness were replaced.

The 'unit system of maintenance' was employed, which meant that each bus was treated as though it was comprised of seven units: 1, the chassis frame; 2, the engine; 3, the front axle; 4, the back axle; 5, the gear box; 6, the steering box; and 7, the bodywork. Spare units were kept in stock at Portslade and could be sent out at a moment's notice to replace any part which had given trouble. The replaced unit would then be sent by return to Portslade, stripped down and rebuilt. The bodywork was (unlike earlier days) not removed from the chassis frame, both being examined and repaired in position. It was not unknown, in an emergency, for such an overhaul to be completed from scratch in 24 hours, the vehicle going out on service the following day.

As each unit was removed from the chassis, it was taken to the 'dirty-wash' where it was stripped down and all its parts thoroughly washed in a spirit-based liquid to remove the mud, oil and grease so that it could be thoroughly examined. All the parts of an engine were carefully boxed during this procedure, prior to its being built-up afresh, tested and sent over to the engine bay where, frequently, it was fitted into another bus of the same type. Other departments dealt with the building-up of gear boxes and back axles, including the worm drive; whilst brakes and brake gear received especially rigorous attention because of the severe strains to which they were subjected.

Portslade personnel could draw upon a list of 243 machine tools, all numbered. But at any one time comparatively few of them were at work: they were kept as an insurance so that it was always possible to make a part if no spares were in stock or could not be obtained from the makers. Southdown actually preferred to see them idle, as it meant that replacements being used had been obtained more economically than the company could manufacture them. By the middle 'thirties also, the works were equipped with electric crack-detection equipment to find flaws not visible on the surface of the piece, thus further reducing unexpected breakdowns.

Whilst the engineers were working with mechanical units 1-6, bodyworkers descended upon the coachwork. All wood components were examined and, if defective, replaced. If a window rattled, it was

Top: A tinsmith at work in the shop specially set up for the purpose. Many craftsmen employed by the company prior to World War II worked at Portslade on a seasonal basis. In the winter they helped repair and maintain vehicles, particularly coaches in their dormant period, and during the summer they transferred to driving, conducting and other duties about the depots. The scheme was introduced in 1934.

Centre: The Central Works at Portslade employed a 'Unit System' of maintenance whereby a bus was divided into seven major parts. A Southdown fitter works on a 'unit 5' – a Leyland gearbox sent to Portslade to be stripped down and rebuilt. If a replacement had already been sent out, on completion of the work it would be placed in store pending fitment to another vehicle. The unit and part numbering system was put into action at all the company's depots to aid standardisation.

Lower: The Bodyshop in action during the 'thirties with 1930 Titans undergoing overhaul, No. 854 (UF 5654) in the foreground. In the days of wooden-framed buses like these, the rear end of Portslade Works incorporated an open-air timber store with battens ready-cut to framework sizes to fit plans of the bodywork for all types then in the fleet. These were printed up on display for the benefit of the coachbuilding staff.

fixed; seats were tested for flaws in legs, backs, springs and cushions; and if a panel needed replacing that was done whilst the engineering work was going on, and given a coat of primary paint. There was a special department which dealt with seat cushions; the men employed there being known as 'trimmers'. Worn moquette was replaced from store, so too were the cushion springs if necessary.

After this work was complete and the bus had been road-tested, it was driven into the paintshop (transferred to Portslade from Park Street in 1929) and repainted inside and out to look like new. In most instances, at one week on average, the painting process took longer to complete than with most other operators, because Southdown took a particular pride in the appearance of its vehicles and when they finally went out, they were expected to display the company's traditional sparkle. For many years, the chosen paint supplier was Dulux (Nobel Chemical Finishes Ltd). The fleetnames and numbers in gold leaf were applied by transfer and each little notice around the bus had to be set out correctly.

The process of painting and lettering was organised such that nearly all the buses were finished on Friday night so that they could be in service on Saturday, when extra custom could be expected. A sub-section of the paintshop was in the hands of signwriters who produced destination and route boards for express coaches, removable slip boards for both coaches and service buses, and various advertisement boards for display at coach stands, offices and depots.

Seasonal Variation

The geographical location of Southdown's operating area meant that to a large extent the company was dependent upon holidaymakers for a large slice of its annual income. Bus operators generally are subject to fluctuations in patronage, from hour to hour of the day, from week-day to week-end, and from season to season. In concert with its neighbouring operators on the south coast, Southdown's summer-season lasted from Whitsun until the end of September, with July and August the peak months. During January 1938, for example, the fleet covered 1,500,000 miles; during August it ran 2,500,000 or two-thirds as much again. At the beginning of April 1938, 467 vehicles of the fleet were licensed; in August, 699. In other words, during the summer months every vehicle capable of earning its keep was on the road.

Basically, the effect of this upon Portslade Works was that a year's overhaul programme had to be compressed into nine months. A basis for the solution to this problem was provided by R. E. Dunhill, appointed chief engineer in January 1934. The company employed fifty versatile men as dual-purpose permanent staff. From the beginning of each summer they worked at various depots as drivers, conductors or perhaps tradesmen. As winter approached they were transferred to Portslade to work as semi-skilled mechanics, whilst other seasonal road staff were stood-off, in the usual way among seaside operators, at the end of the summer.

In planning the overhaul programmes, Portslade officials started with the premise that they could usually handle five overhauls per week in the winter months; that at Easter a number of men would be transferred to the depots, thus reducing the number to four per week; and that after the June exodus of fifty

men the progamme would be further reduced to three buses per week. Every calendar month, programmes were drawn up to decide which buses were to be overhauled. If at any time the yearly programme showed signs of getting out of adjustment it could be moved forward or backward; vehicles would be bought to Portslade when they had travelled 95,000 or 110,000 miles instead of 100,000. The time buses took to complete their 100,000 miles varied from depot to depot; the average at Portsmouth would be about nineteen months, whilst a Worthing-based vehicle might take 22 months to reach that mileage.

Both at Portslade and the depots the general idea was to work on summer vehicles: open-topers and canvas-roofed coaches (which until World War II and their demise Southdown still referred to as 'charabancs'), during the winter months only, and exclusively on service buses during the summer. Service buses covered much the same mileage whatever the season and underwent the same maintenance routine, based on mileage, whatever the time of year.

System of De-licensing

During the summer months, Portslade Works overhauled licensed vehicles. At other times, the buses were de-licensed for the month of the overhaul. Vehicles to be de-licensed for the whole of the winter were selected only according to the type of bodywork fitted. Thus, some 23 open-top double-deckers and 100 'charabancs' were not re-licensed and the remainder of the unlicensed fleet comprised coaches and double-deckers surplus to requirements.

Some of these 'resting' vehicles would be retained in storage at Portslade, but most were returned to occupy odd corners or rows at regional depots. Water was drained off and the batteries removed; wheels were usually kept on, but as far as possible the buses stood on blown-up scrap tyres. Since, in those heady days, the vehicles were all parked under cover, there was no need for any periodical starting of engines.

The Stores Department

The main Southdown stores were at Portslade, with sub-stores at each of the depots. This large and extremely busy department was run, with all the efficiency of a main post office, by Leonard Benstead, chief storekeeper prior to World War II. It took no fewer than 200 men and three women to run the as-yet unextended Portslade Works, all of whom were dependent upon an on-going supply of spares 'on-tap'. The stores occupied two floors and the parts and materials were kept on shelves called 'bins'.

Douglas Mackenzie's numerical expertise extended

Opposite: Erected as 'temporary accommodation' in 1948 on part of the old Paddock, the Unit Store or 'Fridge' as it became known for obvious reasons, was a war-surplus military building bought at a discount. Within, engines, radiators, gearboxes and other units and parts were stored in plastic bags and dutifully inspected from time to time by directors' tours parties. A surviving Titan TD1 open-topper serving as a maintenance vehicle is parked beside it.

to these bins also. Each bore a distinguishing letter and each pigeon hole a number. Southdown part number **E152** therefore could be found in pigeon hole **152** in bin **E**. The bins that contained similar articles at the company's depots had the same numbers, so that a poorly-described part might be quickly identified for despatch, if its bin number were quoted also. Even tins of paint and varnish were known by Southdown part numbers to speed the process of ordering and delivery or collection at Portslade's three stores counters.

Where possible, mechanical spares were grouped according to make and chassis type. The unit groups were arranged in orderly sequence, from front to back of the chassis; clutch spares followed the engine parts, gearbox followed the clutch, transmission followed the gearbox and so on. Bodywork components tended to be considerably more varied and did not lend themselves to such a pattern.

There was nevertheless a section of the stores devoted solely to the body-building side of the works, and there could be found charts and diagrams of all the body types in the fleet, together with fittings, window sizes and standard transfers.

Magnetos, dynamos, batteries, carburettors and fuel pump spares were grouped according to the make and type of **unit** they belonged to rather than the make and type of **chassis** to which they would be fitted. Overhauled and re-assembled units were also held in stock, such as cylinder heads complete with valves and rockers. Gaskets of various types were hung up in batches, each marked with an identifying number.

A stores-plan was displayed above the location of the card index which in turn identified the part numbers and where they could be located. A colour-code system offered further guidance at times when normal stores-staff were off duty.

The main stores at Portslade were also responsible for keeping a replenishment service for sub-stores at the depots. A red PUR form (parts urgently required) would see a service bus or Southdown lorry loaded with the requisite order by return. A stock card system enabled a check to be kept upon local supplies and, if need be, could trigger off an enquiry into why one depot was using many more parts of a certain kind than depots elsewhere.

Presided over by a first-class tailor was the Portslade uniform store. It was Southdown's policy to purchase the best-quality uniforms, and it expected to get three years' service from an overcoat. Stocks of all sizes were held, but the tailor did not make the garments, and spent his time 'maintaining' – altering, storing and issuing them – some 1,000 sets of uniforms and 500 overcoats per year. Seasonal staff's uniforms were inspected, renovated, cleaned, parcelled and labelled ready for re-use the following year; together with the rugs for the 'coach cruise' programme.

World War II and After

Such were the maintenance procedures established by Portslade Works prior to World War II and which formed the basis for its activities thereafter. A first-aid room, canteen and recreation facilities where games were played and dances and concerts held and well-attended at weekends, completed the hive of activity which was Portslade in its formative years.

After September 1939 and the commencement of World War II, Portslade technicians, depleted by military service and participation in Lt Col Alexander Burman's 'Southdown Home Guard' column, were called upon to perform wonders with a fleet lacking in replacements; not least the conversion of 60 saloons to 'standee-type' vehicles with perimeter seating to provide maximum carrying-capacity for the duration of hostilities, and the preparation of Leyland Titan double-deckers to run on producer-gas. Some of the pressure was relieved towards the end of the conflict following the increasing intake of Guy utility double-deckers.

The outbreak of war also saw the transfer from Worthing depot to Portslade of the Ticket Machine Department. The 'TIM shop', as it was otherwise known, grew from a staff of three with 230 machines to a complement of nine by 1953, servicing 921 machines. By that year, the department was servicing 55 to 60 machines a week, making adjustments to a thousandth part of an inch. Whilst their colleagues worked on large bits and pieces of vehicles, this team had to deal with items such as the 3/64 inch ball bearings used in the date unit of the machines in use at the time. The Setright register, which did away with daily inking, automatically wound its own ribbon and issued 50,000 tickets without requiring attention, eased their day, but continuing modifications and increased traffic saw that department move into a larger workshop before the decade was out.

Extensions to the Central Works were undertaken in the late 'forties as returning servicemen and an increased fleet pushed capacity beyond pre-war figures. Seventeen of the utility-bodied Guy 'Arabs' provided the opportunity

between June 1950 and May 1952 for the workforce to expand further to almost 400, as part of the premises was transformed into a coachworks to convert them into permanent open-top form to replace the 1929-vintage Leyland Titans. A special production line, complete with jigs was set up for the task. A further thirteen to a more sophisticated design followed between February 1957 and May 1959.

Folding doors on double-deck Titans, first introduced on service at East Grinstead, quickly became so popular on routes like the 31, Brighton-Portsmouth, that in 1953 another 24 were re-equipped with them at the works, with components and instructions supplied by Leyland. This work was carried out in one of the main extensions to the works. The others were the new paintshops and 'the Paddock' – a now-covered area adjoining the western side of the main works and so-called because it was once an open-space in which old material and vehicles for disposal were deposited. In its new guise it contained the engine test beds and the auxiliary power house.

By 1955, the Central Works were operating at their fullest stretch, the fleet having peaked at its all-time high of just over 1,000 vehicles. The premises now covered an area of 111,104 square feet. Some twenty years later, in the midst of the NBC era, difficulties with new vehicle deliveries kept the works busy, despite inflation, increased competition from private motor cars and a consequent reduction in fleet size (in 1978, for example) to 524 buses and 132 coaches. Keeping the resultant older-than-expected fleet maintained in running order was a Central Works administrative and technical workforce of 231 people, still somewhat greater in number than that of pre-World War II days.

All departments were obliged to keep pace with the rapid technological advances of the 'eighties, perhaps none more-so than the Electrical Units Shop and the Glass Fibre Department. The practice of undertaking contract work for outside customers commenced in the NBC era, as the company's reputation for innovative and thorough work spread beyond the omnibus industry.

The restructuring of Southdown and the sequence of events which led to the establishment of Southdown Engineering Services Ltd based upon the activities of Portslade Works, and its ultimate sale by the National Bus Company in March 1987, are described in Volume I pp 105-8.

One of the more mundane but challenging activities facing the bodyshop was the repair of damaged vehicles. As with most companies who operate double-deckers, contact with a low bridge was an occasional cause of damage. Tempting fate somewhat, Southdown purchased its last bus of lowbridge configuration before World War II. These two post-war models seem to have found some of the comparatively few threatening bridges in the company area.

Above: Always able to feel proud of their labours by virtue of the very special standards attained in vehicle maintenance and presentation, the Portslade workforce had reason to pat themselves on the back for this product, which became a minor classic. Number 451 (GUF 191) was one of 33 Guy Arab utilities rebuilt as permanent open-toppers at Portslade between 1950-59. Highly popular on coastal and scenic routes, when they went at last in 1964 there was no difficulty in selling them.

Right and Below: Portslade works in its final configuration. The first part opened in 1928 was the rectangle immediately behind the main entrance. All the area to the left and rear of that block was known as The Paddock, a place where vehicles for disposal or repair were parked. In the late 'forties, the hangar-like unit-store and the large additional building were put in place, the latter taking on the title of The Paddock. The complex was completed as the 'fifties commenced with the disappearance of the last sizeable piece of open ground. This was the rearward extension of the main block to home the relocated bodyshop and paintshop.

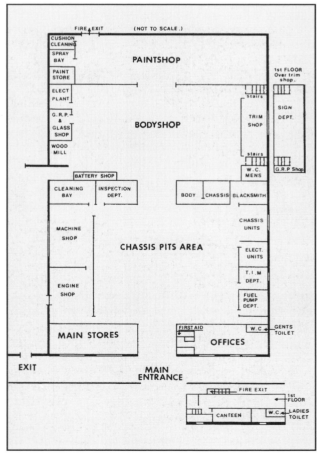

DEPOTS, BUS STATIONS AND OTHER PREMISES

In terms of bricks, mortar and corrugated iron, the legacy inherited from the constituent companies in 1915 varied somewhat. Freeholds from the Brighton, Hove & Preston United Omnibus Company totalled £6,000; from Worthing Motor Services £1,200; and from the London & South Coast Haulage Company, nil. Leaseholds ran in reverse order: from BH&PUOC nil, WMS £50, and L&SCH £1,600. Generally, such assets were not over-generous. Offices, both administrative and public, were small and occupied on the basis of a lease or, in the case of 23 Marine Parade, Worthing, a verbal agreement only. Garages were totally inadequate to deal with the kind of expansion which had been planned from the start. Finding and adapting suitable premises was a major concern of the company in its formative years. Whereas the centre for major overhaul work upon vehicles remained for 70 years in Brighton, early difficulties meant that for well over a decade much of the administrative work in the traffic sector was undertaken by Mackenzie at Worthing.

Unlike its neighbours Maidstone & District who built the first in England, and Hants & Dorset one of the finest, Southdown's basic policy was to eschew bus stations – as distinct from coach stations – wherever possible. Since during its history Southdown built six major and three minor bus stations (and latterly occupied one provided by the local council at Havant), some explanation is necessary as to criteria. It is best given by A. F. R. Carling, Southdown's general manager, writing in March 1953:

'We must of course have a base for our operating staff and facilities such as waiting rooms, lavatories and left-luggage offices for passengers at points where many routes connect. That is expenditure which cannot be avoided and is a fair charge on the travelling public; but we do not want to have to run a single bus on to private property unnecessarily. Our passengers are contributing quite enough to the public highway system through their fares, and should not have to provide extensions to that system as well.

....Lewes is to have a bus station. The fact is we need a base for our operations there, better accommodation for our staff, and more facilities for passengers. Lewes is the county town of East Sussex and a junction of routes. Its high street is narrow, busy, a main traffic artery, utterly inadequate. So we cannot help helping Lewes, thereby subsidising the public exchequer, by running our buses off its main highway ... but that is no reason why we should ask passengers to pay also for expensive substitutes for the roadway at, say, Pool Valley, Brighton or the Carfax, Horsham – places where they can board and alight centrally without being selfish ... to other users of the road. From our point of view, it is another case of 'the higher

the fewer', for new bus stations are very costly. The higher the fares, the fewer the passengers; and we all know what a difference **that** can make !'

Of those subsidiaries having such an officer Southdown was, by BET standards, somewhat late in appointing its first (and last) company architect and providing him with his own department and staff. H. A. F. Spooner was invited in 1954 to take responsibility for continuing Southdown's building development. His *magnum opus* was the supervision of the design and construction of the company's new head office. 'Southdown House' in Freshfield Road, Kemp Town, Brighton, which came into use bit by bit in 1964. In concert with other National Bus Company subsidiaries, his services were dispensed with (in 1975) in favour of the group's NBC Architectural Services.

Earlier, a total of eight depots had been considered sufficiently important to qualify for the status of identifying area-codeletters. A one-inch black letter, engraved on a white disc, was to be found screwed to the interior of the driver's cab in positions which seem to vary according to the depot concerned. During the 'fifties, and until 1970, they were as follows:

PORTSMOUTH	P	WORTHING *	W
BOGNOR	B	(and its subsidiaries:	
which, from 1922 to		Horsham *	WH
1948 had included:		Littlehampton *)	WL
CHICHESTER *	C	BRIGHTON **	A
which then became the		EASTBOURNE **	E
local area office		(combined with Brighton	
		1967)	

*	became part of Central Division 1970
**	became part of Eastern Division 1967

The boundaries of these five principal depots with their constituent subsidiaries, by and large ran at right angles to the south coast. In so doing, they followed coincidentally an ancient law, peculiar to the Sussex coast, in which every parish had to have its due proportion of coast, downland, arable land and woodland, so that each was divided from its neighbour south to north with a comparatively small sea frontage. Thus they may be surveyed neatly west to east.

The following list of property locations, which includes premises occupied subsequent to 1970, is set out accordingly; main depot followed by its subsidiaries in alphabetical order.

PORTSMOUTH & SOUTHSEA (P)

Douglas Mackenzie's early association with Frank Bartlett is described in Vol 1, p23. The traffic then generated had been handled from Bartlett's 67 Commercial Road office (see Vol 1, p13) and another at Clarence Pier. Southdown's attempt to establish itself on the road to Portsmouth in 1916 having been frustrated by a West Sussex County Council attempt to charge 3d per bus mile for the privilege of using its roads, it was not until October 1919 that booking facilities were re-established with Bartlett at his 37 Hunter Road, Southsea address. Early in 1920, Bartlett moved his travel agency to 1 Greetham Street, opposite the Town Hall, and for over two years this office was the official Southdown address in Portsmouth. Up to three Southdown vehicles were open parked the other side of the railway line on Sir H. R. Pink's loading bay at 1-5 Station Street from May 1921 to April 1924.

Several other parking lots in that vicinity had been occupied in turn as the Portsmouth fleet grew until, in 1922, Southdown purchased its own in Hyde Park Road, Southsea. The site contained the remains of the former Portsmouth Female Penitentiary. A garage opened on the plot in 1923 was the company's first in the town and marked the beginning of the extensive development of that depot. Frank Bartlett became local manager for Southdown at that point, and both he and the company moved office there. The local fleet then stood at 20 vehicles; within four years it would rise to 70.

From May 1923 for one year, Southdown had a ticket office in the Clarence Gardens public house, and from May 1924 to October 1925 at No. 70, both in London Road, Portsmouth. With the acquisition of the Southsea Tourist Company on 1st March 1925 came an office opened by STC just over a year previously, built on what had been the Swan Yard at 69 Commercial Road, near the Theatre Royal. This became the principal office for private hire work in Portsmouth and an important location for enquiries and parcels traffic. Also transferred to Southdown were STC's dilapidated garage at 53 Clarendon Road, Southsea; a handsome new building with faience facings of three floors and some 78ft frontage at the apex of London Road and Gladys Avenue, North End, which became the company's local 'Central Offices' known as 'Southdown Buildings' (valued at £6,500 in 1926); a kiosk at South Parade Pier and excursion stands and bus stops on the seafront to the east of the pier. The freehold of both 67 and 69 Commercial Road would be acquired on 28th August 1951.

Further acquisitions and Southdown's own competitive expansion led to the opening in 1934 of a major combined garage and coach station at the junction of London and Military Roads, Portsbridge at the extreme north of Portsea Island. Designed by A. E. Cogswell & Son, the building had a frontage of 270ft and an original depth of 220ft, and provided coverage for 75 buses and coaches, and administrative offices under a roof unsupported by internal stanchions – something of a novelty at the time. It was subsequently the subject of considerable additions and, known as Hilsea East depot, became the largest of the company's operational garages.

Space for a further 43 vehicles at Portsbridge was provided in 1953 by the combination of an additional garage on the opposite side of London Road Hilsea

West, the first of Southdown's buildings to employ the pre-stressed barrel-vault method of construction. It was tucked away behind a commercial garage premises and had no frontage, save access, to the main road.

Company architect, H. A. F. Spooner, was called upon in 1955 to design and supervise the modernisation of the enquiry office at Hyde Park Road together with additional work at the depot. An office at Old Bridge Buildings, 241 Albert Road, Southsea, acquired with the business of Alexandra Motor Coaches in 1935, also received his attention but, despite further acquisition of express and excursion businesses, and some additional land at Hilsea in January 1952, no additional construction work was involved in the city.

Some two months after the acquisitions by Stagecoach Holdings of Portsmouth Citybus Ltd, the ex-municipal undertaking, the operation was given the fleetname *Southdown Portsmouth*. From 1st January 1990 until divestment took effect on 19th January 1991, 'Southdown Portsmouth' operated its Portsea Island-based services from the ex-Corporation depot at Eastney, leased from Portsmouth City Council, and from Leigh Park garage (qv) on the mainland – although the latter remained in Stagecoach use thereafter. Transit Holidays placed Hilsea East on the market and Hilsea West became the base for Portsmouth Transit's *Blue Admiral* fleet as Southdown lost title to all its Portsea Island premises.

ALTON

Curiously, the closure of British Railways' 'Meon Valley Line' in February 1955, which went from Alton to Fareham and Gosport (in Hants & Dorset territory), was compensated for by Southdown with a northward extension of route 38 which, of course, started from Southsea and missed out Fareham and Gosport. Passengers for the latter were obliged, not to reason why, to make use of transfer facilities at Wickham. To complicate matters further, Southdown's 'depot' in Alton (until curtailment of the route at Droxford in 1974) was at Aldershot & District's garage.

CLANFIELD

Acquired with W. E. Pinhorn's 'Meon Valley Services' in 1929 was a garage for four vehicles at North Lane, Clanfield and used in support of service 40 to East Meon. The freehold of additional land followed on 22nd May 1930. The garage was closed by NBC's Southdown in 1972

EMSWORTH

As though mindful of earlier experience in Portsmouth when they fled because they could not afford the garage rent for the local Sussex Motor Road Car Company operation, Mackenzie and Cannon's first depot in the Portsmouth area was a garage rented from Brookside Motors Ltd in 1919 at the respectful distance of Emsworth. The freehold was obtained on

3rd April 1922. The quarter-acre site was in Palmers Road, fronting an unmade lane known as Ford's Road, and the garage made of brick and weatherboard was described in 1926 as 'not well-built, liable to flooding from the River Ems at the rear' .... and the whole site 'worth £900'.

A booking office was opened at 18 High Street in October 1924 but closed, amid local complaint, in 1929 in favour of another farther west in Havant (qv), so much so that a replacement was established at 39 High Street (freehold acquired 5th April 1949) which survived until 1959.

Surprisingly, in view of the large building programme undertaken in Portsmouth over the years, some seven miles to the west, the Emsworth garage was rebuilt and remained in use until it fell foul of a post-MAP revision in October 1981.

FAREHAM

Until 1941, what Southdown referred to as its 'Fareham depot' consisted of crews who lived locally – some having to cycle up to nine miles to Hilsea to collect a bus or, from 1929, west to Warsash outstation. It had no depot of its own in the town and based an overnight bus at Hants & Dorset's Fareham Bus Station. But by this, the second year of World War II, vehicle disposal was deemed sensible and Southdown established its own garage, for six double-deckers, on the east side of the Southern Railway's station approach (it was

extended to take two more in 1949).

Although not its own property, Southdown had already assumed responsibility for all bus and coach services from Fareham Bus Station. In October 1939, the country's division into Emergency Transport Regions had seen Fareham allotted to Portsmouth (ETR Area 6B), with Inspector I. E. Vaughan acting as controller from a Southdown kiosk. Remarkably, the system continued post-war and control was not handed back to Hants & Dorset until 8th April 1956, when that company became agents for Southdown express services and tours from Fareham, reverting at last to pre-war arrangements. Southdown control had NOT extended to those operators at Fareham *not* using the bus station – Provincial (Gosport & Fareham Omnibus Company), Smith Brothers, Glider & Blue and Hants & Sussex.

The Station Approach garage was closed in 1975 and, since Provincial had become an NBC subsidiary, an open parking facility at that firm's Hoeford premises was utilised by Southdown until October 1981. Southdown withdrew eastward completely in January 1991 upon divestment of services operating from Portsmouth depot.

HAMBLEDON

Southdown's garage in West Street was taken over in March 1935 together with the business of F. G. Tanner's 'Denmead Queen Motor Services'. It was employed as the anchor point for what became the 38 and 39 routes from Southsea. Because it was large, it was heightened to take double-deckers and was used also for vehicle storage until the end of the NBC era.

HAVANT

Havant gained a Southdown booking office at the temporary expense of Emsworth (qv) on 27th February 1928. The company's time-table grafted the 'High Street' address at Emsworth on the new one in Havant – and it was not until 1933 that Southdown's publicity caught up with the fact that it was located at 3 **South**

Street (there being no 'High Street' in Havant). The premises were extended to include No. 1 in 1932 and No. 5 South Street in 1936. These were closed in 1962 and replaced with a newly-constructed office and crew facilities at 1 Market Parade, which survived into Stagecoach ownership.

Southdown began parking the occasional bus in Havant railway station yard during World War II and continued to do so frequently thereafter. In 1980, Havant Borough Council decided to construct a bus station in Elm Lane and this was managed on its behalf by Southdown. Because Havant's significance was greatly increased following divestment of Portsmouth in January 1991, the location continues to be an important centre for Stagecoach operations.

HAYLING

Despite Southdown's arrival upon Hayling Island in May 1925, it was not until September 1935 that a freehold garage for saloon buses was occupied at 59 Elm Grove. This was commandeered by the Ministry of Supply in World War II and became a Ministry of Aircraft Production establishment leased to Airspeed (1934) Ltd from 18th October 1940 until 1946. Additional land in Elm Grove was purchased for open-parking in the interim. The garage, which had been extended in 1949, was eventually sold by Stagecoach in October 1992.

What had been the gravel-surfaced Beachlands marshalling area was tarmacadamed in 1947 and took on the status of 'bus station' with a travel booth open in summer only. Stagecoach acquired this also.

HORNDEAN

A 'draw-in', waiting room and enquiry office located at the Ship & Bell hotel opened on 26th January 1926 and the latter was soon a popular 'posting'. In September 1946, a yard on the west side of London Road was concreted over and became Horndean bus station serving, among others, routes to Portsmouth, Clanfield, Havant, Petersfield and, of course, London. A block of flats now stands upon the site.

LEIGH PARK

The City of Portsmouth Passenger Transport Department opened its mainland garage at Leigh Park in the Borough of Havant on 30th September 1956 in support of a Portsmouth 'overspill' development. Since the Portsmouth Area Joint Transport Services agreement was in force, Southdown was able to park two buses there for services 46 and 68. This arrangement ceased in October 1986, following the establishment of the competing Portsmouth City Transport Ltd. One year later, Portsmouth Citybus Ltd, now a Southampton City Transport subsidiary, closed the premises.

When Stagecoach Holdings acquired PCB it was promptly reopened. Following divestment of its Portsmouth operations, Leigh Park – with accommodation for 24 vehicles – remains Stagecoach's only garage in Southdown's former Hampshire territory. For fifteen months, until 2nd April 1992, Leigh Park was nominally a Southdown depot.

PETERSFIELD

Southdown reached Petersfield from Midhurst on 1st April 1924 and one bus stood overnight at the railway station. A garage was build in Station Road the following year and an enquiry office was established at The Coffee House, 27 The Square, in March 1927. The latter also handled the local affairs of the Aldershot & District Traction Co Ltd and Hants & Dorset Motor Services Ltd, the town being the meeting point of all three companies. The unique 'Three Greens' social club united Petersfield personnel who became renowned for their generous support of local charities.

Following acquisition of the excursion licences of George Ewen Ltd in December 1952, the original office proved too small. Southdown purchased the freehold of the site at 8 The Square, on 21st February 1953, where once stood the home of John Small of Hambledon, one of the founders of cricket. As an interim measure, a redundant single-deck Hastings trolleybus was placed on site to act as a tours office. A new office of Georgian village proportions was opened on 11th August 1955 by the chairman of Petersfield Urban District Council.

The garage in Station Road closed in October 1981 and the vehicles were parked in Penns Place until March 1989. Southdown was obliged by divestment to leave Petersfield in January 1991.

PORTCHESTER

Intended as a temporary World War II disposal point and support for increased wartime traffic on service 45, Southdown utilised open parking facilities at East Street, Portchester from 1941. These continued to be used well beyond the war, until 1949, however.

PURBROOK

Park Avenue, Purbrook was the location of a small garage occupied by Southdown from June 1928 in association with the short-lived service 46 from Purbrook Park Gate to Waterlooville via Stakes Hill Road. Traffic proved insufficient at that time. The service was withdrawn on 22nd September 1929 and the garage closed.

WARSASH

Location for forty-seven years (1929-1976) of Southdown's most westerly stage carriage terminus, Warsash was first served by route 41 from Fareham from October 1923 until August 1924. A bus had been parked overnight near the Clock Tower. Hants & Dorset then took over the route.

Circumstances leading to the return of Southdown in November 1929 are described in Vol 1, p43. The

Warsash outstation was Southdown's most westerly garage. It was originally the property of C. J. Newbury & Sons as a strawberry-receiving station set up for the local fruit-picking association when the LSWR removed its special strawberry vans from use at nearby Swanick in 1920. Southdown occupied the premises from 1929 to 1971 – the Southern Railway had returned the vans.

Barn garage in Warsash Road near Fleet End provided room for an initial two double-deckers in support of what was now an extension of service 45 from Portsmouth. The freehold was obtained as late as 25th March 1960. The premises were sold by NBC's Southdown in 1971; and the company withdrew from the route on 1st November 1981 as a result of MAP recommendations.

WATERLOOVILLE

A general enquiry and booking office, for express coach services mainly, was established in the Heroes of Waterloo Hotel, London Road in 1946. The location proved insufficiently productive and the facility was closed after some five years. The old landmark hotel was demolished in 1966.

WICKHAM and NORTH BOARHUNT

As part of its drive to establish a monopoly of services to towns and villages north of Portsmouth, Southdown acquired the Hambledon-Portsmouth route of Blue Motor Services (Southwick) Ltd on 16th September 1935. With it came that firm's garage at North Boarhunt. It was only suitable for saloons however. So, in January 1936, the company moved farther west to a replacement garage in Station Road, Wickham, also on route 38. The freehold of the site was eventually acquired from the British Transport Commission in

1955. It was one of several outstations closed as an economy measure by NBC's Southdown in 1971.

BOGNOR REGIS (B)

When Southdown purchased Arthur Davies' charabanc business in 1915, his booking office at Beach House on The Esplanade came with it. Also temporarily employed, until the first foray into Portsmouth was abandoned on 31st October 1916, was his garage in Chapel Street. With local authorities demanding 3d (1.25p) per mile for the use of their roads, Southdown abandoned a November 1915 advanced plan for a new garage at the junction of Bassett and Argyle Roads. The lasting entry into the naval port made in 1919, it instead purchased Field's corrugated iron garage for £6,369 – at the corner of Richmond and Station Roads, Bognor to support the route. This building was severely damaged by fire in July 1923 and was rebuilt in brick and cement rendering upon the same site. In 1926, it offered 10,480ft super, a 3,000 gallon petrol tank, one inspection pit, and was valued at £9,500.

Beach House acted as local company office, waiting room, enquiry and parcel bureau until the opening of Bognor Bus Station in September 1934. Architects were Clayton & Black of Brighton. The station was built on a 100ft site costing £5,000 at 66-70 High Street, previously the location of the old Bognor Urban District Council offices. It featured a particularly attractive Art Deco facade, well-designed offices and public areas and a recreation room for crews. Following piecemeal acquisition of additional land in John Street, the Richmond Road premises were exchanged, on 30th January 1957 with builders merchants Hall & Co Ltd for their garage in Bedford Street, behind the bus

The unusual art deco facade of Bognor Regis bus station, built in 1934 on the site of the original Bognor council offices in the High Street. Southdown were fortunate in being able to extend the site at the rear and acquire a garage in the same location in an unusual exchange deal with a local firm of builders merchants.

Chichester bus station opened for business in 1956 and the large conveniently-sited garage at the rear combined to make this one of the most efficient property-groupings owned by the company. Nearly forty years later the combined bus station and garage provide Stagecoach South with an important operational and control centre; quite a tribute to the foresight of those who planned this one.

station.

Combined garage and bus station were closed by NBC's Southdown in 1982, the vehicles being transferred to Chichester, to which the area manager's office had removed in 1948. A replacement travel office at 4 York Road was retained by independent Southdown and then Stagecoach.

CHICHESTER (C)

A freehold office costing £125 was established at 18 West Street, near the cathedral, in 1922. When W. G. Dowle's local service was purchased in January 1924 he moved in to run the premises for Southdown. On 27th May 1926, the office removed to larger premises at 11 West Street. Dowle then became Chichester area manager.

Built on land purchased for £3,580 in 1923, the company's first garage in the city, with just 2,240 sq ft of space, was in New Broyle Road, Northgate. The site was that of the Olympic Picture House which had burned down two years previously; but its ornamental facade was retained by Southdown. Until it was ready, the ex-Dowle garage in Summersdale was briefly occupied. Slightly to the south of the first, a larger Northgate garage (8,500 ft super) was built of brick and flint on what had been the local skating rink. It opened in July 1924.

Suitably updated, the Northgate garages were in use until replaced by the garage and bus station complex at Southgate – the company's largest – under construction 1954-56. The culmination of many attempts to create a covered bus station (notably that in October 1942) to relieve the congestion in West Street, the complex was located beside the railway and bestride Basin Road. The garage comprised eight pre-stressed concrete barrel vaults in a row with 85ft beams across the garage at 40ft centres resting on steel frames. The bus station opposite incorporated area administrative and control office, social rooms and a canteen for employees. Passengers got waiting

rooms, enquiry and booking offices, buffet and a restaurant with fully licensed bar. Architect was C. E. Petch and the construction work was overseen by Southdown's own H. A. F. Spooner.

Stagecoach continues to utilise these premises.

COMPTON

Southdown began a service from Chichester Cross to the Coach & Horses, Compton (West Sussex) in January 1930 and built a small garage there to support what initially – and later – was a terminus for route 54. It survived until 1964, when it was one of BET Southdown's several economy cuts.

EASTERGATE

Following acquisition by Southdown of his Silver Queen Bus Service, Cecil Walling transferred the freehold of his premises in Fontwell Avenue to the company on 5th April 1945. The Eastergate garage was employed by Southdown until 1961.

MIDHURST

Midhurst was reached on 1st April 1924 with the then service 39 from Chichester to Petersfield. To provide an intermediate staging-post, the tenancy of a wooden garage was obtained that year in North Street. The leasehold was acquired in October 1946 and more substantial premises were built there two years later. An enquiry office at the same location dated from 1930. Both premises closed in early NBC days, but a crew room behind what had been the office remained to support vehicles kept overnight on a public car park.

PETWORTH

Service 22 from Brighton Aquarium to Steyning was extended to Petworth Square on 18th June 1921 and a freehold brick garage of 1,600 sq ft was brought into use in 1924 on what used to be a stonemason's yard

Douglas Mackenzie's 'counting-house' in its original condition as acquired by Southdown from Worthing Motor Services Ltd. Located on Marine Parade, the first floor was extended outward to the line of the pavement as a booking office so that Mackenzie's traffic department could hold sway there, until he was finally coaxed to Brighton.

in Angel Street. It was valued at £1,100 in March 1926. An enquiry and booking office at Streeter & Co's premises in The Square was in use by 1927. Socially this outstation was paired with Midhurst. The garage was one of those which went in the 1971 round of closures.

SELSEY

Started in July 1920 as service 32 (52 later) from Chichester Station to the Marine Hotel, Selsey, the route covered some seven miles. This was thought sufficient to establish a small garage on land at the New Inn, Selsey, leased from the brewers Henty & Constable in January 1923. It lasted in company service until 1964.

SINGLETON

When Southdown acquired Dowle's Chichester to East Dean service in January 1924, it was some months before his parking place in the village of Singleton was given up. A garage in the parish, which includes Goodwood Racecourse, was in operation by 1927. It became one of those closed by Southdown in 1954.

WALBERTON

Walberton's first Southdown bus service was the No. 6 from Worthing to Bognor Regis starting on 18th June 1921. For a few months in 1922 a bus was based in the village, it is thought in a rented garage.

WEST DEAN

The displaced Singleton bus and its crew were re-located at West Dean from 1924 until Southdown established its garage back at Singleton, the next village to the east. The vehicle was housed in a rented building.

THE WITTERINGS

Albert Frederick (Alf) Trickey's service from Chichester to the Witterings was acquired in 1923. Trickey's West Wittering garage, next to the post office, was part of that deal. The company next acquired the leasehold of a garage at Longlands Farm, East Wittering on 13th October 1924, gaining the freehold of that and an adjoining shop on 13th May 1946. Land beside it was added the following September. The premises survived in Southdown ownership until 1965.

WORTHING (W)

Worthing Motor Services Ltd bequeathed the Ivy Arch garage on the Broadwater Road to the new company, the freehold being obtained on 19th November 1915. Considered by many in Southdown to be 'the place where it all began', it remained in company ownership until after a more commodious garage with suitable maintenance facilities was opened in 1920 (see below). The Ivy Arch garage was then sold, on 22nd July 1921, to a horticultural agent.

The premises based upon James Town's 'Steyne Hotel Mews', the Steyne garage (not to be confused with Steine Street in Brighton) came to the company from Brighton, Hove & Preston United Omnibus Co Ltd, the freehold being confirmed on 1st February 1916. This substantial brick building measured 160ft x 67ft and was valued at £8,700 in 1926. Located in Library Place, it was destined to become Worthing coach station.

Immediately behind this, the North Garage, which was equipped for servicing the local fleet, was built on leasehold land and opened in 1920. By means of piecemeal demolition of such buildings as Bedford House and Lamports Cottage (in 1937) and purchases of gardens of houses about to become shops on the south side of Warwick Street, the Bedford Row garage, used exclusively for accommodation, was bought into use the following year beside the western wall of the North Garage. It stood behind the Dome Picture House, forming a neat complex of three garages not physically attached but in immediate proximity to each other.

Arguably, the most important ex-WMS building in Worthing was Douglas Mackenzie's 'counting house' at 23 Marine Parade, initially held on a verbal agreement only at £75 per annum. The freehold was obtained on 11th November 1922. In 1916, with accommodation at the company's registered office in Brighton (qv) becoming inadequate, Mackenzie happily returned the traffic department to this familiar building where he'd carried out similar work for WMS – thus putting some eleven miles between that section and the nominal headquarters. What was supposed to be a temporary measure lasted until 1926, when he reluctantly agreed to go back to Brighton. Until then, this was also the office from which new vehicles were ordered, including those for Wilts & Dorset Motor Services Ltd (see also Vol 1, p47).

Over the years, Southdown opened offices for enquiries and excursion and express bookings at several locations in Worthing – one of the earliest 86 High Street in August 1915. The ex-BH&PUOC office at 5 South Street (long before that Richard Walker's London stagecoach booking office) was incorporated into the Arcade Buildings and was joined by No. 4 inherited from Fairway Coaches in December 1933. The first floors of Nos. 9-11 South Street had been occupied from November 1932. Also held on a lease from July 1935 was a shop at 2 The New Broadway, Tarring Road, West Worthing – and from 24th December 1936, a basement at 45 Marine Parade. A replacement for this was opened at 20 Marine Parade in July 1954 which survived until 1967.

The 'counting house' and the three-garage complex continue in Stagecoach use.

ARUNDEL

A booking office and waiting room were established in November 1925 in a High Street shop leased from the Duke of Norfolk. The premises were closed and replaced by similar facilities at a new bus station for four vehicles in River Road, opened on 6th May 1951. In the early 'seventies, NBC's Southdown declared it surplus to requirements.

BARNS GREEN

Following the conflagration described in Vol 1, p48, W. H. Rayner's remaining bus and services based on Barns Green, Itchingfield were sold to Southdown in January 1935. Since his garage had been destroyed, Southdown built another in the hamlet, some four miles south-west of Horsham, on freehold land purchased (not from Rayner) for £80. The plot measured 50ft x 275ft. The garage was closed in 1954.

DIAL POST

Dial Post garage was a one-bus affair at the Benson Lane corner of the A24 Worthing-Horsham road. *Tweenus* (November 1953, p10) reports that 'when Arthur Davey joined Southdown on 25th June 1924 his first job was to cycle to Dial Post garage where his service 2 bus bedded down nightly'. Well, there's no evidence of short workings to Dial Post at that time and the service was numbered 5 until 24th May 1928 – June 1928 seems a more likely opening date. The freehold was purchased on 17th April 1931. There's no doubt about the year of its closure – 1966.

HANDCROSS

Forever associated in road transport history as the place where in 1906 ten passengers on a *Vanguard* Milnes Daimler were swept from the top deck by a tree

branch and killed, Handcross saw Southdown establish a connection with the East Surrey Traction Company in April 1916. This was withdrawn the following year and was not re-established until 18th June 1921 (for Crawley and Croydon). The company straightway opened a garage on the west side of London Road (A23). Additional leasehold land was acquired in January 1937 and title to the property was maintained until 1965.

HORSHAM (WH)

On 12th July 1919, Southdown sent three employees and one bus to Horsham to establish service 17 to Brighton. For several weeks until the No. 5 (2, from 1928) route from Worthing was established, the vehicle was parked at Messrs Rice's premises in Worthing Road. Springfield Road was the next location until the first of two garages in Denne Road off East Street came into use at livery stables in September 1924. It could house four buses – five with a little juggling. In 1926, the plot still comprised a brick built garage worth £1,625, a yard paved in blue brick, a three-stall stable, two coach houses and a cottage rented out by SMS. The freehold site of the second, farther along the road, was acquired on 18th January 1935. It was extended in 1948 to accommodate 55 buses. An up-to-date clubroom was opened there in 1951 and by the next year there were 111 Southdown employees based in Horsham.

Southdown's first office in Horsham was rented at 22 Richmond Terrace in 1923, with a staff of one inspector and one regulator. The lease was obtained on 30th July 1925. Aldershot & District and the East Surrey Traction Companies shared the premises, which moved in 1933 to refurbished rooms at 23 The Carfax; the freehold being acquired by Southdown on 31st August 1944.

Horsham garage blended beautifully with the landscape; it was covered in summertime with Virginia creeper. It had been extended to accommodate over 50 buses in 1948 and was an important centre of operations in Southdown's northern area. The building was both closed and demolished during the territorial retreat of 1987.

At its peak in the early 'fifties the Carfax office was handling some 100 Southdown arrivals and 100 departures with up to 30 duplications each day; London Transport (as successors to East Surrey) 50 and Aldershot & District 16. With Basil Williams' Hants & Sussex office next door, The Carfax was living up to its meaning – 'the meeting of four ways '. The joint office was given a further updating, Spooner fashion, in 1958. From January 1935, coach bookings had been taken also at 4 Park Street.

Horsham depot became an early victim of independent Southdown's retreat from its northern territory, closing as an active unit in January 1987 and becoming briefly a repository for redundant vehicles awaiting sale. As other operators moved in, Southdown's presence in the town was reduced to buses running in from elsewhere. The Carfax office was given up in December of that year.

LITTLEHAMPTON (WL)

Littlehampton depot began equally humbly with two service 31 vehicles parked overnight on a site in River Road in 1921. The following year an office was rented in the Dolphin Yard, Surrey Street, where Inspector R. Howe supervised local traffic. In January 1924, the purchase of South Coast Tourist brought offices at Seagate Cottage, Beach Road. The suite was a very small office on the ground floor and another at the top of some rickety stairs. Nevertheless, it was in use until 1926 when a freehold garage worth £9,500, was opened in East Street. On a site of 9,700ft super which included enquiry, paying-in and timekeepers' offices, it provided accommodation for 20 vehicles and included inspection and catchpits and interceptor – and a 3,000 gallon petrol tank. Five small houses on site, including the aptly named Cannon Cottage, were let to employees. In 1931 an additional office for coach bookings at 65 High Street and a kiosk at The Parade were brought into use.

By 1952 the depot's complement had risen to 29 vehicles and it was handling a good deal of coach traffic and a summer-season town service in addition to its rural routes. The increase had been steady rather than spectacular.

The depot gained its own area code in the 'fifties but, like Horsham, remained a subsidiary of Worthing. It became a victim of the 1971 round of sevice closures. NBC's Southdown moved into a replacement office opposite the site of the garage. It survives.

PULBOROUGH

Historically the terminus of the Sussex Motor Road Car service from Worthing, Pulborough gained a Southdown garage in London Road in 1927. That year, service 9 – Littlehampton-Pulborough-Horsham – was renumbered 69 although short workings to Pulborough had been in place from 1st May 1926 on that route only. The garage was another which closed in 1971.

STEYNING

Southdown's route from Brighton Aquarium to Steyning commenced on 1st June 1915. A garage was constructed on a site at the rear of the Star Inn, initially on a 21-year lease from 24th June 1921. What had been service 15 became No. 22 that year and was later extended to Petworth, Midhurst and Petersfield. The garage survived as a Southdown outstation until, and despite its traditional attachment to Worthing, it passed to the reactivated Brighton Hove & District on 1st January 1986.

STORRINGTON

One of the original leasehold buildings taken over by Southdown from Worthing Motor Services Ltd at the foundation in 1915, the small garage at Amberley Road comprised the western end of Adela Powell's 'Southdown Garage'. This name predated its eventual use by the company (see Vol 1, Ch3) and may well have prompted French and Clark to come up with the famous alternative. The freehold was purchased for £533 on 26th October 1926. Separated from the rest and modernised over the years it nevertheless grew no larger, but survived into Stagecoach ownership.

WASHINGTON

The Sussex Motor Road Car Company's traditional association with licensed premises was taken up by Southdown on 9th March 1923 when land for an enquiry and booking office was purchased at the Frankland Arms. Washington lay at the crossroads of the company's routes from Brighton to Petworth, and Worthing to Horsham. Worthing-based Inspector R. G. Stocker was in charge 1945-50. It did not survive beyond the days of BET's Southdown.

BRIGHTON (A)

At Brighton, Southdown inherited the right, established by Worthing Motor Services Ltd in 1912, to park its vehicles in the stable yard of the Royal Mews, Steine Street. Also from WMS came a booking office at 58 Eastern Road, Kemp Town (freehold was obtained 21st July 1925). From the Brighton, Hove & Preston United Omnibus Company came a share in No. 6 Pavilion Buildings which for some months was Southdown's head office; a plot of land between Park Street and Freshfield Road, Kemp Town; and the Mark Lane Mews at 19 Upper St. James's Street that still housed the equine establishment of F. J. Mantell. Walter Flexman French's London & South Coast Haulage Company contributed the leasehold garage and office at 73 Middle Street, formerly occupied by Anne & William (Jolly Jumbo) Ecclestone – in turn briefly the registered office of Southdown, 1916-17; and L&SCH's head office at 8-10 Ditchling Rise, the latter soon dispensed with.

These premises were neither large enough nor able to provide suitable maintenance facilities for

Left: Pool Valley bus station, Brighton in the late 'thirties. Southdown had established leasehold offices in the Royal York Buildings in 1929 and gained a well-sighted terminus free from general road traffic right on the seafront in the centre of town, and that at minimum cost to the company's budget.

Below left: Southdown's own architect, H. A. F. Spooner designed the new headquarters of the company which came into use in 1964. From a functional point of view it was a whole lot more efficient than the rambling but charming Steine Street complex, but externally it was not the kind of building likely to gain the approval of the Prince of Wales. 'Southdown House' in Freshfield Road, Kemp Town, ceased to be Southdown property on 31st December 1985.

Brighton's share of a fleet now past the 50 mark at the end of 1915, particularly since covered accommodation was deemed essential for starting vehicles in the forthcoming winter. Even a coal yard in West Street had been pressed into service as a parking lot that September. Southdown engaged C. E. Clayton, architect of several buildings in Brighton and Hove (including the Conway Street garage of BH&PUOC) to design a new garage, central overhaul and maintenance depot to be built on the land at Freshfield Road. This would house most of the then Southdown Brighton-based fleet from 1916 (see page 15 this volume). The company continued to develop and expand the site – at Park Street from November 1915 to February 1923 and in December 1920 by the purchase of stabling and land in Freshfield Road proper.

The search for centralised office accommodation focused on Steine Street. James Stuart-Smith, ex manager of WMS and proprietor of the Royal Mews, lived at No. 5. On 23rd August 1915 he became clerical supervisor-cum-manager for Southdown and let the ground floor of his house to the company. In 1918, he moved his family to a house opposite enabling the whole of No. 5 to be occupied and take on the role of head office.

Meanwhile, the 'Southdown Kiosk' for booking and enquiries for excursions had been opened on 11th November 1915. It was in Madeira Walk beside the Aquarium and faced the Palace Pier. A waiting room was added in April 1921. Southdown's first attempt to build a bus or coach station, at Brighton Aquarium in 1922, is described in Vol I, p53. The Kiosk remained,

however, and for several years a lady employee on shiftwork functioned there like a regulator, booking in the buses as they arrived from Freshfield Road and out as they left on service.

A tenancy agreement for an additional booking office at 14 West Street came with the excursion business of White Heather Motor Services in August 1921. This removed to 69 Grand Parade from April 1924 to October 1925 and then to West Street Shelton Hall – the 'Kings Road' office active until World War I.

Following the burgeoning 'head workshops' role of the Freshfield Road complex, land at 5-8 Edward Street was purchased in April 1924, purely for accommodation purposes. The brick and timber garage built there initially had a boarded roof and wooden sliding doors. It offered 16,880ft super and in 1926 was valued at £21,000, then the company's most valuable property. Extra land fronting Sun Street was added in September 1936.

Central maintenance at Brighton and at Portslade central works (opened 1928) is the subject of a separate section of this volume.

The nearest thing to a bus station in Brighton was established courtesy of the corporation on 1st July 1929. A company office was set up in the triangle which is Pool Valley, just off the Grand Junction Road; all public parking was barred, and departure bays for stage-carriage services were established on two sides of the triangle. This became the terminus for Brighton-bound Southdown buses. It narrowly escaped becoming a public car park in 1962, but was latterly a coach station – as the buses moved to Churchill Square – until the end of NBC control when Brighton became the preserve of re-emergent Brighton Hove & District.

The premises in Steine Street grew over the years 'much like a patchwork quilt' by the piecemeal addition of further properties. Across St. James's Street, land in George Street and Little George Street was added. On the east side and running parallel to Steine Street, from 1931 onwards, Manchester Street gave up most of its addresses, a large part of which became the express coach station with associated booking office. An open-plan tours office opened there in 1955 on the site of the publicity department, now removed to Freshfield Road. On the west side 'Travel Corner', founded originally in March 1930, was developed at the junction of Old Steine and St. James's Street – a sizeable enquiry office which lived to be updated in NBC days. Another, for tours and excursions, had occupied a shop and basement at 5 Marine Parade from March 1931 – the 'Albemarle office'. The last development in the area was eastward into Charles Street, 1961-63.

H. A. F. Spooner's first 'big work' for Southdown in Brighton was the new 'accommodation' garage at Moulsecoomb, built to relieve the pressure upon the Lane, Vicarage (1938) and Park Street garages of the Freshfield Road complex. Office work too had reached saturation point and his second – and last – was the new head office at Freshfield Road, which left the rambling Steine Street premises to concentrate upon coach traffic. Moulsecoomb opened in 1957; 'Southdown House' in 1964.

Responsibility for the day-to-day running of Brighton Hove & District, assumed on 1st January 1969, brought with it that firm's properties in Hove (qv) and its Whitehawk garage near Brighton Racecourse. When BH&D was reactivated from 1st January 1986, Southdown relinquished to it title to all properties in Brighton save Southdown House and the adjoining Vicarage garage – which were acquired for sale by National Bus Properties Ltd.

This building at East Grinstead was once the Southdown garage which extended from Chequer Road through to Cantelupe Road. That had been achieved by knocking-together the original Southdown premises at 24 Chequer Road and joining it up with Sargent's garage at the rear in 1955. The premises were closed and sold by Southdown in 1972 – an early NBC era disposal.

BOLNEY

The company had a crew and vehicle stationed at Bolney, on a road worked by service 14 'milk-churn buses', from 1916. The lease for a garage site was obtained in December 1920; the freehold on 4th September 1923. Situated in London Road, the building of corrugated iron with sliding doors, measured 30ft x 24ft and in 1926 was valued at £350. It remained in use until September 1963.

BURGESS HILL

Service 28, Brighton Aquarium to Burgess Hill started on 1st July 1922 and a bus was outstationed at the

latter – it is believed in the open near the 'Kings Head'. The service closed on 30th September of that same year, and the outstation went with it.

CHELWOOD GATE

The rented garage at the 'Red Lion', Chelwood Gate, Fletching had its origin in the terminus established in 1920 with the then service 29 from that village to Brighton. The site was acquired on 19th September 1928. Its importance increased in July 1933 when service 30 from Brighton was extended (for one year) to East Grinstead as was, more lastingly, service 92 from Eastbourne. The standing area was extended in July 1952. BET's Southdown closed the garage in 1967, still little more than a shed in a field.

COWFOLD

Cowfold, some three quarters along the distance from Brighton to Horsham on route 17, was the location for a small rented garage opened and closed within the year 1923 as Southdown tested the traffic. Henfield (qv) proved the more convenient.

Quite an imposing structure with an ecclesiastical appearance, Haywards Heath bus station was one of the later additions to the Southdown inventory, being built in the middle 'fifties at the same time as the bus station at Lewes. The Haywards Heath depot was quickly in trouble following deregulation and both bus station and garage were closed by independent Southdown.

CRAWLEY

The opening of Crawley Coach Station at County Oak, to the north of the village, in 1931 is described in Vol 1, pp83-4. Increased local traffic led to the construction of an adjoining garage in 1959 and the opening of an office in Three Bridges Road on 6th July 1958. Crawley depot closed in the NBC era cuts of 1971, the freehold going to the Ministry of Transport. Currently 'Astral House' the premises now on the site of the coach station were previously 'Caledonian House', the headquarters of British Caledonian Air Lines from nearby Gatwick. When Southdown was in its infancy, the latter was famous only for its racecourse.

EAST HOATHLY

A small garage in East Hoathly, half way between Hailsham and Uckfield, was opened in 1923 in support of service 29 from Eastbourne. This is the one case where 'ancient Sussex law' was not followed; for despite its geographical location, East Hoathly became a Brighton area, rather than Eastbourne responsibility. It was closed in 1966.

EAST GRINSTEAD

Southdown's association with East Grinstead started in July 1933 with the commencement of a four-stage take-over of H. J. Sargent's business, finally completed in March 1951. Very much an outpost on the northern fringe of the company's territory, where connections with London Transport Services were established, East Grinstead depot began with a garage at 24 Chequer Road whose freehold was acquired on 9th January 1934. One of its buses ran to Eastbourne, the other to Brighton. Private hire work started in 1935 and was enhanced by the purchase of Sargent's excursion licences in May 1938. By the outbreak of World War II there were seven Southdown vehicles based in the town.

A booking office was rented at 11 High Street from 2nd December 1937, to be replaced by one on a lease at No. 33 from 4th October 1938. Excursion work was halted during World War II and the loss of a local cinema, which lessened stage-carriage traffic in the evenings and weekend, set the depot back somewhat – until 1947, when licences for tours were restored.

Post-war acquisitions from Sargent (qv), both stage and additional excursion, brought a total of 15 vehicles to the town. Sargent's garage at 32 Cantelupe Road, purchased on 22nd March 1951 and conveniently at the rear of Southdown's Chequer Road, was included in the last of these deals. They were 'knocked-through' and enlarged in 1955.

East Grinstead depot closed in 1972 in continuation of NBC Southdown's nationalisation programme.

HASSOCKS

A garage in the railway station approach was utilised by Southdown from 1952 as a result of increased traffic at what had become an important crossroads in the company network. It was closed during the latterday NBC era.

HAYWARDS HEATH

For those living within reach, Haywards Heath has long been the main railway station for commuters to London, prime minister Harold MacMillan among them. Southdown service 14 reached the station from Brighton in June 1918 and stands nearby were quickly established. A garage was built on freehold land acquired in Gordon Road for £1,251 on 14th August 1926; and a kiosk at the railway station followed, with a licence to stand omnibuses on its forecourt being granted in October 1932.

Haywards Heath was one of six locations deemed appropriate by Southdown for the construction of a major bus station. The site, at Finch's Corner in Perrymount Road was bought in January 1952 on the basis of its relative proximity to the railway. No new garage was involved, but the layout of the accommodation on two floors resembled that being built simultaneously at Lewes, but with the addition of two shops. The terrain sloped, however, and the lower end of the building had a certain ecclesiastical look about it. Stands on the west side featured bays in echelon, the concept for which was imported from the United States. The bus station, which cost £51,000, opened for business on 1st May 1956. That was not the end of construction in the town; the garage, whose standing area was increased in 1955, was extended in 1963.

The depot came under threat in the competitive environment post-deregulation on 26th October 1986. Almost to the day, independent Southdown closed the garage two years later, the bus station having been put up for sale previously.

HENFIELD

Half-way house between Brighton and Horsham, a garage for four double-deckers was built in Lower Station Road, Henfield in 1923. The freehold was purchased for £559 on 1st September 1930. The fortunes have smiled upon it, and it survives into Stagecoach ownership and use.

HOVE

In March 1930, Southdown acquired John Poole's 'Royal Red Coaches'. With that enterprise came its tours offices at 7 St. Aubyns Gardens in Hove, the 'proud to be different' neighbour of Brighton. Poole remained in charge of that office for Southdown until his retirement in September 1950.

The original building which stood here was the old Lion Steam Brewery in Pevensey Road, Eastbourne. Southdown acquired the lease of that property as early as April 1916, initially building two garages there. Then a bus station was built instead and came into operation in 1929. It is seen here in the 'fifties at the height of its usefulness.

It was not until control of Brighton Hove & District passed to Southdown on 1st January 1969 that the company acquired further property in the Borough of Hove. The head office of BH&D and its West and East Garages in Conway Street came into the fold. This arrangement lasted until 1st January 1986 when BH&D awakened from its dormant state and reclaimed its premises in Brighton, Hove and more besides.

In the interim, and in conjunction with Southdown, the National Bus Company occupied managerial offices in Wilbury Road, Hove.

HURSTPIERPOINT

A short-lived tenancy agreement for a garage at Mansion House, Hurstpierpoint was signed on 1st April 1939. Occupancy did not survive World War II.

LEWES

Lewes, eight miles north-east of Brighton, had already been served by the London & South Coast Haulage Company, so it enjoyed a Southdown bus presence from the beginning. It was not until 1922, however, that an enquiry and booking office was rented at 54 High Street. This removed to No. 182 on 17th September 1923 and, again, to No. 174 in 1930.

Land at Eastgate Street, purchased in December 1948, was cleared in 1952 for the construction of Lewes Bus Station together with a garage for 19 vehicles (see introduction, this section). It opened on 30th May 1954.

Lewes remained a subsidiary of Brighton until NBC's 'restructuring' of Southdown and Philip Ayers' choice of the town as the company's new headquarters from 1st January 1986. They were located in rented accommodation at Walwer's Lane. In 1991, Stagecoach moved house to the Lewes Enterprise Centre, 112 Malling Street and, as the group continued its remarkable expansion in the south of England, it became also the head office of Stagecoach Group subsidiaries providing local bus services from Andover (Hants) in the west to Broadstairs (Kent) in the east.

So, hilly and delightful Lewes became the southern bastion of the plebeian bus, which seems appropriate for a place where Simon de Montfort won the battle (1264) which ensured the survival of parliamentary democracy.

NEWHAVEN

The tenancy of an office at the Old Brewery House, 1 Bridge Street came to Southdown from Worthing Motor Services Ltd in 1915. The leasehold was acquired on 15th March 1916. It underwent numerous changes and improvements over the years, one of the more important in 1954, and maintained a very useful presence at the junction of routes from Brighton, Lewes and Eastbourne until the end of the BET era.

SCAYNES HILL

An outstation was set up at Scaynes Hill, 2° miles east of Haywards Heath on land acquired in September 1921. It comprised a freehold corrugated iron garage on a plot 50ft x 150ft, which cost a total of £363. Its initial purpose was to cover short journeys to Haywards Heath on service 21, Brighton-Cuckfield. It survived until 1935.

SHOREHAM

A booking and enquiry office was established in leasehold premises at 86 High Street, Shoreham on 11th August 1915. It proved extremely long-lived, and was eventually acquired by Brighton Hove & District at the partition of Southdown on 1st January 1986, on the grounds that it was in the BATS area.

WIVELSFIELD

A small garage at Wivelsfield, two miles south of Haywards Heath, was occupied (in support of service 23 Brighton-Handcross and 29 Brighton-Haywards Heath via Plumpton) from 1931. It was declared surplus to requirements in 1950, curiously before the notorious Finance Act of that year had had a chance to bite.

EASTBOURNE (E)

Just before the launch of Southdown, Worthing Motor Services Ltd started running a stage-carriage service, in May 1915, from the Royal Mews, Brighton to Eastbourne via Seaford – only one return journey per day initially. From such a humble beginning grew Southdown's association with gracious Eastbourne. There were still only two journeys per day going right through to Eastbourne when, on 11th April 1916, the company acquired the lease of the former Lion Steam Brewery in Pevensey Road, from the Kemp Town Brewery Company. The freehold was purchased in March 1919 for £3,000; the attraction being the covered yard which previously housed the drays. The central (tower) portion of the building was leased to the Scenic

Eastbourne bus station became a possibility following purchase in the middle 'twenties of land at Royal Parade East. Here was built the Royal Parade garage with a 110ft frontage and room for most of the 1927 Eastbourne fleet. There was sufficient land available at the rear to cope with further expansion and, until the NBC era, the premises provided an important covered parking and maintenance facility at the eastern end of the company's area.

Restaurant Services Ltd from May 1920 until January 1928 when it returned to Southdown. In the interim, the resultant two garages (on the north side of Pevensey Road) had been known as: No. 1 Garage, some 30 yards east of Terminus Road with 38ft frontage and 53ft deep and valued at £2,500; and No. 2 Garage, with 11ft entrance and another 20ft wide in Langney Road, at £2,000 – both fitted with roller-shutter doors.

Re-establishing occupation of the whole premises was part of a large plan for the construction of a covered bus station on the site. It came into operation in 1929. The 35 plus vehicles for which Eastbourne was now responsible would be garaged at the junction of Beach Road and Royal Parade East (to the north-east of The Redoubt) built on land bought from the Eastbourne Ice & Cold Storage Company on 21st October 1924. In its original form, this garage, of brick with sliding doors, had a 110ft frontage with 82ft depth, offered 6,600 feet super, workshops, stores and a yard. The contract price was £6,984 and it was valued at £8,100 prior to its opening in 1927.

The company's first booking office in the resort was in a rented room at 4 Grand Parade in March 1923. Excursion work which came with the acquisition of Stretton's 'Cavendish Coach & Car Company' on 9th February 1925 brought with it his under-let office at 1 Cavendish Place and some nineteen months' use of his garage and parking lot in Bayham Road. Further parking facilities were obtained on 10th April 1929 with the assignment of Ernest Piper's leasehold premises, capable of housing at least two vehicles, in Langney Road – at £200 per annum. His 'Red Saloon' buses had been based there.

When Southdown purchased the business of Chapman & Sons (Eastbourne) Ltd on 1st March 1932, the deal did not include that firm's premises, which were initially retained to rent out as accommodation for coaches visiting Eastbourne. Chapman's relented, however, and Southdown gained title absolute to its large garage complex on 21st January 1933. This comprised Nos. 11 and 13 Susans Road and the entrance between them to the Victoria Garage, which was linked by an open yard to the Ceylon Garage with access to the parallel Cavendish Place. Further access to these garages was provided by a driveway from Pevensey Road. Numbers 32 and 34 Cavendish Place were also included in the purchase price of £16,000. The complex became Southdown's Eastbourne Coach Station.

With Pratt & Pearce's 'Little Vic Orange Coaches' came another booking office for excursions at 15 Grand Parade on 14th March 1933. Although not all, a very large proportion of Eastbourne-based coach traffic was now in Southdown hands and a clear distinction was made between premises. The Royal Parade Garage dealt exclusively with stage-carriage vehicles and the low-height Cavendish Place complex with the more glamorous side of the business.

A large extension and face-lift for the coach station was completed in 1953 which almost doubled the covered accommodation at 52 vehicles. The raising of the roof enabled double-deckers to gain access for the

Uckfield garage was of medium proportion and provided facilities for both Southdown and Maidstone & District vehicles coming into the town from the east. Two M&D vehicles flank No. 685 (285 AUF) a Leyland Leopard of 1963 on a sunny March day of the following year. The premises survived to become Stagecoach property.

first time, the booking office was improved including a glazed canopy outside it, and a new private hire office was constructed on the first floor. The premises were updated and extended once again in 1961.

The Royal Parade Garage was closed by NBC's Southdown in 1979; booking offices had started to go earlier, in 1968, with 1 Cavendish Place, and the Pevensey Road Bus Station followed suit. The Cavendish Place garage and offices complex, however, survives in Stagecoach ownership.

ALFRISTON

Alfriston, then a village of some 500 souls, got its first Southdown service of three return journeys each day from 1st June 1922 as an offshoot of service 27. On 17th November 1929, when this had become the 26 from Seaford to Berwick along the beautiful Cuckmore Valley, Southdown rented a small outstation garage in West Street, Alfriston. It survived until 1954; like Barns Green (qv) an unusual date for a closure at a time of increasing traffic.

CROWBOROUGH

For many years a no-man's-land between Southdown and Maidstone & District, thanks to the presence in the town of Beacon Motor Services, Crowborough came at last into the Southdown orbit on 16th September 1949 when the company gained control of the local firm. With it (on 24th September) and transferred to the newly-formed subsidiary of Southdown, Beacon Motor Services (Crowborough) Ltd came proprietor L. B. Atkins' garage at Homedale, Jarvis Brook, to the south of the town. A booking office for Beacon Tours was opened by Southdown at The Broadway on 25th May 1952. When, on 30th March 1954, the subsidiary was fully absorbed by Southdown, the Beacon Tours name was retained for wider use. The garage was closed by NBC's Southdown in 1980.

HAILSHAM

Inspector Vic Fugler was sent to Hailsham in September

1929 to take charge of Southdown's leasehold office 45 High Street which had opened the previous June. It was not until 1957, however, with traffic at its peak, that a garage to cover short workings was built in Mill Road and the office removed to the same location. The freehold was acquired on 25th October 1963, but both premises were closed by independent Southdown in 1987.

HEATHFIELD

Heathfield was first served by Southdown on 1st April 1920, when route 18 from Brighton Aquarium to the Royal Oak, Hawkhurst was established. Between 15th July and 2nd September 1953 an additional journey each day was made between Brighton and Heathfield Post Office. During that period a bus and crew were outstationed at Heathfield. It was the opening of service 91 from Eastbourne to Uckfield via Heathfield on 1st May 1927 which justified the provision of a freehold garage costing £1,314 in Tilsmore Road. Increased wartime traffic in the area necessitated the opening of an enquiry office at Langston's Cafe in the High Street on 10th February 1944. The standing area for the garage was increased in March 1949. It was closed by NBC's Southdown in 1971.

SEAFORD

Inherited from Worthing Motor Services 'Sussex Tourist Coaches' operation in 1915, was a booking office on the Esplanade, Seaford. It proved to be an important staging post in the later establishment of Southdown in Eastbourne (qv). The original office closed on 1st April 1923, in favour of a freehold premises valued at £1,200 at 5 Clinton Place and purchased on 13th November 1922.

Land in Richmond Road was leased to the company on 20th December 1924, and a garage designed by E. A. Chilton was erected upon the site. The later Dane Road garage was built upon a parcel of land purchased from the Southern Railway for £2,000 on 21st October 1931. As traffic on the south coast road and from Seaford itself generated more custom, a larger garage was built in 1957 at Claremont Road. The latter garage outlasted the office, which was closed by NBC's Southdown, and was leased by independent Southdown to 'The Old House Antiques'. Stagecoach continue to utilise the open-parking rights secured as part of that agreement.

UCKFIELD

Service 19 from Brighton Aquarium to Uckfield was in operation by June 1920 with four journeys each way daily. A garage was constructed on leasehold land acquired in Mill Road in December of that year. It was Southdown's meeting point with the East Surrey Traction Company and Autocar Services of Tunbridge Wells. With the population of Uckfield approaching 3,000, in 1931 a booking office was opened in the High Street. Freehold land on the west side of that street was purchased in February 1935 to provide a bus station for both Southdown and Maidstone & District vehicles. Both garage and bus station remained in use to be transferred to and utilised by Stagecoach.

UPPER DICKER

On 1st May 1929, service 92 – Eastbourne to Uckfield and Chailey – had its frequency increased and a three-hourly diversion to Upper Dicker added. This new short working justified the creation of an outstation in the hamlet that year. The rented accommodation lasted until 1967.

All the above locations, save three, may be found on the 1939 route map in Vol 1, pp4-5. Those missing from that official map are:
1. Leigh Park – one third of the way north between Havant and Rowlands Castle.
2. Eastergate – the number 64 sits on its position between Tangmere and Yapton.
3. Barns Green – located near Horsham on route 75 between Itchingfield and Coolham.
In addition Southdown supported its coaching activities with express and tours booking facilities in:

LONDON

Over the years from the middle 'twenties, many Southdown coach drivers were native or adopted Londoners, based in the capital and who built for themselves an honourable record of getting their passengers back to the metropolis come flood, snow, traffic jams or *Luftwaffe*. Southdown standards were nowhere better maintained.

London-based crews were controlled initially by an inspector on roadside stands. On 22nd January 1925, Southdown leased a ground floor room at 76 Lower Belgrave Street, Pimlico as its own booking office, but title was passed to the newly-established London Coastal Coaches Ltd on 12th August of that year. Nevertheless, it remained listed as a Southdown booking office until the opening of Victoria Coach Station on 10th March 1932. From that date until Southdown's identity was subsumed

A vehicle or a property? Rather in the same way that the exact nature of Southdown's hovercraft of 1962 was never satisfactorily established, so this 'enquiry office and waiting room' caused some doubt as to identity – save that it was once a Hastings trolleybus. Towed about to wherever it was required, its longest tour of duty was at Petersfield Square from 1953-55 pending the opening of a new building there.

under the National Express banner, the company maintained its own office at Victoria. As a back-up for its maintenance and refuelling requirements a licence for the use of the Chimes Garage, 253 Streatham High Road was obtained on 23rd September 1932.

With the business of Chapman & Sons (Eastbourne) Ltd came the tenancy of that firm's 17 Ebury Street, Buckingham Palace Road tours office. Owned by Hotel Belgravia Ltd, the company paid £300 per annum for the privilege of the address until, on 20th December 1937, it was given up in favour of the ground floor and basement of 27 Princes Street, Hanover Square. That office was manned until 15th February 1940, by which time a hoped-for quick ending to the war was clearly out of the question, and all tours and excursion work ground to a halt. Victoria Coach Station became an outsize National Fire Service depot during the blitz on London. Post World War II, from 1946 onwards, Southdown tours reservations in the capital were made through the agency of London Coastal Coaches Ltd, now at Victoria Coach Station, and seven other well-known travel service firms.

Between 1915 and the end of the BET era, Southdown acquired title to numerous other lease and freehold properties, ranging from cottages on land purchased for development to desirable residences in prime Sussex locations. It was company policy to rent the former to local crew members and provide accommodation for senior officers in the latter. Other residential properties held pending acquisition of neighbouring land were rented or sub-let to members of the public. From 1950 onwards, as prices began to rise, there was a noticeable increase in the company's efforts to gain the freehold of such properties, both as an insurance against changed plans and as investments. Changed plans there were; the company purchased land at places as varied as Ford Aerodrome, Middleton-on-Sea and the Tilsmore Estate at Waldron, to say nothing of the aborted 1915 garage site at Bognor Regis. Similarly, numerous rooms, offices and other commercial properties were let or underlet to various retail organisations pending planning decisions or eventual sale. There is nothing to suggest that Southdown made a loss on any of these transactions. The establishment of NBC's National Bus Properties put an end to such home-grown initiatives.

TICKETS

Second only to methods of numbering, tickets held great interest for Douglas Mackenzie the hobbyist. Thanks to him, a magnificent collection of specimen tickets survived as a record of Southdown's methods of fares-collection, each batch carefully annotated in his own hand. It included specimens from the Isle of Wight Express Motor Syndicate, Kent Motor Services and Western Motor Coaches (all undertakings which he had managed) and Brighton & Shoreham Tramways, Worthing Motor Omnibus Company, Brighton, Hove & Preston United Omnibus Company, London & South Coast Haulage Company and Hants & Dorset Motor Services, among others. The following information is culled largely from these notes and from his 'Reminiscences' in *Tweenus*, the Southdown house magazine.

On 1st April 1915, the ticket stock taken over by South Coast Motor Services Ltd (renamed Southdown on 2nd June 1915) included Isle of Wight values 8d, 1/4 and over; Sussex Motor Road Car and Worthing Motor Services tickets of all kinds; London & South Coast; and values over 6d of the Brighton, Hove & Preston United. From L&SCH came also a supply of charabanc tickets, which Southdown used for excursions from Brighton seafront, labelled *'Brighton Queen' Char-a-Banc: A. W. Ecclestone, Kings Head Garage, West St, Brighton and Middle Street.*

When 4°d tickets were required in 1916, the need was first met by using old Isle of Wight Express Motor Syndicate returns. It was intended to use only sage green tickets, but so many sets were found necessary that all the Isle of Wight stock was used, with hand-written stickers covering inappropriate wording (see also Vol. I, p38 for ticket system inherited from Arthur Davies of Bognor in 1915).

The initial inherited stock amended and used up, Southdown adopted a policy of having tickets printed for each route with named stages in order down each side – the so-called 'geographicals'. Tickets for 1d and values up to 1/- were of different colours but plain, whilst for °d values the lefthand side only was coloured. For other values of over 1/- a coloured stripe (not *red* from 1929-36; see below) was overprinted down the centre of the ticket. All return tickets had two coloured stripes, overprinted down the edges – a practice which would become the basic Southdown standard until 1939 and as late as 1971 for 'through' tickets. In effect, it proved extremely difficult to keep all the colours distinct and they were adjusted when they were found too similar; but generally conductors found the colours helpful and frequently saved them from issuing the wrong ticket.

World War I conditions however led to frequent alterations also in fares in 1916, so the company abandoned geographicals, for the remainder of the war, on all routes save the Worthing town services and used 'emergency' tickets instead. These featured numbered stages in sequence instead of naming the stops. Although the Norfolk Bridge over the River Adur at

Shoreham was closed to bus traffic at this time (see Vol 1, p35), an attempt was made to hold the existing custom by the issue of through tickets of all values. Tickets issued on the Brighton side of the bridge had, for administrative purposes, no stripes.

Whilst special tickets were designed for issue to the public from the Seaford and Newhaven offices, tickets for surviving excursions from the Kiosk at Brighton Aquarium were made up with books of 32, to match the capacity of the largest charabancs then employed.

In 1919, temporary single tickets were prepared for joint use with Maidstone & District on service 15 between Eastbourne and Hastings and, in January 1923, when return tickets were first issued between Brighton and Lewes, Maidstone & District – who were sharing service 18, Lewes to Hawkhurst – objected to the SMS style of return, so an unusual-for-Southdown perforated tear-in-half type was printed to meet the company's views.

Some interesting additional variations from the Southdown standard included the stock taken over with W. G. Dowle's 'Chichester & Summersdale Motor Services' in 1924, in which a different colour of ticket was issued for each conductor; the geographical tickets inherited from the Southsea Tourist Company on 28th February 1925, which listed so many stages that they were named on the best part of the back also, but which continued to be issued on ex-STC vehicles, by conductors still in their STC grey uniforms, until the stock was exhausted; and special tickets for use on Portsea Island for joint services with Portsmouth Corporation during a truce which began on 1st January 1930.

Through tickets with Hants & Dorset Motor Services Ltd, introduced following the curtailment at Fareham on 1st March 1926 of services which previously ran through from Portsmouth to Southampton and to Winchester, were raised in 1928 'following a change of traffic manager at Hants & Dorset' – which gives some idea of the early power of these officers – when two tickets for such a journey became necessary, one through and one transfer from the respective company according to direction of travel. They were updated once again in 1932 with the bold message on the reverse CHANGE BUSES AT FAREHAM. Similar arrangements were made with the Aldershot & District Traction Co Ltd for services beyond Petersfield and Horsham, although it was not unknown for the occasional printer's error on the obverse to tell passengers in that area also to 'change at Fareham' – impossible, need one add.

From 1929-36, a red stripe down the middle (instead of a red diagonal which earlier tended to conceal some of the stages) identified an exchange ticket – a ticket given to the conductor in *exchange* for a *transfer* ticket to make the complete single journey. Other colours were also used later. Such a facility existed *within* the company's area itself also. For instance, since 1925 there had been two routes through Portsmouth between North End and South Parade Pier, Southsea. A passenger arriving at the former on a Commercial Road-routed vehicle could transfer at North End to a Fratton Road route destination (or vise-versa) on a bus coming in from elsewhere, rather than wait at his original boarding point for a vehicle routed via his desired destination. From 1936, transfer tickets were marked with a prominent 'T' for issue at the point of boarding on the second bus.

In that year also, 'dated' return tickets were introduced, numbered down the edges 1-16 or 17-31, to be 'punched' in the appropriate box, the tickets being changed on the evenings of the 16th and 28/29/30th or 31st of each month.

Virtually all of the tickets mentioned so far were of Williamson's 'Punch' type, held in a wooden rack with clips and 'punched' or cancelled by a simple machine (on a strap over the conductor's tunic) which gave an audible 'ping' and collected the resultant small disc of coloured card within its metal case whence the discs could be retrieved and counted if necessary. In association with this type of machine, Southdown employed a method of operation different from other operators. The general practice elsewhere was to issue conductors with enough tickets to last one day, in no case less than 100 of a set value, then the next day

From 1915 until the last was phased out of use in May 1940, Southdown conductors were issued with Williamson Punch-type ticket machines and a wooden rack with coloured card tickets of various values held in place with spring clips. Illustrated is a conductor's waybill, a Williamson machine, several sets of tickets from that era and a pair of conductor's cancellation clippers used to indicate that a passenger had commenced his return journey.

The machine that gave its name to the TIM department at Portslade Works, the TIM (Ticket Issuing Machines) Major, winner of a Southdown comparative trial of machines in the late 'thirties. This TIM (or P-type) became the standard Southdown ticket machine in 1939, was used throughout World War II and survived until the last was phased out in the 'fifties. The machine printed its own tickets on plain paper rolls inserted as necessary by the conductor, sometimes en route.

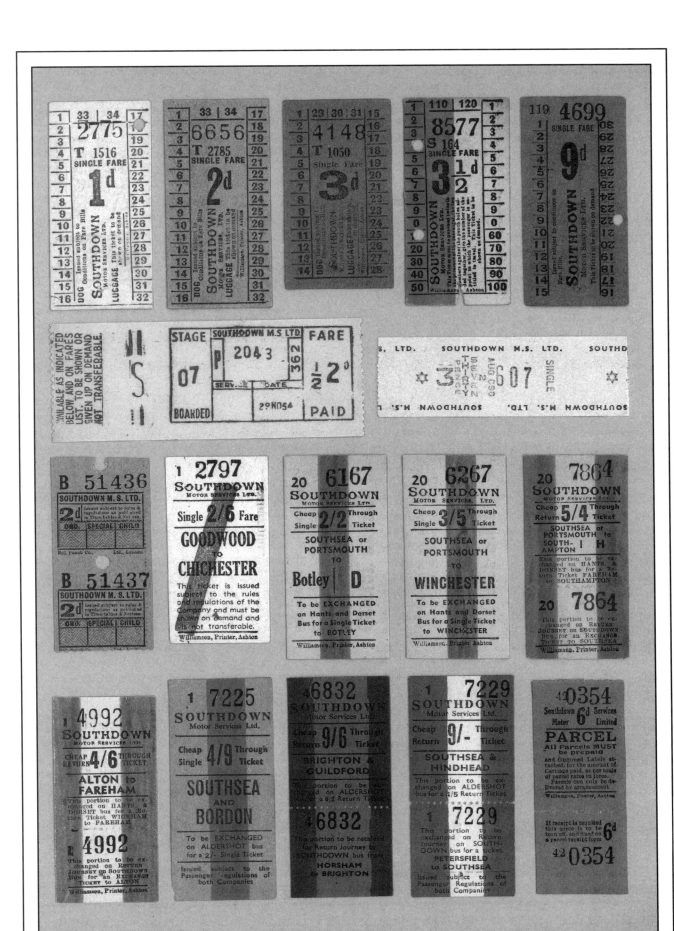

these were replenished from general stock with the next numbers *in store*, not the next *in sequence*. Thus a conductor could find No. 3399 followed by 2700 onwards, which meant he had to write out most of his values twice during the day, doubling also the work of the cashiers. Southdown, in contrast, issued tickets through to No. 9999 and then tried to ensure that each conductor went on to 0000, so that each followed on continuously (though the serial numbers might vary with different thousands). This made the work more simple and lowered the risk of errors. The disadvantage (for one there always is) was the need to keep a much larger stock of tickets.

From November 1934, experiments were made with Ticket Issuing Machines (TIM), which printed the tickets on a roll inserted into the machine, the conductor tearing them off against the serrated mouth of the metal front.

Trials with Setright machines were conducted in 1935, with tickets held in a clipboard and inserted one by one to the depth of an inch at the base for details dialled by finger and printed at the turn of a side-mounted handle. Further tests followed in 1938 with Setright 'Short Range' machines – a forerunner of the Speed Setright adopted twenty years later. By 1939, the choice of a replacement system had been narrowed to two; the TIM Major and the Clayton-Harris Verometer ticket printing machines. Six of the latter were tried out in October 1939, the ticket roll being inked by a typewriter ribbon. Unfortunately, fares over one shilling (5p) required two tickets – a shilling on the first (or top ticket) and pence on the next, making a combined vertical ticket 6° inches in height. In contrast, the horizontally printed TIM Major happily produced S – single, R – return, WR – workman's return and, only for some more expensive journeys MR – the quaintly-named 'married returns', not for husbands and wives but two tickets side by side to make up the fewer combinations of shillings and pence an individual ticket couldn't handle. The TIM Major proved the winner and became the Standard Southdown ticket-machine throughout World War II and for over a decade afterwards. As a back-up in the event of machine-failure, the inappropriately named Automaticket was issued to conductors, its details filled in by pencil and a carbon copy retained.

Once that decision had been made in 1939, increased members of 'emergency' punch tickets, rather than geographicals, were used so as to reduce the stock of tickets that would become useless when TIM machines were generally adopted. Because of World War II shortages, the last Williamson Punch tickets were both thinner and, at 2° inches, shorter than before. Many carried on the reverse the hopeful advice: Whar can I do on Holiday in Wartime? HAVE A RIDE ON A SOUTHDOWN BUS ! – somewhat out of step with the Ministry of War Transport's stern IS YOUR JOURNEY REALLY NECESSARY? poster campaign. With the exception of 'through' tickets, the final rack-type ticket was issued on 6th May 1940.

British phlegmatism reigned supreme on 14th May 1940 when, despite what was happening just across the channel in France, Lewes Races were held as usual – and Southdown used the occasion to try out a special green TIM ticket roll for the races traffic. It was not adopted.

Southdown did not employ 12-journey weekly tickets until July 1941, when the wartime coalition government agreed to pay the cost of transport above 3/- (15p) per week

in certain cases, usually where the passenger was deemed to be engaged upon essential 'war work'. To see what they looked like before its own was designed and issued, Southdown asked for and received specimens of such tickets for study from Midland Red, Northern General and Hants & Dorset, who already used them.

The last new TIM Major machines entered service in 1947. The following year the Speed Setright register began to be phased in, one depot at a time. In effect, this produced a slimmer, neater but more substantial version of the previous ticket, printed on a cream ground colour. Then, during 1949, Southdown purchased a batch of an effort to match it by TIM, the '3' series, such that by the end of 1952 there were four different types of ticket machine in regular use, known respectively as: TIM Majors (or P type), TIM Minors (A type), TIM '3' (N type) and Speed Setright registers. The latter had replaced the TIM equipment by the end of the decade.

In the late 'seventies and under National Bus Company control, Southdown withdrew the Speed Setright machines and replaced them with Almex one-man-operator equipment fitted next to the driving position. At the same time, Lamson Paragon ticket-issuing units continued in use at the company's booking offices. Then, under independent Southdown management in the second half of the 'eighties, Timtronic machines were phased in on all services. And when, in turn, Stagecoach took control, it extended their use by replacing the Almex Magnet system previously used on Portsmouth Citybus with Timtronic for use by 'Southdown Portsmouth', until divestment of Portsmouth operations in January 1991.

Return tickets at reduced fares had been issued on certain routes from the beginning in 1915; but at first only from the country to the big towns, to encourage country residents to 'come in' regularly for shopping. There had soon been an outcry from those passengers who wished to go from town into the country instead. So the next concession was to provide return ticket facilities from either end. After that, return fares for sections frequently used but not necessarily ending in a big town were introduced. Season Tickets followed soon after.

'Free Passes', issued to 'important' people like chairmen of licensing committees, police superintendents, company officers, family friends of the management, and others who surely didn't need them, preceded all and were inherited from a custom first set by the Sussex Motor Road Car Co Ltd in 1904. Parcel-carrying, which ceased in the 'seventies with conversion to one-man-operation under NBC, was undertaken on all routes and grew to such proportions by the early 'twenties that most Southdown saloons were fitted with roof luggage racks and ladders to reach them, so that more passenger room and less damage to seats resulted. By the 'thirties, internal racks above the seats had replaced them. Parcels on double-decked buses were always carried beneath the staircase. Separate series of parcel tickets were issued by parcel agents appointed at retail premises in practically every town and village served by Southdown over the years. Sign of the times, it was only the fear of what could happen to a momentarily unattended vehicle which caused the withdrawal of the facility when buses became one-man-operated.

The largest single section of this volume is devoted to a summary of Southdown vehicles operated from the foundation of the company in 1915 until the name 'Southdown Motor Services Ltd' was formally dispensed with in 1992. The accumulated total of vehicles purchased new, second-hand, acquired, transferred or otherwise numbered within the fleet at one time or another precludes the publication here of full details, so the categories listed are in each case under the following headings:

Fleet No.   Registration   Chassis   Body Type   Date New

Additional details on each individual vehicle are to be found in the joint PSV Circle and The Omnibus Society fleet history of Southdown 2PK 1 : Part 1 – 1915 to 1935 and 2PK 11 : Part 2 – 1936 to 1974, wherein may be found Company Body Numbers, Manufacturers Body Numbers, Body Changes, Notes on Engine Changes and other details, Dates of Withdrawal, Disposals and Subsequent Histories. From 1974 onward, the reader is directed to the annual Fleet List of Southdown (and other local operators) published by the Southdown Enthusiasts Club (original Edition 1954), and to the club's annual reviews from 1984 onwards.

When the company's first fleet was brought together in the difficult days of World War I, following the pooling of interests by Worthing Motor Services Ltd, the London & South Coast Haulage Co Ltd and the 'country' services of the Brighton, Hove & Preston United Omnibus Co Ltd, vehicles were referred to, for the purpose of identification, solely by their registration numbers. In the case of Worthing Motor Services Ltd, Douglas Mackenzie had established a rudimentary system of sequencing whereby the **letters** tended to be ignored and the vehicle identified by its registration **numbers** only. With that firm, any second-hand vehicle Mackenzie could lay hands upon was re-registered in Brighton (CD) or from his office retained at Ryde, Isle of Wight (DL) in such a way that the numbers rose upwards (rather than falling here and there), even if in leaps and bounds. That system had reached near perfection when Mackenzie discovered (in 1914) that the County of Armagh was prepared to grant him whole sequences of rising numbers (following their identification letters IB) to be taken up over a period of time.

Writing from memory in 1938, Douglas Mackenzie related:

'...it was obvious that such a system could not last for long, so that early in 1916 they were all properly [fleet] numbered, a separate ten being given to each make or class. At that time there were 56 buses altogether, and the numbers 51 to 59 were allotted to Tilling Stevens petrol-electrics. After the war petrol electrics were ordered in about equal quantities with Leylands, and the Tilling Stevens numbers went from 51 to 100, the Leylands started at 101 and went ultimately to 199, whilst further Tilling Stevens were numbered 201 to 257 ... We have .... been worried by the rolling stock that we took over from various small proprietors. At first they were numbered in the 300 [range], but afterwards they have been put in any odd places where we knew the numbers would not be reached by the class to which that 100 was allotted. At present, the numbers 1 upwards are 'Cubs', 1 to 5 being 14-seaters, 7 to 12 are 26-seaters, 13 to 26 are 20-seaters for one man working. Then 30 to 58 are 20-seater coaches on 'Cub' chassis. The double-deck buses were originally numbered from 801 to 975, but we then realised that we should want a lot more, and we had already allocated 1,000 upwards to 'Tiger' chassis, so as the 100s and 200s were then vacant, we started again with 100 in 1935 ...'

He then listed the classes in order and concluded: '... many of our staff may have wondered why we have not filled in all the back numbers. I think from this they will realise the enormous advantage of keeping classes in groups, so that directly you hear the number you can tell to what class it belongs. This prevents mistakes in ordering spare parts and generally facilitates routine work.'

What Douglas Mackenzie didn't mention in this account is something for which he should be given credit to add to his other achievements. Visiting the company's Portslade Works in early 1936, 'Knight-Errant', a correspondent for the Leyland Journal, noted that Southdown employed a novel system whereby the local authority cooperated in the provision of registration numbers for Southdown which allowed the last two digits to match the last two numbers of the vehicle's company fleet number. Had he really only just noticed? Attempts to do just that had been made at the outset of fleet numbering in 1916, thanks to Mackenzie's fascination with numbers. Several municipalities took this up later, but the fashion did not become widespread among territorial companies until the National Bus Company era commenced in 1969.

From 1915 until 1974, when a national revision of registration marks awarded to the Brighton Local Vehicle Licensing Office an additional range of letter-couplets, all buses and coaches purchased new by Southdown (which were all registered in the County Borough of Brighton) received combinations of CD or UF. In the early days a registration number was frequently re-issued to the company for a replacement vehicle (usually of a different make), but this had ceased by 1920. Prior to 1974, any Southdown vehicle displaying some other combination of letters was either a second-hand acquisition or a demonstrator still technically the property of its manufacturer.

In describing the type of body fitted to each vehicle, the following codes are used:

Numbers refer to seats fitted : on double-deckers the number before the diagonal refers to the top deck; the one after, the lower deck. A number following a + sign refers to the permitted number of standing passengers if this is greater than the 'norm'.

Prefix **letters** to seating capacity : **Suffix** letters to seating capacity

Ch	Charabanc	F	Front entrance
C	Coach	R	Rear entrance
ChB	Charabus (convertible)	RO	Rear entrance, open stair
B	Saloon (single-deck) bus	RD	Rear entrance with doors
O	Open top double-deck bus	C	Centre entrance
H	Highbridge double-deck bus	D	Dual door
L	Lowbridge double-deck bus		
CO	Convertible open-top double-decker		
F	Full-fronted front-engined vehicle		
DP	Dual-purpose (coach or bus)		

It is worth noting that until World War II in Southdown parlance, both written and spoken, any coach with a roll-top canvas centre-section was still called 'a charabanc', despite its fixed front and rear roof sections. Normally, in the rest of the trade, such a vehicle would have been called 'a sunsaloon' but, for the purpose of this summary, it is categorised as 'a coach'. During the same period, in a hang-over from the early 'twenties when each vehicle was identified by a small number in a circle on the front chassis frame, fleet numbers were referred to in Southdown work sheets and correspondence as 'ring-numbers' – although that format had long been discontinued. Failing that, they were called 'car numbers', for at Southdown a PSV was never, thanks to Douglas Mackenzie, a **bus**; it was always a **car**. In deference to him, a single-deck bus is here referred to as a **saloon**.

Cut down from its proud day when it provided transport for the Sussex Territorials 'motor dash' to Newhaven in 1909 – when it was a double-decker – Milnes Daimler DL 383, saw service with Southdown as the new company's delivery van. Anything from an excess of parcels to spare parts needed in a hurry became its province, for which it was provided with a longer rebuilt radiator. Despite its relegation to the works department, the vehicle was still graced with a fleet number – 83.

Initial fleet acquired at formation, 1st April 1915

(1) from Worthing Motor Services Ltd

FLEET No.	REG'N	CHASSIS	BODY	TYPE	DATE NEW
84	CD 338	Milnes Daimler	Harrington	Ch23	1905
85	CD 361	Milnes Daimler	WMS	C20F	?
82	DL 371	Milnes Daimler	WMS	C20F	?
81	DL 381	Milnes Daimler	WMS	C20F	?
	DL 382	Milnes Daimler	chassis only		?
83	DL 383	Milnes Daimler	bus used as van		?
49	DL 493	Leyland X	Dodson	023/16R O	1913
29	DL 621	Straker-Squire U	Dodson	018/18RO	1912
51	IB 551	Tilling-Stevens TS3	Newman	022/18RO	1914
52	IB 552	Tilling-Stevens TS3	Newman	022/18RO	1914
1	IB 701	Daimler CB	Strachan & Brown	B26R	1914
2	IB 702	Daimler CB	Strachan & Brown	B26R	1914
7	IB 707	Daimler CC	Dodson	018/18RO	c1913
9	IB 709	Daimler B	Hora	C30F	1914
10	IB 710	Daimler B	Hora	C30F	1914

Principally because these vehicles were known intimately by Mackenzie and Cannon, some of them incorporating personally-supervised amendments and improvements, they lasted longer in the service of Southdown than those from the other two constituent companies. All bar DL 382 were still in stock in 1916 to receive fleet numbers. In addition, a Humber platform lorry was taken into stock from this source (DL 404) and eleven assorted spare saloon and coach bodies. The Tilling-Stevens double-deckers were to survive with Southdown until 1928. Total value of the vehicles which were acquired from WMS was £9,003 16s 4d.

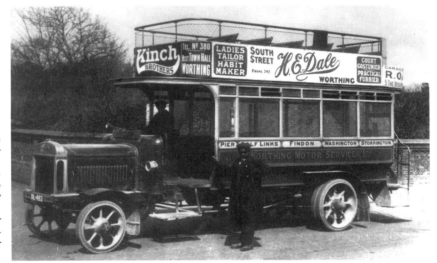

Worthing Motor Services passed on to Southdown DL 493 which became the company's No. 49. By the standards of the day, it was a big vehicle and, with no seats beside the driver, offered good cargo-carrying capacity as well. It was a Leyland X, the first association with the products of that manufacturer and historically important because, from that moment onward, the company was never without representatives of the make in the fleet – and, indeed, it far outnumbered all others. Number 49's open-topped bodywork was by Dodson.

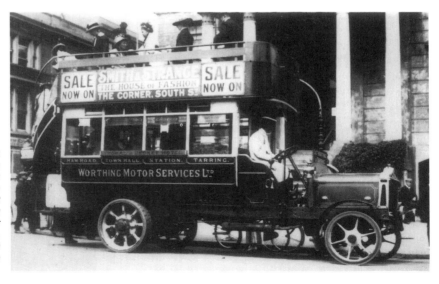

The Dodson lines are again evident, but on this occasion providing no protection for the driver, on Daimler CC IB 707, which became Southdown's No. 7. For the company to have retained six large Daimlers at this stage of World War 1, suggests that the military must have found something unacceptable about them. That speaks volumes for the efforts of the dedicated crew (whose names, remarkably we know – see Vol 1 p26) at the Ivy Arch garage, to keep them rolling in service; like this one pausing at Worthing Town Hall.

(2) from Brighton, Hove and Preston United Omnibus Co Ltd

	CD 397	Milnes Daimler	Dodson	C30F	1905
	CD 465	Milnes Daimler	Dodson	C30F	1906
	CD 476	Milnes Daimler	BH&P	C30F	1906
	CD 477	Milnes Daimler	Dodson	C30F	1906
	CD 495	Milnes Daimler	BH&P	C30F	1906
	CD 509	Milnes Daimler	Dodson	C30F	1906
27	CD 1441	Straker-Squire U	Dodson	C30F	1911
28	CD 1681	Straker-Squire U	Dodson	C30F	1912
	CD 2570	Daimler	?	Ch11	1914
	CD 2816	Daimler	Dodson	Ch11	1914
	LE 5408	Daimler	Dodson	Ch11	1914

In addition, the new company was obliged to take a 32-seat saloon body, a 25-seat coach body, six 30-seat coach bodies, six torpedo charabanc bodies and the following horse-drawn vehicles: purchased by BH&PUOC from F. J. Mantell, July 1914 – Sixteen landaus, Licence No. 106, 174, 198, 209, 280, 333, 376, 379, 388, 429, 430, 458, 492, 494, 496, 525; two victorias – 130 and 169; three horse charabancs – 21, 45, 46; two 16-seat charabancs, 'The Queen', No. 42; 'The Little Wonder', No. 13; three 24-seat charabancs, 'The Queen' (sic) No. 6; 'the Old Times; No. 18 and 'The Skylark', No. 28 – plus one four-horse coach (unlicensed) and one light covered van: from Collison, August 1914 – one horse-charabanc. Tractive effort for these vehicles was to be provided by 19 horses at £17. 10s 0d each (£17.50p). A Unic and two Darracq taxis completed the contribution.

Whilst the Milnes Daimler had gone within the year and the Daimler Unic and Darracq vehicles were sold almost immediately, the horse-drawn carriages were used throughout the 1916 season by Southdown. And when the mechanically-propelled vehicles came to be fleet-numbered in 1916, only the two Straker-Squires remained to represent the BH&PUOC contingent. Total value of vehicles acquired from BH&PUOC was £5,262 10s 6d.

Straker Squire U, No. 28 (CD 1681) was one of Brighton, Hove & Preston United's contributions to the new company – the Brighton to Worthing route coming under the category of an appropriate 'country service'. The sophisticated glazed and enclosed coachwork on this chain-driven U-type, almost identical to those employed by WMS, suggests that Dodson the builder was in no way constrained by Mackenzie's claim to have invented the concept of the slipper-style elevated seating. Whatever, he got his hands on the BH&PU examples.

The scramble for replacement war-time vehicles led to some marginally obscure makes entering the fleet. CD 3326, with an enamelled St. Andrews cross on the radiator, was a Caledon 4-tonner with second-hand Brush bodywork. We are fortunate that a friend with a camera caught this crew relaxing at Lewes on 8th October 1915 because the vehicle didn't remain around long enough to receive a fleet number – and the same applied to three more of the same manufacture also ordered that same year.

(3) from London and South Coast Haulage Co Ltd

93	CD 2031	Durham Churchill 2 ton	Harrington	Ch18	1914
94	CD 2155	Durham Churchill 2 ton	Harrington	Ch22	1914
95	CD 2485	Durham Churchill 3 ton	Harrington	Ch27	1914
96	CD 2537	Durham Churchill 2 ton	Harrington	Ch22	1915
	CD 3089	Straker-Squire CO2	Brighton MC Works	B35R	1915
	LH 8977	Leyland 806A/S	Cremmen	B26R	1913
	LN 9931	Leyland 806A/S	Cremmen	B26R	1907
	?	Daimler CD *	?	?	?

Additionally there were: purchased from William and Anne Eccleston, July 1914; four Fiat 24/40 chassis, one fitted with lorry body, plus four torpedo bodies to fit; one Fiat 16/24 chassis with touring car body. From French's Garage & Motor Works Ltd – one Panhard 11/13 van. The schedule also included one Star 10/12 van and one Overland with unidentified body, plus five saloon bodies to fit B and CD type Daimlers, and one new torpedo body to fit the same make. The collection was completed by two 11-seater torpedo charabanc bodies. *The unidentified Daimler CD chassis was probably fitted with saloon bodywork by Brush or Dodson – a survivor from the attentions of the military requisition teams of World War I. Ironically, by far the largest collection of spares from the BH&PUC source was for Daimlers. Only the four Durham-Churchill charabancs remained in service to receive Southdown fleet numbers in 1916. Total value of vehicles acquired from L&SCHC was £8,790 4s 1d, making a grand total of £23,056 10s 11d for the fleet at foundation. LH 8977 is illustrated in Vol 1, p29.

Various new vehicles, purchased 1915

	CD 3321	Ensign-Tylor	Harrington	Ch27	1915
22	CD 3322	McCurd	BH&P	B36R	1915
23	CD 3323	Romar	BH&P	Ch32	1915
24	CD 3324	Romar	BH&P	C30F	1915
25	CD 3325	Romar	BH&P	C30F	1915
	CD 3326	Caledon 4 ton	Brush	B32R	1915
21	CD 3327	McCurd	Dodson	C30F	1915
	CD 3328	Caledon 4 ton	Birch	B32R	1915
	CD 3329	Ensign-Tylor	Harrington	Ch32	1915
30	CD 3330	Straker-Squire COT/5	Beadle	B29R	1915
31	CD 3531	Straker-Squire COT/5	Dodson	C30F	1915
34	CD 3534	Straker-Squire COT/5	Dodson	C30F	1915
53	IB 553	Tilling-Stevens TS3	Newman	O22/18RO	1915
	IB 611	Ensign-Dorman	WMS	C30F	1915
41	IB 612	Straker-Squire CF	Hora	C30F	1915
42	IB 613	Straker-Squire CF	Hora	C30F	1915
	IB 614	Caledon 4 ton	fitted with van body		1915

Deprived of those vehicles manufactured by companies whose products were deemed by the War Office to be suitable for military use, the fledgling company was obliged to cast about for less-vulnerable purchases. The process had already been started by Worthing Motor Services Ltd who had paid the £408 6s 8d deposit on the two McCurd chassis, which were now delivered to Southdown and taken into account as part of the agreed value of WMS at the formation. The pair proved rather more durable than the three Ensigns (two with Tylor engines, one with Dorman) and three Caledons – the latter firm also a victim of the war, Scottish Commercial Cars Ltd of Glasgow, previously a dealer and unable to obtain further supplies of Commer chassis. Both types had proven unsatisfactory within a year of entering service. Serving with the McCurds in the 1916 introduction of fleet numbering were three Romars and five dependable Straker-Squires. All were purchased as chassis plus engine in order to use the large collection of spare bus and coach bodies inherited by the company and, in the case of Tilling-Stevens No. 53, to be bodied elsewhere by Newman. The latter far-outlasted its contemporaries; retiring in 1929.

Various second-hand vehicles purchased 1915

3	IB 703	Daimler CB	Harrington	Ch27	?
8	DU 2789	Daimler CC	?	Ch24	?
	B 2113	Leyland X	?	Ch 27	?
	KT 5291	Leyland X	Dodson	B31R	?
26	CD 3083	Straker-Squire CO	Birch	Ch26	1915

Indicative of the 'needs-must' policy adopted by the company at this early stage is that three makes are represented in these piecemeal purchases; that charabancs were not ideal for the stage carriage work which awaited them; and that the Straker-Squire CO (range introduced that year) can have been the only one with few 'miles on the clock'.

Acquired from Arthur Davies, Bognor, May 1915

97	BK 2237	Commer WP1	Bayley	Ch27
98	BK 2245	Commer WP1	Bayley	Ch27
99	BK 2299	Commer WP1	Bayley	Ch27

Purchased primarily with an eye upon expansion westward and an eventual 'recapture' of Portsmouth for Mackenzie and Cannon, Davies 'Motor Garage' was acquired in 1915. In addition to the three Commer charabancs, the deal involved an additional charabanc body – which was not used by Southdown – a licence for a stage carriage service from Bognor to Portsmouth, via Chichester (not made use of until 4 April 1916) and the services of Arthur Davies as Bognor manager. For further details see Volume I pp 32, 38.

New vehicles, purchased 1916

32	CD 3532	Straker-Squire COT/5	Dodson	B31R	1916
33	CD 3533	Straker-Squire COT/5	Harrington	Ch32	1916
35	CD 3535	Straker-Squire COT/5	Harrington	Ch32	1916
36	CD 3536	Straker-Squire COT/5	BH&P	C30F	1916
37	CD 3537	Straker-Squire COT/5	Dodson	C30F	1916
	IB 615	Caledon	Dodson	B31R	1916

Walter Flexman French was the common factor which enabled Southdown, Bournemouth & District and The Maidstone & District Motor Services Ltd to obtain Straker-Squire chassis during the difficult times of World War I. The Caledon was the residue of an order for four of that manufacture. It saw even less service with Southdown than the rest of the batch.

Second-hand vehicles, purchased 1916

	IB 708	Daimler B	Harrington	Ch32	
	?	Daimler B	Maule	B32R	
92	IB 805	Scout	Dodson	C30F	

The purchase of Daimlers in the midst of World War I was a rarity indeed. IB 708 was probably acquired and re-registered by Mackenzie in August 1916 and the unidentified Daimler was acquired from the Cleveland Omnibus Company of Middlesbrough but probably snapped up by the War Department soon afterward. The chassis of the Scout was transferred in April 1916 from Wilts & Dorset Motor Services Ltd in which Mackenzie and Cannon had acquired an interest.

Acquired from Thomas Tilling Ltd, Brighton, January 1917

54	IB 614	Tilling-Stevens TS3	Tilling	Ch22	1913
55-7	IB 615-7	Tilling-Stevens TS3	Tilling	Ch27	1914
58	IB 618	Tilling-Stevens TS3	Tilling	Ch27	1916

These charabancs were rebodied, and re-registered as above by Mackenzie upon acquisition, having previously been LH 8926, LN 7126, LH 8885, LP 9667 and LH 9038 respectively. In December 1918 the chassis were re-registered again to IB 854-8 respectively – and yet again in 1919 to CD 4854-8. As such, they survived to be fitted with pneumatic tyres in 1927/8. LH 8926 is illustrated in Vol 1, p73

Acquired from Crosville Motor Services Ltd, Chester in January/February 1918

59	IB 619	Tilling-Stevens TS3	Tilling	O18/18RO	1914
60	IB 620	Tilling-Stevens TS3	Tilling	O18/18RO	1914

Originally registered LH 9432 and M 5731, these were previously Nos. 2 and 1 in the Crosville fleet, the former having been originally intended by Tillings for use in London. At the end of 1918 they were re-registered IB 859/60, and again (in August 1919) to CD 4859 and (December 1920) to CD 4860, respectively.

Southdown was still looking for buses, wherever they could be found, in 1918. This Tilling-Stevens TS3 is an historically interesting one in that when Crosville Motor Services Ltd purchased it from Ward Brothers of Crewe – in whose livery it is seen here – it was Crosville's first double-decker, suitably given fleet number 1 by that company. Southdown acquired both it and a sister TS3 as being representatives of a make increasing in number within the ranks. It was re-registered IB 620 and given the fleet number 60 by Southdown.

Acquired from George Town, Worthing, November 1918

26	CD 3083	Straker-Squire CO		O22/18RO	1915
91	LN 4588	LGOC X type	Dodson	O18/18RO	1910
90	LN 9967	LGOC X type	Dodson	O18/18RO	1910

The Straker-Squire chassis was previously in the Southdown fleet (as No. 26) in 1915. Southdown fitted it with the body ex 51 (IB 551), but it was retired at Hove the following year. Town had acquired the X types from the London General Omnibus Company where they had been Nos X59 and X50 respectively. Two spare bodies, one a double-decked open-topper and the other a charabanc were included in the purchase.

At the time the World War I Armistice was being negotiated, Southdown were engaged in humbler talks with George Town for the purchase of his Worthing local services and the three vehicles he employed to maintain them. This one, LN 9967 which became No. 90 in the company fleet, was one of a pair of London General Omnibus Company X-type double-deckers involved in the transaction which followed. The X-type had been designed as LGOC's first standard bus and was the forerunner of the more famous LGOC B-type.

Leyland N vehicles, 1919-21

101	CD 3531**	Leyland N	Bayley	Ch32	1919
102	CD 3532**	Leyland N	Brighton MC Works	B35R	1919
103	CD 3533**	Leyland N	Dodson	B31R	1919
104	CD 3534**	Leyland N	Harrington	Ch32	1919
105	CD 3535**	Leyland N	Dodson	B31R	1919
106	CD 3536**	Leyland N	Harrington	Ch32	1919
107	CD 3537**	Leyland N	Dodson	O22/20RO	1919
108	CD 5108	Leyland N	BH&P	B32R	1919
109	CD 349*	Leyland N	Bayley	Ch27	1919
110	CD 5110	Leyland N	Harrington	Ch32	1919
111	CD 5111	Leyland N	Harrington	Ch32	1919
112	CD 5112	Leyland N	Dodson	B--R	1919
113	CD 5113	Leyland N	Harrington	Ch32	1919
114	CD 5114	Leyland N	Hora	C30F	1919
115	CD 5115	Leyland N	Dodson	B31R	1919
116	CD 5116	Leyland N	lorry body		1919
117	CD 5117	Leyland N	lorry body		1919
118	CD 5118	Leyland N	Dodson	O22/20RO	1919
119	CD 5119	Leyland N	Dodson	B31R	1919
120	CD 5120	Leyland N	Harrington	Ch32	1919
121	CD 5121	Leyland N	Harrington	Ch32	1920
122	CD 5122	Leyland N	Harrington	Ch32	1920
123	CD 5123	Leyland N	Harrington	Ch32	1920
124	CD 5124	Leyland N	Harrington	Ch32	1920
125	CD 5125	Leyland N	Harrington	B33R	1920
126	CD 5126	Leyland N	Harrington	B33R	1920
127	CD 5127	Leyland N	Dodson	O44RO	1921
128	CD 5128	Leyland N	Harrington	Ch32	1921
129	CD 5129	Leyland N	Goodman	B36-	1921
130	CD 5130	Leyland N	Harrington	Ch32	1921

*   re-registered CD 5109 in February 1920
**   re-issued registration numbers

Soon after the Armistice had brought World War I to a close, Douglas Mackenzie took it upon himself to visit the Lancashire town of Leyland, home of the eponymous commercial vehicle manufacturer. There he was shown plans for the mass production of a worm-driven version of the Leyland M lorry, suitable for passenger-carrying work. Impressed, he placed an order for an initial thirty – a very large number for those days – to be delivered as they became available. He then travelled to Maidstone and visited the Tilling-Stevens factory, placing a similar order for that firm's well-tried TS3 model (qv). That done, he then informed his board of directors. Their reactions go unrecorded. The Leyland N was powered by a reliable 36-40hp 4-cylinder engine giving an admitted top speed of 16 mph. The wheels were cast steel tubular spoked and a feature of the pressed steel chassis was the adjustable truss rods beneath. For the first time a small supplementary pump recorded on the dash the oil level in the sump. When deliveries of the initial Leyland order were complete, half of the chassis had been fitted with charabanc bodywork – a fair indication of the weather prospects at the time and the popularity of the open vehicle. This is in marked contrast with Southdown's western neighbour Hants & Dorset, all of whose Leyland N chassis finished up with saloon-bus bodywork – all, save one, Christopher Dodson's CD-19 type. Only five of these were represented in this Southdown batch, although – unusually – there were three double-deckers by that coachbuilder, on a chassis intended for single-deck bodywork. There was much rebodying of these vehicles in the 'twenties, some with open-topped double-decks, and all were refitted to run on pneumatics towards the end of that decade.

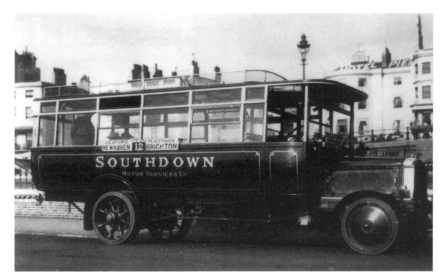

The first substantial post-war order placed by Mackenzie went to Leyland Motors for thirty of that manufacturer's reliable N-type – a worm-axle driven version of the already-successful M-type lorry. Delivered in June 1919, No. 102 (CD 3532) was originally fitted with BMC bodywork. In this view at the Aquarium, Brighton MC on 21st October 1922, the vehicle is fitted with Christopher Dodson's standard CD19-type 31-seat saloon – at that time one of the best-selling bodies in the provinces. The front disc wheels are rather unusual.

The lines of the original Harrington 32-seat charabanc bodywork are still evident on No. 104 (CD 3534), rebuilt in 1925 with armchair seats, a full set of pneumatic tyres and a remarkably well-designed covered top. The problem of what to do with the spare wheel had been solved by Harrington at the time by incorporating it boldly into the design. This proud display was at Eastbourne's Pevensey Road premises – the office would open at 9.15am on Sundays, but don't expect the first bus to leave on service until 10.00am.

Steine Street, Brighton during the railway strike in September 1919; and Southdown got the message about sending regular coaches to London. Number 110 (CD 5110) is among the vehicles providing a necessary service to the capital for otherwise stranded passengers. They are survivors, they have lived through the worst war in history, and seem pleased to pose for the camera. The large gentleman with cane and attache case in the foreground is thought to be F. J. Mantell. The vehicle's coachwork is again by Harrington.

Daimler vehicles, 1919

15	CD 1750	Daimler Y		Lorry	?
4	CD 3323	Daimler Y	Maule	B32R	?
5	CD 3325	Daimler Y	Hora	C30F	?
6	CD 3326	Daimler Y	Hora	C30F	?
13	CD 3391	Daimler Y	Dodson	B31R	?
14	CD 5214	Daimler Y	Dodson	B31R	?
12	CD 2485	Daimler W	Bayley	Ch27	?
11	CD 3321	Daimler B	WMS	C30F	?

All eight chassis are likely to have been ex-army vehicles released by the War Department. Number 12 is known to have come to Southdown from the Abdulla Cigarette Company and 13-5 via the District Car Company. The registrations of 4-6, 11/2 had been transferred from earlier vehicles. Numbers 11-3 were re-registered CD 6011-3 in November 1920 and 15 to CD 5215 in April 1920.

Tilling-Stevens TS3, 1919-20

61	IB 861*	Tilling-Stevens TS3	Tilling	O23/18RO	1919
62	IB 862*	Tilling-Stevens TS3	Harrington	Ch32	1919
63	IB 863*	Tilling Stevens TS3	Harrington	Ch32	1919
64	IB 864*	Tilling Stevens TS3	Harrington	Ch32	1919
65	IB 865*	Tilling-Stevens TS3	Birch	B32R	1919
66	IB 866*	Tilling-Stevens TS3	LGOC	O22/18RO	1919
67	IB 867*	Tilling Stevens TS3	Harrington	Ch32	1919
68	CD 4868*	Tilling-Stevens TS3	Dodson	O18/18RO	1919
69	CD 4869	Tilling-Stevens TS3	Harrington	Ch32	1919
70	CD 4870	Tilling-Stevens TS3	Dodson	O18/RO	1919
71	CD 4871	Tilling-Stevens TS3	WMS	C30F	1919
72	CD 4872	Tilling Stevens TS3	Dodson	O18/18RO	1919
73	CD 4873	Tilling Stevens TS3	Harrington	Ch32	1919
74	CD 4874	Tilling-Stevens TS3	Dodson	O18/18RO	1919
75-7	CD 4875-7	Tilling Stevens TS3	Birch	B29F	1920
78-80	CD 4878-80	Tilling-Stevens TS3	Birch	B29F	1920
81	CD 1581	Tilling Stevens TS3	Harrington	Ch32	1920
82	CD 5642	Tilling Stevens TS3	Harrington	Ch32	1920
83	CD 1583	Tilling-Stevens TS3	Brush	B30F	1920
84	CD 2184	Tilling-Stevens TS3	Brush	B30F	1920
85	CD 2485	Tilling-Stevens TS3	Brush	B30F	1920
86-90	CD 5586-90	Tilling-Stevens TS3	Harrington	Ch32	1920

* re-registered CD 4861-7 in 1919/20

These vehicles represent the result of Mackenzie's unauthorised visit to Maidstone after World War I, following his similar trip to Leyland to order the same number of Leyland N chassis (qv). The TS3 was the classic petrol-electric chassis, its transmission system controlled by two levers each side of the steering column. The purpose of this was to make the vehicle easier to drive – the effect similar to today's automatic transmission. As with most innovations, there was a disadvantage – in this case the extra weight caused by the additional dynamo and motor. Progress tended to be just that little more noticeably ponderous when pneumatics were fitted and speeds legally increased to 20 mph.

That this vehicle was built with opening doors on the offside initially – at least until the panelling stage of construction – may be seen from the numerous pieces of beading in the appropriate shape and proportion (for reason, see caption for No. 64 overleaf). When this photograph was taken in 1926, Tilling-Stevens No. 67 had been re-shod with pneumatic tyres and long since re-registered from IB 867 to CD 4867 – the Brighton local authority having come into line with Mackenzie's registration requirements from 1919 onwards.

The ultimate development of the enclosed Mackenzie slipper is carried by No. 62 (IB 862) – although in those days of multi-body swaps, the original body is noted as a 32-seat Harrington charabanc. The chassis is one of the order placed with Tilling-Stevens in 1919 for 30 vehicles to balance the similar order for Leylands. It is one of the unspectacular but reliable petrol-electric TS3 models. The photograph is a Southdown official one, with the vehicle posed beside a list of company telephone numbers.

Tilling-Stevens TS3 No. 64 (originally IB 864, but here re-registered CD 4864) fitted with its original Harrington 32-seat charabanc coachwork. Originally, such charabancs were equipped with hinged doors on both sides of the bodywork, but legislation following a series of accidents nationwide had decreed that all those upon the offside should be permanently screwed shut where already fitted and not included in future building. If the canvas were folded properly, the cape-cart hood could be raised in minutes.

Second-hand vehicles, purchased 1920

48	CD 5648	Tilling-Stevens TS3	LGOC	O18/18RO	?
49	CD 349*	Tilling-Stevens TS3	LGOC	O18/18RO	?
50	CD 2150	Tilling-Stevens TS3	lorry		?
16-8	CD 5216-8	Daimler Y	Dodson	B31R	?
19	CD 2719	Daimler Y	lorry		?
20	CD 5220	Daimler Y	Hora	C30F	?
21-2	CD 5221-2	Daimler Y	Dodson	B31R	?
23	CD 3023	Daimler Y	lorry		?
24-6	CD 5224-6	Daimler Y	Dodson	B31R	?
150	PA 9572	Leyland X	Dodson	O23/16RO	?

* re-issue of registration number

Second-hand purchases of chassis of which it is recorded that 16 was acquired from the District Car Company, 17-8 from Walter Flexman French's United Service Transport Company, 21/4/5 and 48-50 from Brownwood Garage Ltd, and 19, 20/2/3 from the British Automobile Traction, Maidenhead branch. Number 150 was in service for less than one year.

Among fifteen second-hand chassis purchased by Southdown at various times in 1920 was No. 20 (CD 5220), a Daimler Y. This came to the company, with two others, from the British Automobile Traction Company's Maidenhead office whose operations founded the Thames Valley Traction Company. Originally fitted with a 30-seat Hora coach body, it is instead here equipped for stage-carriage work with an example of Dodson's CD19 type saloon bus body to seat 31 passengers and driver.

Leyland G7, 1921-26

131-132	CD 6541-2	Leyland G7	Dodson	B31R	1921
133	CD 6543	Leyland G7	Dodson	O44/RO	1921
134-135	CD 7044-5	Leyland G7	Harrington	Ch27	1921
136-137	CD 7136-7	Leyland G7	Tilling	Ch26C	1921
138-141	CD 7138-41	Leyland G7	Tilling	O27/24RO	1921
142-144	CD7142-4	Leyland G7	Harrington	Ch30C	1921
145	CD 7145	Leyland G7	Harrington	B33D	1921
146-148	CD 7723-5	Leyland G7	Harrington	Ch30C	1923
150-152	CD 7720-2	Leyland G7	Harrington	Ch30C	1923
153-156	CD 7713-6	Leyland G7	Tilling	O27/24RO	1923
157-159	CD 7717-9	Leyland G7	Tilling	O27/24RO	1923
160-163	CD 8060-3	Leyland G7	Harrington	Ch30C	1923
164-165	CD 8064-5	Leyland G7	Tilling	O27/24RO	1923
166-167	CD 8376-7	Leyland G7	Harrington	B37R	1924
168-170	CD 8378-80	Leyland G7	Harrington	Ch30	1924
171-174	CD 8381-4	Leyland G7	Harrington	Ch30	1924
175-176	CD 8900-1	Leyland G7	Harrington	Ch30	1924
177	CD 9877	Leyland G7 special	Harrington	Ch30R	1925
181-184	CD 9881-4	Leyland G7 special	Harrington	Ch30R	1925
181-184	CD 9881-4	Leyland G7 special	Harrington	Ch30R	1925
192-194	UF 92-4	Leyland G7 special	Harrington	Ch30R	1925
195-199	UF 995-9	Leyland G7	Tilling	O27/24 RO	1926

In February 1920, Leyland decided to supersede the passenger-carrying N chassis in production with the G range. With a wheelbase of 15ft 1°in and chassis length of 23ft 7°in, the G5 was 5 inches shorter than the N in both measurements. The G7 was correspondingly larger: Southdown already being Southdown, the G7 chassis was selected as the standard for the next five years. From 1921, Tilling gained the ascendancy as the firm to be entrusted with the construction of double-decked bodywork from new. All were refitted with pneumatic tyres and in 1928, a minor re-bodying programme shared between Tilling and Short Brothers added a further nine 51-seat double-deckers to the batch – Nos 131-5/45/53-5. CD 7045 in later double-decked form is illustrated in Colour Section 1.

Dodson is again the builder of the major part of this open-topped bodywork fitted to No. 133 (CD 6543) of 1921. The forward part of the structure has been extended by Southdown to incorporate a large goods space beside the driver, thus creating an example of that mixed-blessing – a milk-churn bus. Service 14, and its variations to Hurstpierpoint was a suitable route for such a capability for this Leyland G7 – a development of the previous N type, with longer wheelbase and chassis.

Leyland G7 No. 141 (CD 7141) awaiting departure for Lindfield at Brighton Aquarium on the 18th November 1922. The vehicle carries a Tilling body which for many years was a classic, built under licence also by other firms – wider window-frames necessitating the provision of a shorter bay. That, and the Tilling-style beading would be thus featured in work carried out by such firms as Brush and Short Brothers, as well as the Tilling company's own factory at Wren Road, Camberwell. Southdown too would be long associated with it.

Acquired from W. C. Taylor (White Heather Motor Services) Brighton, August 1921

7	CD 6524	Daimler Y	Harrington	Ch27	?
30	CD 6353	Thornycroft J	Harrington	Ch32	?
31	CD 5379	Thornycroft J	Harrington	Ch28	?
32	CD 4711	AEC Y	Harrington	Ch27	?
33	CD 4710	AEC B	Harrington	Ch27	?
149	CD 5260	Leyland X4	?	Ch32	?

The dates of the original construction of the vehicles remain unknown, largely because the majority would seem to have been refurbished ex-War Department chassis. Most, if not all, of the coachwork was built locally at Hove between 1919 and 1921. The Diamler survived in Southdown service until 1929, the others went much earlier.

Something of a rarity in the Southdown fleet. Among the vehicles acquired with the business of White Heather Motor Services of Brighton in 1921 were two AECs; both fitted with rather more usual Harrington charabanc bodies. No. 32 (CD 4711) was an AEC 'Y' model, the other a 'B'. Allowing for the fact that AEC and Daimler bits and pieces were interchangeable and liberally applied to either during post-war rebuilds, an AEC radiator on a Southdown was a most unusual sight at any stage of the company's history.

Tilling-Stevens 3A, 1922-6

91-6	CD 6891-6	Tilling-Stevens TS3A	Tilling	O27/24RO	1922
97-100	CD 6897-900	Tilling-Stevens TS3A	Tilling	Ch26	1922
201-2	CD 6834-5	Tilling-Stevens TS3A	Tilling	O27/24RO	1923
203-12	CD 7703-12	Tilling-Stevens TS3A	Tilling	O27/24RO	1923
213-6	CD 8013-6	Tilling-Stevens TS3A	Tilling	O27/24RO	1923
217-24	CD 8417-24	Tilling-Stevens TS3A	Tilling	O27/24RO	1924
225	CD 9225	Tilling-Stevens TS3A	Tilling	O27//24RO	1925
240-1	CD 9640-1	Tilling-Stevens TS3A	Tilling	Ch26C	1925
242-7	UF 42-7	Tilling-Stevens TS3A	Tilling	O2724RO	1925
248-57	UF 748-57	Tilling-Stevens TS3A	Tilling	O27/24RO	1926

Featuring minor modifications to the transmission system, the TS3A model was, for all intents and purposes, a continuation of the TS3 series of open-topped double-deckers, saloons and charabancs, purchased as part of the company's policy decision, at this stage, to keep a balance between Leyland and Tilling-Stevens additions to the fleet. The large number of double-deckers represented reflects the rapidly increasing network of routes and the related weight of custom. Numbers 95-6/9 were severely damaged in the garage fire at Bognor in July 1923. The chassis frames of all three were retrieved, restored, re-engined and re-bodied with Tilling 51-seat open-topped coachwork; and re-entered service the following year as CD 8295-6/9.

A full charm of schoolgirls has been recruited to enact the role of passengers for this substantial-looking Tilling-Stevens TS3A parked near Chichester Cathedral in 1922. The poses, from coy to impish, look remarkably like those of today. The conductor's precarious position reminds us that there were three steps to go before one reached floor level and the foot of the staircase – one really had to watch what one was doing, those days. The bus is Tilling-bodied No. 94 (CD 6894).

Vulcan VSD, 1922

171-4	CD 7101-4	Vulcan VSD	Harrington	Ch18F	1922

An unusual purchase new by Southdown was that of a batch of small capacity vehicles built by Vulcan Motor & Engineering Co of Southport, Lancs. That manufacturer enjoyed something of a boom at this time, particularly with orders from seaside operators. The VSD's comparatively low-loading configuration was seen as appropriate for less-agile tourists on short-distance excursions.

To cope with small groups of middle-class customers wishing to make up their own parties, Southdown made what at first was an unusual purchase for the company – a quartet of Vulcan VSD chassis, fitted from new with pneumatic tyres on the front wheels only. Their low-loading characteristics made them also popular on short excursions for the elderly. All four were fitted with Harrington 18-seat bodies – as No. 172 (CD 7102) demonstrates.

Vulcan 2T, 1923

176-8	CD 8106-8	Vulcan 2T	Vulcan	B21F	1923

At two tons apiece, the Vulcan 2T was slightly heavier than the VSD model and therefore capable of seating 21 passengers on more taxing stage-carriage work over country roads, many of which were still unmetalled (not yet coated with tarmacadam). The saloons were standard Vulcan products throughout, including the bodywork, which featured the usual 'baker's -van' oval window behind the driver's off-side door.

Acquired from Albert F. Trickey ('Sapphire'), Birdham, Chichester, June 1923

175	BP 7485	Vulcan VSD	C. F. Rymer	B23R	1921

Whilst its previous owner was taken on as an employee of Southdown, for whom he was to work at Portsmouth for over forty years, this vehicle was garaged at Bognor where, within days, the bus bodywork was severely damaged in a fire at the depot. It returned to the road refurbished as a charabanc. Vulcans 171-178 were renumbered 301-308 in 1923.

Acquired from E. Higgins ('De Luxe') Brighton, August 1923

8	CD 6521	Daimler Y	Harrington	Ch26	1916

The vehicle's chassis was originally ex-War Department, but the registration number dates from 1921. Still with some life in it, No. 8 transferred to Wilts & Dorset in 1928.

Acquired from C. G. Shore ('Royal Blue Services') Bognor, November 1923

321	BP 6985	Guy B	?	B--F	1921
322	BP 5965	Guy B	?	B21F	1920
323	BP 5963	Guy B	?	B24F	1920
331	BP 9685	Ford 1 Ton	?	B14F	1923
332	BP 9687	Ford 1 Ton	?	-14-	1923
333	BP 9683	Ford 1 Ton	?	-14-	1923

Delivered on solid tyres, the humble 4-cylinder Guy saloons of Shore's Royal Blue Services represented Southdown's introduction to the make. They were a far cry from the 'Arab' double-deckers which would feature large in the company's fleet a quarter of a century later. In contrast, the small capacity Ford saloons had been delivered on pneumatics.

When C. G. Shore's Royal Blue Services of Bognor Regis were acquired in 1923, two makes new to the company entered the fleet. Number 323 (BP 5963) was a Guy B saloon dating from 1920 and seating 24 passengers. Despite the proclaimed 12 mph speed limit, a Guy bus was one which had a fair turn of speed and therefore could not be 'chased' with automatic success if its driver put his foot down. On that score alone, gaining the three Guy's involved was a sensible move.

The second make involved in the take-over of Royal Blue of Bognor was Ford. Three new 1-Ton 14-seaters were included in the sale and entered the Southdown fleet for one year's service. This is the kind of vehicle which some big companies purchased to 'chase' such independent operators – and found that they couldn't keep up with a Guy, let alone overtake it, which must have amused Shore, who'd had both. Number 331 (BP 9685), a representative of the three from Royal Blue is parked beside Bognor station.

Daimler CK22, 1924

35	CD 8569	Daimler CK22	Dodson	ChB28R	1924

Originally delivered on solid tyres, but later fitted with pneumatics, this was a one-off purchase, designed to sample the concept of the 'charabus' which had entered service with neighbouring Hants & Dorset Motor Services Ltd and other operators. The bodywork, based by Dodson on its 'CD 19' saloon body, was an attempt to combine the functions of the open charabanc and the closed bus in one vehicle. Windows plus frames were stored under the offside of the vehicle, and the canvas 'roof' rolled up to a central beam which carried the internal lighting. In practice, if a sudden heavy shower occurred the passengers got soaked before it could be put together again – although the vehicle was retained by Southdown as a 'special' until the end of 1930.

A thorn among the roses. Useful for model-makers perhaps, a rear three-quarter view of Dodson's patent 'Charabus', the only one purchased by Southdown. In good weather like this, the canvas roof rolled up to the central beam and the windows went into that wooden box behind the rear wheel. Before committing themselves to buy any more Southdown discovered the major fault: assembling it in a downpour resembled a War Office Selection-Board puzzle. Number 35 (CD 8569), the chassis involved was a Daimler CK22.

Acquired from W. G. Dowle (Summersdale Motor Services), Chichester, January 1924.

309	BP 7489	Vulcan VSD	?	B24R	1921
310	BP 8429	Vulcan VSD	Vulcan	B21F	1922
334	BP 5177	Ford 1 Ton	Cutten	B14F	1920

With Dowle's two Vulcans added, Southdown had accumulated quite a little fleet of the make, totally unpredictable some three years earlier. The Ford 1 Ton saloon had been bodied locally for Dowle.

As well as his garage at Summersdale, Chichester, which the company used briefly in 1924, W. G. Dowle provided Southdown with three additional vehicles when his business in that city was acquired. Two of these were Vulcan VSD models. Number 310 (BP 8429) was that Southport manufacturer's standard all-Vulcan product with its typical baker's van window oval beside the driver. This one was a 21-seater dating from 1922. Dowle had the pleasure of watching its continued employ nearby as he became local manager.

Acquired from Frank Plater and Norris Brothers (South Coast Tourist Company Ltd) Littlehampton, January 1924

34	BK 2962	AEC Y	?	Ch27	1919
341	BK 2879	Dennis 3 Ton	?	Ch27	1919
342	BK 2880	Dennis 3 Ton	?	Ch27	1919
343	BK 4505	Dennis 3 Ton	?	Ch27	1920
344	BP 8603	Dennis 2° Ton	?	ChB20	1922
345	BP 8799	Dennis 2° Ton	?	ChB20	1922
346	PX 155	Dennis 3 Ton	Edmunds	B30F	1923
347	PX 157	Dennis 3 Ton	Edmunds	B30F	1923

Always something of a figure in the local communities in which he lived, Frank Plater was nothing if not persistent. After South Coast Tourist at Littlehampton was acquired by Southdown, he transferred all the mechanical expertise he excelled in to the running of the Southsea Tourist Company, his larger Portsmouth-based concern. When that too was purchased by Southdown the following year, he took himself off across the Solent and concentrated upon the day-to-day affairs of his Isle of Wight Tourist Company. What became Southdown's No. 34 was one of a pair of war-surplus AECs (the other went to Southsea Tourist). Those apart, absolutely every other chassis ordered by Plater was built by Dennis Brothers Ltd at Guildford. These were the first to come into the Southdown fleet and a new number series commencing at 341 was introduced to accommodate them. The registration numbers show that there was a joint purchase policy for both mainland Tourist companies. The two saloon buses had been operated on SCT's Littlehampton-Arundel-Angmering stage-carriage service, relieved occasionally by coaches from the touring fleet.

Despite the fact that Guildford, the home of Dennis Brothers Ltd, is not a million miles away, it was not until the company purchased the business of the South Coast Tourist Company at Littlehampton that the first Dennis took on Southdown colours. Of the eight vehicles involved, seven were Dennis. Number 347 (PX 157) is the nearer of a pair of Dennis 3 ton saloons with 30-seat bodywork by Edmunds, newly repainted in Bognor's rebuilt garage. In 347's case, the bonnet still needs the brush.

Southdown's first forward-control vehicles (the driver beside the engine) were purchased in 1925. The batch comprised fourteen Tilling-Stevens TS6, the first eleven of which had double-decked bodywork by Tilling – the extra length of this model having lost that firm's characteristic short-bay. The massive bulk of these vehicles was spoiled somewhat by spindly wheels, until pneumatics replaced solid tyres by 1928. Number 228 (CD 9228) is posed at Brighton with crew, prior to going into service on the flagship route 31 to Portsmouth.

Tilling-Stevens TS6, 1925

| 226-36 | CD 9226-36 | Tilling-Stevens TS6 | Tilling | O27/24RO | 1925 |
| 237-9 | CD 9837-9 | Tilling Stevens TS6 | Tilling | B35R | 1925 |

Forward control vehicles – those with driving position on the offside of the engine, rather than behind it – first entered the Southdown fleet in 1925, thus introducing also the half-width cab which would survive in service until the Bristol Lodekka was phased out half a century later. The design permitted either four extra seats upstairs in a double-decker or, as with Southdown, a more spacious layout of seats, thus making the eleven double-deckers ideal for long-distance stage carriage work. The comfort factor had been increased by 1928 when all 14 'TS6' vehicles had their solid tyres replaced with pneumatics.

Leyland SG11, 1925

185-6	CD 9711-2	Leyland SG11	Tilling	B35R	1925
187	CD 9817	Leyland SG11	Tilling	B35R	1925
188-91	UF 88-91	Leyland SG 11	Tilling	B35R	1925

Leyland's contribution to forward control was the SG series of chassis. Although not the first variant to be produced by Leyland, the SG11 was nevertheless Southdown's first 'side type' by that maker – 'side type' was the Leyland term for a forward control vehicle. No further order for the SG11 was placed by Southdown however and further 'normal control' G7 chassis were purchased the following year (qv).

Acquired from Cavendish Coach and Car Company, Eastbourne, January 1925

40	HC 603	Napier	?	Ch17	?
41	HC 1819	Napier	?	Ch28	1920
42	HC 1601	Napier	?	Ch9	1919
43	HC 1037	Napier B72	?	Ch22	?
44	HC 1627	Studebaker	?	Ch10	1919
45	HC 2381	Unic	?	Ch14	1921
46	HC 2745	Crossley	?	Ch14	1921
47	XL 1815	De Dion	?	Ch19	1922

Among south coast seaside resorts, Eastbourne seems to have attracted a larger number of operators of excursions and tours than most. Many of these, however, owned no more than one or two vehicles, so the Cavendish C & CC was quite large by local standards (if Chapman & Sons are discounted) when its business was acquired by Southdown in time for the 1925 season. The mixed bag of vehicles suggests that Stretton, the proprietor, had himself bought out some of the opposition in his time.

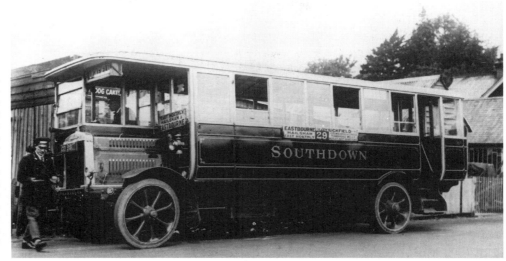

Not quite in keeping with its even-handed policy 'twixt Tilling-Stevens and Leyland, Southdown ordered only seven forward-control models from the latter. These were of that firm's SG11 type, fitted with Tilling 35-seat saloon bodywork which also entered service in 1925. They were big beasts, and the conductor appears to be inspecting his smacked hands after starting No. 187 (CD 9817) at Uckfield on 23rd August 1926 in preparation for a run to Eastbourne on service 29 with through passengers from Tunbridge Wells.

'So now we're working for Southdown'. Among the five different makes of vehicle acquired with W. Stretton's 'Cavendish Coach & Car Company' at Eastbourne was No. 47 (XL 1815) a De Dion-Bouton 19-seat charabanc, then some three years old. By any standard it was an impressive looking creature. But for the inevitable spares problems created by a solitary representative in a larger 'unit-based' fleet, it would probably have been retained rather longer than the two seasons for which it continued to be employed by Southdown.

Acquired from Southsea Tourist Company Ltd, Southsea, Portsmouth, February 1925

36	BK 2975	AEC Y	?	Ch28	1919
348	BK 2211	Dennis 3 ton	?	Ch28	1914
349	BK 2881	Dennis 3 ton	?	Ch28	1919
350	BK 2883	Dennis 3 ton	?	Ch28	1919
351	BK 2884	Dennis 3 ton	?	B25	1919
352	BK 4051	Dennis 3 ton	Bartle	B25F	1919
353	BK 4294	Dennis 3 ton	?	Ch28	1920
354	BK 4378	Dennis 3 ton	?	Ch28	1920
355	BK 4432	Dennis 3 ton	?	Ch28	1920
356	BK 4379	Dennis 3 ton	?	Ch28	1920
357-8	BK 4394-5	Dennis 3 ton	?	B27R	1920
359	BK 4433	Dennis 3 ton	?	Ch28	1920
360	BK 4530	Dennis 3 ton	?	Ch28	1920
361-2	BK 4500-1	Dennis 3 ton	?	Ch28	1920
363	BK 4434	Dennis 3 ton	?	B30-	1920
364	BK 4502	Dennis 3 ton	?	Ch28	1920
365	BK 4504	Dennis 3 ton	London Lorries?	B30R	1920
366	BK 4503	Dennis 3 ton	London Lorries?	B30R	1920
367	BK 4435	Dennis 3 ton	?	Ch28	1920

368	BK 6585	Dennis 1° ton	London Lorries	Ch/B20F	1922
369	BK 6648	Dennis 2° ton		Ch/B20F	1922
370	BK 6682	Dennis 3 ton		Ch26	1922
371	BK 6709	Dennis 2° ton	London Lorries	Ch/B20F	1922
372	BK 6747	Dennis 2° ton		Ch/B20F	1922
373	BK 6760	Dennis 2° ton		Ch/B20F	1922
374	BK 4348	Dennis 2° ton	London Lorries	B25F	1920
375-6	TP 29-30	Dennis 4 ton	Hickman	O26/24RO	1924

Prior to 1925, if one took a charabanc trip from Portsmouth and Southsea it is highly likely that it would have been run by one of the french-grey cars of Frank Plater's second 'Tourist' company, Southsea Tourist Company Ltd. The remarkable standardisation of the fleet and the fact that fifteen vehicles were added to it in 1920 alone, gives some idea of the post World War I traffic potential on Portsea Island. For a few years after the Southdown purchase there was scarcely enough money to repaint the vehicles and the ex-Plater staff happily clung to their smart grey uniforms, such was the reputation they had built for themselves.

If ever Southdown's presence in Portsmouth was in doubt, it was confirmed by the purchase of Frank Plater's 'Southsea Tourist Company' in 1925, together with 30 vehicles. As with his South Coast Tourist firm, all bar one of those were Dennis charabancs and buses. The exception was this AEC Y charabanc, BK 2975, which became No. 36 in Southdown ownership, thus joining an exclusive club within the company's ranks, its fleet number following on from the Daimler charabus and the three previous AEC vehicles recently acquired.

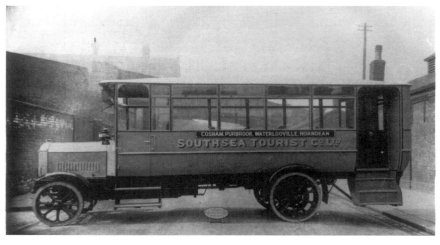

Representative of the saloon buses acquired with the Southsea Tourist Company is this Dennis 3 ton model. The photograph, taken in 1920, is thought to be of one of the pair BK 4504-3 (which became Nos. 365-6 in the Southdown fleet). Taken at Kentish Town, it is the bodybuilder's, London Lorries Ltd, official record. With the exception of possibly two by Bartle and another pair by Hickman it would probably be a safe guess that practically all the other charabancs and buses were bodied by London Lorries.

Just one vehicle was taken with the business of Miskin & Strong of Littlehampton and that another Dennis 3 tonner to join the recently acquired fleet of this make. This vehicle, another bearing evidence of planned offside doors in its Harrington body, had been used both for excursions and stage-carriage service to Slindon by Miskin & Strong from their Victoria Terrace headquarters – although only the former activity was taken into account by Southdown. CD 5095 was allotted fleet number 377 for service with the company.

Acquired from Miskin and Strong, Littlehampton, May 1925

377	CD 5095	Dennis 3 ton	Harrington	Ch28	1920

Having already acquired a large second-hand fleet of Dennis vehicles this additional charabanc of the same make proved to be a worthwhile purchase. So much so that its chassis frame was lengthened and a Dennis E engine fitted in November 1926. It was rebodied at the same time and served until late 1929.

Tilling-Stevens B9B, 1926-8

401-10	UF 1001-10	Tilling-Stevens B9B	Harrington	Ch30R	1926
411	UF 2011	Tilling-Stevens B9B	Harrington	Ch29R	1927
412	UF 1814	Tilling-Stevens B9B	Harrington	Ch29R	1927
413	UF 1813	Tilling-Stevens B9B	Harrington	Ch29R	1927
414-30	UF 2014-30	Tilling-Stevens B9B	Harrington	Ch29R	1927
431-7	UF 2031-7	Tilling-Stevens B9B	Tilling	Ch29R	1927
438	UF 2038	Tilling-Stevens B9B	Harrington	Ch29R	1927
439-44	UF 2039-44	Tilling-Stevens B9B	London Lorries	Ch30R	1927
445-50	UF 2945-50	Tilling-Stevens B9B	Harrington	C30R	1928
451-9	UF 2951-9	Tilling-Stevens B9B	Harrington	C30R	1928
480-3	UF 3080-3	Tilling-Stevens B9BL	Harrington	C20R	1928

In 1926, came the first Tilling-Stevens vehicles which were not of petrol-electric configuration. The prefix 'B', in Tilling-Stevens usage until 1933, denoted a vehicle fitted instead with a gearbox and conventional transmission. The resultant reduction in weight was timely: these – and all subsequent first-hand deliveries – were fitted with pneumatic tyres from new. Type B9B was powered by the new 'Express' Ricardo engine, but was still of normal control layout. The four B9BL 'Devon Tourers' were the first Southdown vehicles fitted with power-assisted brakes.

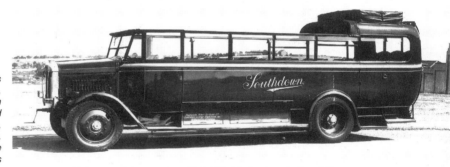

A Tilling-Stevens B9B with London Lorries coachwork, No. 442 (UF 2042), is shown, right, as rebuilt from charabanc configuration to sunsaloon form, although Southdown would never have called it that. The second vehicle, below, is a Harrington-bodied example – No. 454 (UF 2954) in original condition. They were part of an order for 63 Tilling-stevens coaches and charabancs placed in 1926.

Above: The last quartet of the order, delivered in 1928, were the Tilling-Stevens B9BL model, which incorporated the mechanical advances of its companions, but had a considerably shortened wheel base for 20 passenger use. They also had the advantage of power brakes, ideal for their 'Devon Tourer' role. This Publicity Department photograph records upon the back that having been sold to a Jersey firm in 1937, No. 483 (UF 3083) was 'carried away by the Germans in 1944'. 'Kindly return to Southdown Motor Services Ltd' says the stamp which follows.

No. 423 (UF 2023), after a more extensive rebuilding which brought it up to early 'thirties standards with such refinements as an enclosed front as well as rear canopy and destination display together with glass-panelled company-identity provision.

Acquired from S. Foard, Eastbourne, December 1926

27	LP 8233	Daimler CB	?	Ch22	?
378	CD 6203	Dennis 3 ton	?	Ch28	1922
41	HC 5003	Berliet 20hp	?	Ch14	1925
37	HC 5507	Berliet 20hp	?	Ch14	1925
38	HC 6625	Morris 30cwt	?	Ch22	1926

Proof of the continuing importance placed upon the acquired Dennis fleet was that 378 was another vehicle of that make and type to have its chassis frame lengthened and a Dennis E engine fitted, before entering service with Southdown, with whom it served until 1929. The smaller vehicles, however, continued their trade from the seafront for a similar period.

Acquired from W. Stride, Hayling Island, December 1926

30	TP 4102	Morris 30 cwt	Wadham	B18F	1926

Probably because it was a service bus rather than a charabanc, this equally new Morris vehicle found less appropriate work and was sold after just a few months' service.

Dennis 30 cwt, 1927-8

501-18	UF 1501-18	Dennis 30 cwt	Short	B18R	1927
519	UF 1519	Dennis 30 cwt	Harrington	B19R	1927
520	UF 1520	Dennis 30 cwt	Short	B19R	1927
522-6	UF 3022-6	Dennis 30 cwt	Short	B19F	1928

The reliability of its acquired Dennis fleet led Southdown to place its first order for chassis of that make direct from the manufacturers. Whilst

No. 519 was of composite (metal and wood) construction, the remainder introduced all-metal construction to the company, a year before Short Bros came up with a double-decked version. The 30 cwt was powered by a 4-cylinder Dennis engine.

Having sampled the delights of Dennis in some considerable measure, the company now purchased some direct from the Guildford manufacturer. Twenty-five 30 cwt chassis were ordered in 1927 for use with lightly-trafficked headways on both main and rural routes. The initial batch of eighteen was provided with 18-seat all-metal bodywork by Short Brothers. Number 501 (UF 1501) was the first. The view was taken in March 1927 for record purposes.

The last five Dennis 30 cwt of this order were of a 19-seat front-entrance layout and included No. 526 (UF 3026), but were again of Short Brothers all-metal construction. Consequently, they were as durable and hard-wearing as a Land Rover and would probably have gone on for ever, were it not for the need to retain an up-to-date image. An example of the earlier rear-entrance type is another project for restoration to 'as-new condition' being carried out by the remarkable team of preservationists working at Amberley Museum.

Tilling-Stevens-Southdown, 1927

| 54 | UF 2199 | Tilling-Stevens-Southdown | Short | B25F | 1927 |
| 200 | UF 2200 | Tilling-Stevens-Southdown | Short | B25F | 1927 |

The chassis of these two saloon buses were constructed by Southdown, under the direction of the new chief engineer, R. G. Porte, using Tilling-Stevens units. Sadly no picture of the resulting vehicles has survived, yet both 54 and 200 (renumbered 80 in 1931) served Southdown until 1933.

ADC 802, 1927 and 1928

| 28 | UF 2638 | ADC 802 | Short | O60RO | 1927 |
| 29 | KO 5702 | ADC 802 | Short | O60RO | 1927 |

Interest in six-wheeled buses was strong in the late 'twenties and the Associated Daimler Company was hoping for great things from its 802-type double-decker, also known by the LGOC type letters LS ('London Six'). ADC was, in effect, a sales marriage of AEC and Daimler and most 802 models, including the above, had Daimler 35 hp 6-cylinder 5.7-litre sleeve-valve engines of the type being used in contemporary limousines and, later, in the Daimler CF6 chassis. Originally both ADC demonstrators, Southdown took delivery of No. 28 in October 1927, Maidstone & District Motor Services Ltd took KO 5702. M&D transferred theirs to Southdown in February 1928 when it joined 28 on the Brighton-Portsmouth route. After what was clearly a year's trial operation, both went back to AEC at Southall and Southdown took no further interest in the type.

The pair of then-giant ADC 802 six-wheeled double-deckers which were on extended trial with Southdown in 1927-8, must rank among the more remarkable vehicles to appear on service in Southdown colours. Not surprisingly, they saw service upon such core routes as the 31, Brighton-Worthing-Chichester-Portsmouth run. Of all-metal construction and powered with six-cylinder engines they provided notice that if something special were around Southdown would at least give it a fair trial. Number 28 (UF 2638) is illustrated.

A comparatively cheap source of reliable stop-gap vehicles was found in 1927 when Birmingham Corporation had a dozen Daimler Y-type chassis with Brush open-topped bodywork on offer. They were put to work in and around the Brighton area pending new purchases. Number 317 (OB 2103) demonstrates the configuration of pneumatic tyres on the front only, the state in which they all operated for Southdown. It is running on the short-lived service 13B between Brighton and North Moulsecoomb at Easter 1929; and the spelling shown is curious.

Acquired from Birmingham Corporation Transport, June 1927

311	OB 1572	Daimler Y	Brush	O26/26RO	1916
312	OB 1571	Daimler Y	Brush	O26/26RO	1916
313	OB 1570	Daimler Y	Brush	O26/26RO	1916
314-5	OB 1573-4	Daimler Y	Brush	O26/26RO	1916
316	OB 1569	Daimler Y	Brush	O26/26RO	1916
317	OB 2103	Daimler Y	Brush	O26/26RO	1916
318-9	OB 2101-2	Daimler Y	Brush	O26/26RO	1916
320	OB 2105	Daimler Y	Brush	O26/26RO	1916
321	OB 2104	Daimler Y	Brush	O26/26RO	1916
322	OB 2106	Daimler Y	Brush	O26/26RO	1916

After purchase of what became No. 316 in April 1927 for trial purposes, the first of the batch of twelve was acquired through the dealership of the Associated Daimler Company. All the vehicles had been fitted with AEC engines and at least one had an AEC radiator. Each was fitted with Brush bodywork in 1922 and later improved – and Southdown reduced the seating capacity to 48 before entry into service. They had been converted to pneumatic tyres on the front axle before arrival in Sussex, but retained solids on the rear; and proved a useful stop-gap for two years during a period when purchases of new double-deckers by Southdown had virtually ceased.

Acquired from F. Bevan (Golden Butterfly Coaches), Brighton, November 1927

521	UF 1182	Dennis 30 cwt	Harrington	Ch14F	1926

Another trusty Dennis brought into the fleet and put to work in its familiar role for a further four seasons.

Acquired from C. H. Williams (Pullman Services) Hove, November 1927

43	XF 4067	Unic	?	Ch14	1921
44	XH 4004	Unic	?	Ch14	1922

Based at Williams' Imperial Garage at Hove, these vehicles had been engaged on local excursion and private hire work. The purchase also included a Leyland which remains unidentified and did not enter the Southdown fleet. The Unics enjoyed just one season with the company before sale locally.

Not untypical of the many excursion firms which sold out to the company over the years was that of C. H. Williams' Pullman Services of Hove. Two diminutive French-built Unic 14-seat charabancs which came with it were, in contrast, very unusual additions to the Southdown fleet in which they plied their trade for the company during the 1928 season. XF 4067 became No. 43 for that short period. Unic, however, remained better known for the provision of taxi-cabs in the capital at that time.

Acquired from Unique Coaches, Brighton, November 1927

29	?	Daimler CB	?	?	?

Very little is known about this vehicle other than its make and type. Despite being allotted a Southdown fleet number, it was sold in chassis only form to Norris Brothers of Littlehampton within two months of purchase.

Dennis G, 1928-9

527-31	UF 3027-31	Dennis G	Short	C18R	1928
532	UF 4532	Dennis G	Short	C18R	1929

The Dennis G, first introduced in 1927, was evolved from the earlier 30 cwt model but dedicated by the manufacturers solely to passenger-carrying work. It was somewhat longer and had an improved braking system but the engine was the same 4-cylinder Dennis unit as before. All six coaches had roll-back canvas hoods for local excursion work.

When Southdown discovered a requirement for half a dozen light coaches in 1928 it turned again to Dennis. The G type derivative of the earlier 30 cwt was the obvious choice since it had been specially produced by Dennis for the passenger-carrying trade rather than general commercial traffic. The bodywork, in rear-entrance 'sunsaloon' style with canvas fold-back hood, was by Short Brothers, and the finish in two-tone green – or three if the canvas too is counted. Number 529 (UF 3029) is pictured before entry into service.

Tilling-Stevens 'Express' B10A2, 1928-31

461-79	UF 3061-79	Tilling-Stevens B10A2	Short	B32R	1928
484	UF 3584	Tilling-Stevens B10A2	Tilling	B32R	1928
485	UF 3585	Tilling-Stevens B19A2	Harrington	B32R	1928
486-91	UF 3586-91	Tilling-Stevens B10A2	Tilling	B32R	1928
492-4	UF 3592-4	Tilling-Stevens B10A2	Harrington	B32R	1928
495-7	UF 3595-7	Tilling-Stevens B19A2	Tilling	B32R	1928
620-1	UF 3824-5	Tilling-Stevens B10A2	Harrington	B30R	1928
622-3	UF 3822-3	Tilling-Stevens B10A2	Harrington	B30R	1928
638	UF 3826	Tilling-Stevens B10A2	Harrington	B30R	1928
639-40	UF 4239-40	Tilling-Stevens B10A2	Harrington	B30R	1929
600	UF 4300	Tilling-Stevens B10A2	Short	O24/24RO	1929
641	UF 4641	Tilling-Stevens B10A2	Harrington	B32R	1929
642	UF 4642	Tilling-Stevens B10A2	Short	B31R	1929
643	UF 4643	Tilling-Stevens B10A2	Harrington	B32R	1929
644-63	UF 4644-63	Tilling-Stevens B10A2	Short	B31R	1929
644-71	UF 5064-71	Tilling-Stevens B10A2	Short	B31R	1929
672-7	UF 5972-7	Tilling-Stevens B10A2	Harrington	B31R	1929
678	UF 5678	Tilling-Stevens B10A2	Harrington	B31R	1930
679	UF 5679	Tilling-Stevens B10A2	Short	B31R	1930
680-1	UF 5680-1	Tilling-Stevens B10A2	Harrington	B31R	1930
682-5	UF 5682-5	Tilling-Stevens B10A2	Short	B31R	1930
686-8	UF 5686-8	Tilling-Stevens B10A2	Harrington	B31R	1930
689	UF 5689	Tilling-Stevens B10A2	Short	B31R	1930
690-9	UF 6590-9	Tilling-Stevens B10A2	Short	B31R	1930

1200-1	UF 6600-1	Tilling-Stevens B10A2	Short	B31R	1930
1202-9	UF 6802-9	Tilling-Stevens B10A2	Short	B31R	1930
1210-5	UF 7310-5	Tilling-Stevens B10A2	Short	B26R	1931

A new generation of full-sized forward-control single-deck buses first appeared in 1928 based upon the Tilling-Stevens Express B10A2 chassis, which had a lower frame level than the B9 series. Short Brothers, Harrington and Tilling (ten vehicles only) shared the body contracts. Ultimately there were 115, delivered 1928-31. In a period when bus body design was passing through, in some instances, an unhappy transition in styles, this Southdown 'standard' was notably well-proportioned and the large but neatly shaped destination box was ahead of most operator's ideas. The first batches were initially 461 upwards, but were soon renumbered 601 up; the series overflowing after 699, the last sixteen becoming 1200-15. Although buses, some were equipped to a rather more coach-like specification with reduced seating. Although not as lively as their name suggested, these 4-cylinder vehicles were very reliable – and, except for the 1928 batch, all remained in service until the commencement of World War II and then helped shift the troops with other operators after disposal by Southdown. Numbers 1210-15 were lightweight examples for Hayling Island.

The interesting 'odd-man' among these vehicles was No. 600. The fleet number, placed retrospectively in front of the single-deck versions of the same model, suggest that this open-topped double-decker was merely considered an interesting experiment. Ahead of its time, Short Bros built its metal-framed body. If more attention had been paid to that advanced technology, the large rebodying programme Southdown were obliged to have carried out post-World War II may well have been avoided.

Tilling-Stevens new B10A2 'Express' was a welcome addition to the ranks, offering new levels of passenger comfort based on its lower load-line. Over a four year period from 1928, 133 saloon bus examples of the type were purchased, involving the work of three stalwart bodybuilding firms, Short, Tilling and Harrington. The name 'Express' was the manufacturers, rather than Southdown's although the latter actually pressed some – like No. 639 (UF 4239) – into service on express routes to the capital; not their ideal role, as it turned out.

Whilst No. 639 was a Harrington-bodied example, No. 647 (UF 4647), posed here in a bodybuilders' photograph, was by Short Brothers of Rochester. The latter seem to have nosed ahead with detail refinements, such as window corners and fillers – spin off no doubt from that firm's recent experience with all-metal construction. All these saloons, however, were built to Southdown-specified standard and incorporated successfully the firm's notion of what a large but neatly-shaped destination box and indicator should look like.

The one-off all-metal No. 600 (UF 4300). The only wood used in this vehicle's construction had been the upper-deck seat slats and the non-slip battens on the walkways.

Tilling-Stevens 'Express' B10B2, 1929-30

701	UF 4001	Tilling-Stevens B10B2	Harrington	C30R	1929
702-10	UF 4502-10	Tilling-Stevens B10B2	Harrington	C30R	1929
711-5	UF 4511-5	Tilling-Stevens B10B2	Harrington	C20R	1929
716-8	UF 4825-7	Tilling-Stevens B10B2	Harrington	C30R	1929
719-22	UF 5019-22	Tilling-Stevens B10B2	Harrington	C30R	1929
723	UF 5423	Tilling-Stevens B10B2	Harrington	Ch30R	1929
724-33	UF 5827-36	Tilling-Stevens B10B2	Harrington	Ch30R	1929
734	UF 5734	Tilling-Stevens B10B2	Harrington	Ch30R	1929
735-46	UF 5837-48	Tilling-Stevens B10B2	Harrington	C30R	1930
747-63	UF 6347-63	Tilling-Stevens B10B2	Short	C30R	1930
764	UF 6664	Tilling-Stevens B10B2	Harrington	Ch28R	1930
765	UF 6665	Tilling-Stevens B10B2	Harrington	Ch30R	1930
766-7	UF 6666-7	Tilling-Stevens B10B2	Harrington	Ch28R	1930
768-9	UF 6668-9	Tilling-Stevens B10B2	Harrington	Ch30R	1930

Work horses in the Southdown coach fleet in the 'thirties were the 69 representatives of the normal-control version of the low-loading Express model – the B10B2. All but seventeen, which were bodied by Short Brothers, received coachwork by Harrington, although the charabanc bodies of 723-34 and 764-9 had previously been fitted to earlier vehicles in the Southdown fleet. Both batches received new Harrington coach bodies in 1934 – in the latter case extending the vehicles' Southdown careers until 1940. Modernisation to others included the addition of a front roof panel and fleet identification and destination display box, thus giving the type's low radiator an even more pronounced 'ground-sniffing' effect.

The normal-control coach equivalent of the Tilling-Stevens B10A2 was the B10B2, also known as the 'Express' by the maker. The batch again contained a few 'Devon Tourers' with greatly shortened wheelbase and chassis length. This time there were five, again bodied by Harrington with rear-entrance 20-seat 'sunsaloon' bodies and indeed, so far as that firm was concerned, probably represented a 'follow-on' part of another order. The lower bonnet line was the most noticeable difference, as shown by No. 714 (UF 4514).

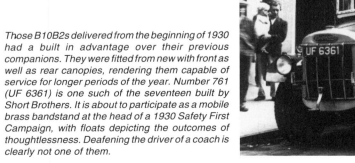

Those B10B2s delivered from the beginning of 1930 had a built in advantage over their previous companions. They were fitted from new with front as well as rear canopies, rendering them capable of service for longer periods of the year. Number 761 (UF 6361) is one such of the seventeen built by Short Brothers. It is about to participate as a mobile brass bandstand at the head of a 1930 Safety First Campaign, with floats depicting the outcomes of thoughtlessness. Deafening the driver of a coach is clearly not one of them.

Leyland Titan TD1, Tiger TS1 and 2 models 1929-31

801-23	UF 4801-23	Leyland TD1	Brush	O27/24RO	1929
824-29	UF 5424-29	Leyland TD1	Leyland	L24/24R	1929
830-41	UF 5530-41	Leyland TD1	Leyland	L24/24R	1929
842-65	UF 5642-65	Leyland TD1	Leyland	L24/24R	1930
866-77	UF 6466-77	Leyland TD1	Leyland	H24/24R	1930
878-81	UF 7078-81	Leyland TD1	Short	H24/24R	1931
882-932	UF 7382-432	Leyland TD1	Short	H26/24R	1931
1001-2	UF 5741-2	Leyland TS2	London Lorries	C26D	1930
1003-5	UF 5803-5	Leyland TS2	London Lorries	C26D	1930
1006-8	UF 5806-8	Leyland TS2	Harrington	C26D	1930
1009	UF 5809	Leyland TS2	London Lorries	C26D	1930
1010-5	UF 5810-15	Leyland TS2	Harrington	C26D	1930
1016-21	UF 6616-21	Leyland TS2	Harrington	C26D	1930
1022-8	UF 6922-8	Leyland TS2	Harrington	C26R	1930
1029	UF 7329	Leyland TS2	Harrington	C30R	1931
1030	UF 7330	Leyland TS2	Hoyal	C30R	1931
1031-3	UF 7331-3	Leyland TS2	Harrington	C30R	1931
1034	UF 7334	Leyland TS2	Hoyal	C30R	1931
1035-6	UF 7335-6	Leyland TS2	Harrington	C30R	1931
1037-41	UF 7337-41	Leyland TS2	Hoyal	C30R	1931
1042-55	UF 7342-55	Leyland TS2	Harrington	C30R	1931
1056-60	UF 7856-60	Leyland TS1	Hoyal	C30R	1931

The Leyland Titan TD1 double-decker, together with the corresponding Tiger TS1 of similar mechanical design was introduced to an admiring road passenger transport industry at the 1927 Commercial Motor Show. Both were of low-loading configuration and had a new 6.8-litre 6-cylinder overhead camshaft petrol engine known as the T type which was to form the basis of a whole family of engines used in full-sized Leyland models up to 1942. The extra power and reliability this offered helped eventually to kill off Southdown's love affair with the products of Tilling-Stevens and its successor TSM. Wheras the Titan TD1 contributed much to the early demise of the urban electric tramcar, its enclosed version (by Leyland and Short in Southdown's case) was seen by the territorial operators as a splendid weatherproof method of shifting larger loads of passengers between towns and all the villages along the way. Furthermore, Southdown, although not beset by too many low bridges in its territory, saw the advantage initially in investing in Leyland's lowbridge version in order to minimise roof damage from trees aplenty – until permission was granted to lop freely as seen necessary.

Since Southdown was already in the midst of equipping itself with a large fleet of Tilling-Stevens Express saloon buses, the only Tigers to enter the fleet in this batch were bodied as coaches. For the same reason, the other forward-control model available at the time, the 4-cylinder Leyland Lion LT series, did not attract an order from Southdown. Both Tiger TS1 and TS2 had a wheelbase of 17ft 6in, but the latter had a shorter rear overhang beyond the back axle. Only the last five Tigers delivered in this batch were of the 'long-tailed' TS1 type. UF 4813 is illustrated in Colour Section 1.

The double-deck fleet was given a firm step forward with the arrival of the first 23 Leyland TD1 Titans. The type had been in production over a year and was already a great success nationwide, particularly among municipalities. These first examples were bodied by Brush at Loughborough and No. 804 (UF 4804) is pictured there before delivery. The Tilling ancestry of the design is evident in the short-bay centre-frame, a feature reproduced also by Short Brothers in their similar 'Highbury' type for Maidstone & District and Hants & Dorset.

Acquired from W. E. Pinhorn (Meon Valley Services), Catherington, August 1929

533	TP 6947	Dennis 30 cwt	Strachan & Brown	B19F	1928
534	TP 7563	Dennis 30 cwt	Strachan & Brown	B19F	1929
535	TP 7196	Dennis 30 cwt	Wadham	B14F	1928
391	TP 7485	Dennis E	Dennis	B32D	1929

Four little-used Dennis saloon buses joined the fleet following this purchase and, save 391, saw a considerable number of years in Southdown service.

An open-top option was in some ways a curious one for Southdown to continue to take up when Leyland's all-enclosed lowbridge double-decker (with body also built by Leyland) was already available on line. Leyland had produced an open-staired version which neighbouring companies took, but Southdown passed by. Number 863 (UF 5663) of 1930 had its Publicity Department picture taken in the usual place on Dyke Road. The lowbridge version had seats in rows on the top deck with an offside gangway sunken into the lower saloon.

If the Leyland Titan double-decker 'killed off the British tramcar' as is claimed, it was one of its saloon counterparts, the Leyland Tiger, which in Southdown's case ended the company's long association with Tilling-Stevens. From the delivery of the first Tiger TS2 model in 1930, Southdown was hooked primarily on the products of Leyland and would remain so until the dawn of the NBC era, given a few exceptions here and there. Number 1005 (UF 5805), an express coach by London Lorries, helped set the ball rolling.

Once the Tiger was available, Harrington seemed to reach for new heights. Although in the main constructed of materials light as possible, the result nevertheless combined expressions of solidity, sleekness and comfort never before reached. It was achieved with the mixture of old-fashioned touches like deep moquette, curtains at the windows and polished veneers; and of modern clean straight lines with all features tucked neatly away behind flush panels. Only the roof rack offers drag on No. 1010 (UF 5810), a dual-door 26-seater.

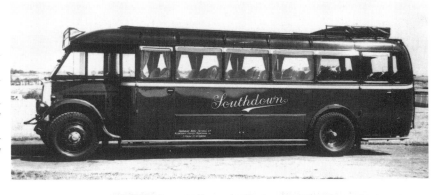

'Height' was practical as well as metaphorical in the construction of later examples of Harrington's bodywork, particularly where the vehicles were intended primarily for express work. The combination of low floor and an extra few inches to the ceiling gave such coaches good headroom. At the same time, the seating was raised to 30 by the elimination of the front door, plus some internal rearrangement. Number 1044 (UF 7344), marked for London (by the Publicity Department's artist) depicts evolution at work.

Acquired from H. J. Twine, Eastbourne, September 1929

381	HC 9385	Graham Dodge TDS	?	B20-	1928
382	JK 88	Thornycroft A6	Strachan & Brown	B22R	1929
383	HC 9159	Thornycroft A2	?	B20-	1928
392	JK 210	Dennis E	Strachan & Brown	B31F	1929

Twine's stage carriage services had been operated from Eastbourne although his garage was actually at Hailsham. Not surprisingly, the Dennis outlasted its earlier companions in the Southdown fleet.

The company remained active throughout in the continuing acquisition of small rival businesses as and when they came up for sale. One such at Eastbourne was the stage-carriage work, plus four vehicles, of H. J. Twine in September 1929. One of these was a Thornycroft A6, JK 88, with bodywork by Strachan & Brown, in whose works photograph it is seen in London before delivery to Twine. Suitably painted into Southdown colours, it became No. 382, and added another make to the company's inventory.

Leyland Lioness LTB1, 1930 and 1933

301-6	UF 5849-54	Leyland LTB1	Harrington	C20R	1930
307-11	UF 6507-11	Leyland LTB1	Harrington	C20R	1930
312-7	UF 8826-31	Leyland LTB1	Harrington	C20R	1933

Southdown remained faithful to the traditional 'tourer' concept for its extended tours until the mid-'thirties. The Leyland Lioness LTB1 fitted this bill perfectly and Harrington built the coachwork with a spacious layout of just twenty seats. The original batch of eleven, delivered in 1930, also known as the Lioness Six, set the standard. The six delivered in 1933 featured a more solid-looking structure at the top of the window line, but the roof was still of the canvas folding type. These incorporated new features such as a fully-floating rear axle and a deeper Tiger style radiator. The seventeen Lioness' were rebuilt with glass quarter lights in the late 'thirties and were renumbered 1801-17, most surviving until 1951-2.

Even production of the traditional normal-control coach passed to Leyland with Southdown's order for 27 Lioness LTB1 coaches in 1930. 'Coach-cruise' was their intended purpose and to this end no effort was spared to make them as much like large luxurious private cars as was possible. Harrington provided the bodywork and the designer seemed to revel in the opportunity to produce just one more batch of 'cabriolets'. Number 314 (UF 8828) is one of six which were not delivered until 1933 – already dated, but extremely elegant.

Acquired from F. & J. Poole (Royal Red Coaches), Hove, March 1930

29	PN 3091	Chevrolet LQ	?	Ch14	?
31	BH 8896	Fiat	?	Ch14	?
32	PM 583	Fiat	?	?	?
33	BP 6649	Fiat	?	?	1921
34	XK 6897	Fiat	?	?	?
384	PN 3456	Thornycroft A2	Redhead	Ch20F	?
500	PM 9170	Dennis 30 cwt	Baker	Ch14	?

A mixed fleet, from which the Fiats quickly disappeared and the Dennis survived until 1933, outlasting all the others.

Acquired from A. Potts (Potts Coaches) Brighton, June 1930

28	CD 6879	Daimler Y	?	Ch26	1922
30	PC 9910	Fiat	?	Ch14	1923
36	CD 4909	Daimler CK	?	Ch23	1920
393	UF 4501	Dennis F	Duple	C30	1929
394	UF 4516	Dennis F	Duple	C30	1929
395	UF 4925	Dennis F	Duple	C30R	1929
396	UF 1832	Dennis F	Duple	C25	1927
536	UF 4847	Dennis GL	Harrington	Ch18R	1929
537	UF 4848	Dennis GL	Harrington	Ch18R	1929

Once again, the newer Dennis vehicles outlasted the others, 537 until 1937.

Potts Coaches of Brighton came into the fold in 1930, bringing with them nine vehicles, six of which were of Dennis manufacture. Of these, two were the handy GL model suitable for 18-seater coachwork provided, in the case of No. 537 (UF 4848), by Harrington – hence it looked very much at home in the 'thirties colours of Southdown's coaches which now included a primrose waistband. This little vehicle was dependable and popular and was utilised for seven summer seasons on private hire work.

Demonstrator on extended loan from AEC Ltd, August 1930 – March 1931

10	HX 1091	AEC Regent 661	Short	H59R	?

Allotted a fleet number and in full Southdown livery, the vehicle did not encourage an order for the type.

Caught swinging at some speed into Brighton's Old Steine is a unique vehicle – an AEC double-decker in full Southdown colours. Number 10 (HX 1091) was a Regent 661 model on extended loan to the company, 1930-31, from AEC Ltd, and was fitted with Short Brothers then-standard Vee-front enclosed bodywork, this one seating 59 passengers. 'Unusual for Southdown' features include the route between Brighton and Horsham painted along the waistrail and the route number, stencilled white on black on the broad cantrail panel.

TSM C60A7, 1931

200-2	UF 8030-2	TSM C60A7	Harrington	C30R	1931

When Tillings severed the connection with Tilling-Stevens in 1930, the associated operating companies' business with the Maidstone concern virtually collapsed overnight. However, Southdown did take three of the new C60A7 6-cylinder model in 1931, starting a new 200 series of fleet numbers.

Tilling-Stevens having become TSM in 1930, following the withdrawal of the Tilling organisation from its directorship, the outlook became bleak for the Maidstone concern. Southdown purchased three of the revamped TSM firm's C60A7 model in 1931 and had them bodied with 30-seat express coach bodies by Harrington to the same pattern as those for current Leyland Tigers. Number 202 (UF 8032), although marked for service on the South Coast Express, is in fact up on the Dyke Road having its 'for sale' photograph recorded.

Leyland Titan TD2 double-deckers, 1932-3

933-43	UF 8373-83	Leyland TD2	Short	H26/24R	1932
944-9	UF 8844-9	Leyland TD2	Short	H26/24R	1932
950-4	UF 8850-4	Leyland TD2	Short	H26/24R	1933
955-9	UF 9755-9	Leyland TD2	Short	H26/24R	1933

The TD2 was, in effect, an updated heavier-duty version of the TD1 with a larger capacity, 7.6-litre version of what was basically the same 6-cylinder petrol engine. Other engineering modifications were incorporated, notably the design of the rear-hubs, but generally the appearance and dimensions of the chassis were altered only in detail. Southdown again favoured Shorts with the bodywork order to the design which featured their vee-screen outline at the front of the upper deck.

Already well-established as the standard Southdown double-decker, Leyland's Titan in its uprated TD2 guise was a natural choice for additions. The Short Brothers 'Vee-front' body design was all that seemed to impress the company about the borrowed AEC, and some had been featured on the latter TD1 examples; so that manufacturer's product was selected for the 1932-3 deliveries. Number 933 (UF 8373) was the first and this photograph by the manufacturer was featured in the bodybuilder's publicity material thereafter.

Leyland TS4 coaches, 1932-33

1062-73	UF 8832-43	Leyland TS4	Harrington	C32R	1932
1074-85	UF 9774-85	Leyland TS4	Harrington	C32R	1933

The Tiger TS4 retained the 17ft 6in wheelbase of the TS2 model but, at 27ft 6in overall, was 1ft 6in longer. It was fitted with a redesigned and deeper radiator, a 7.6-litre engine and had triple servo braking, fully floating rear axles and rear-shackled front springs. The Harrington coachwork was basically similar to that upon the earlier TS2 examples. All were taken by the War Department in September 1940, but some were eventually returned. Of these, 1084/5 served with Southdown until 1957. Number 1071 had a full-length luggage rack on the roof and was used as a 'bandwagon', with the rack carrying the instruments of military and other brass and silver bands.

'Whitewall' tyres – an idea imported from America: they soon looked messy in touristy cow-pat country – on a Leyland TS4 this time. Tiger No 1071 with Harrington 32-seat coachwork features one of those board displays which permitted another for, say, express route working to be secured over the top of the original at short notice, thus making the vehicle readily available wherever it was resting. Number 1071 (UF 8841) was, however, the 'bandwagon' with extra-length luggage rack on the roof.

For many years 1071 was the exclusive coach of the Band of the Royal Marines, Eastney Division. If you liked Sunset and Prelude to the Morning, this is where those gentlemen with pith helmets sat on the way to the next concert.

Demonstrator on extended loan from TS Motors Ltd, January 1932

700	KJ 2919	TSM E60A6	Short	H24/24R	1931

Although not quite the last of the company's association with the products of the Maidstone manufacturer, this 6-cylinder 'Express Six' version of the coach chassis purchased by Southdown the previous year, was the last double-decker from that source – no follow-up order forthcoming. Portsmouth Corporation, however, took ten of the type.

Acquired from Southern Glideway, Eastbourne, March 1932

30	JK 857	GMC	?	C13	1929
31	HC 9153	ADC 416	Duple	C23	1928
32	JK 1064	Morris Viceroy	?	C20	1930
37	JK 1911	Gilford 168OT	Duple	C28D	1931
38	JK 1273	Gilford 168SD	Duple	C26D	1930
39	JK 1065	Gilford 168SD	Duple	C26D	1930
40	JK 473	Gilford 168SD	Duple	C26F	1929

371	HC 9817	Dennis F	Hoyal	C20	1929
1000	JK 1098	Leyland TS2	Duple	C28D	1930
1061	JK 1266	Leyland TS2	Duple	C28D	1930

Although the smaller of the two concerns acquired at Eastbourne in 1932, Southern Glideways' express fleet included twice as many makes of vehicle. The Leyland Tigers were separated by the fortunes of war: 1000 went to the War Department in 1940, 1061 served Southdown until 1955.

Looking for a moment like an attempt at a model of something else, is No. 700 (KJ 2919), a TSM E60A6 on loan from TS Motors Ltd in 1932, but in full Southdown colours. On this occasion, slip-boards are used to give the vehicle greater mobility on the Southdown system, but again the chosen route is the 17 between Brighton and Horsham – and the bodywork was again the same 'vee-fronted' design (of 48 seats this time) by Short Brothers. Unfortunately for TSM, the demonstration succeeded only for Shorts, and no chassis orders were placed.

Acquired from Chapman & Sons (Eastbourne) Ltd March 1932

41	HC 7507	Lancia Pentaiota	Park Royal	C18	1927
42	HC 7509	Lancia Pentaiota	Park Royal	C18	1927
318	HC 6075	Maudslay ML4	Duple	C22	1926
319	HC 9129	Maudslay ML4B	Duple	C22	1928
320	HC 9995	Maudslay ML4B	Hall Lewis	C22	1928
321-3	JK 20-2	Maudsley ML4B	Hall Lewis	C22	1928
324-6	JK 23-5	Maudslay ML4B	Hall Lewis	C22	1928
327	JK 26	Maudslay ML4B	Hall Lewis	C22	1929
328-9	JK 27-8	Maudslay ML4B	Hall Lewis	C22	1928
330	JK 655	Maudslay ML7A	Duple	C28D	1929
331	TD 5458	Maudslay ML2	Knape	Ch18	1926
332	TD 5460	Maudslay ML2	Knape	Ch18	1926
333-4	JK 1002-3	Maudslay ML4B	Park Royal	C26R	1930
335	JK 1004	Maudslay ML3B	Park Royal	C26R	1930
336	JK 1005	Maudslay ML4B	Park Royal	C26R	1930
337	JK 1006	Maudslay ML4B	Park Royal	C25	1930
338	JK 1007	Maudslay ML4B	Park Royal	C26	1930
339-40	JK 1207-8	Maudslay ML4B	Park Royal	C22	1930
341	JK 1209	Maudslay ML6B	Duple	C26	1930
372	HC 2347	Dennis 4 ton	Park Royal	C25	1921
373	HC 2349	Dennis 4 ton	Park Royal	C26	1921
374	HC 2351	Dennis 3° ton	Park Royal	C22R	1921
375	HC 2833	Dennis 3° ton	Park Royal	C22R	1922
376	HC 4141	Dennis 2° ton	Dennis	Ch22	1924
377	HC 4143	Dennis 2° ton	Park Royal	C22	1925
378	HC 4145	Dennis 4 ton	Park Royal	C30	1925
379	HC 5059	Dennis 4 ton	Park Royal	C30	1925
380	HC 5385	Dennis 3° ton	Park Royal	C22R	1925
381	HC 2837	Dennis 3° ton	Park Royal	C22R	1921
382	HC 6077	Dennis 30 cwt	Dennis	?	1926
383	HC 6079	Dennis 2° ton	Park Royal	C22R	1926
385-6	DB 2209-10	Dennis C	Park Royal	C22R	1921
387	DB 2212	Dennis C	Park Royal	C22R	1921
388	HC 9131	Dennis F	Park Royal	C26	1928
389-90	JK 1008-9	Dennis GL	Park Royal	C14R	1930

In addition to express workings to London from Eastbourne, Chapman's had built up an extremely good reputation for Continental tours to Switzerland etc, and were among the first to make this feasible by the fitment of 'balloon' tyres to its then (the 'twenties') fleet of Dennis charabancs. Needless to say, it was a Dennis GL (390) which in 1938 was the last survivor of this fleet in the Southdown ranks. Circumstances leading to the purchase of this business are described in Morris, Colin *Regional History of British Bus Services, Vol 1: South East England* TPC 1980 and *Southdown Vol 1: The History* Venture 1994.

There was nothing brand-new in the large fleet which came into Southdown ownership following the purchase of Chapman & Sons' business at Eastbourne in 1932, despite the very great reputation the firm had built up in the resort since horse-drawn days. Apart from the dependable Dennis models to which Southdown was well-used, there were some rather exotic machines involved. What became No. 41 (HC 7507) was one of a pair of Lancia Pentaiotas, the six-cylinder model – another first for Southdown.

Among the 22 Maudslays included in the absorbed Chapman's fleet was No. 330 (JK 655), a one-off ML7A model with forward-control and a 28-seat 'sunsaloon' body by Duple. It is pictured at the centre of the Cavendish Place complex in Eastbourne in full Southdown rig including a chrome 'Southdown' badge on the radiator. The double-door format for coaches was already becoming thought of as something of a seat-loser and the company set about replacing it fairly quickly.

Number 333 (JK 1002) was one of several Maudslay ML4B models – a typical latter-day Chapman type – included in the sale. Of normal-control layout, it conformed to the earlier 'twenties ideal of the proper way to travel in the long hot summertime. Those summers were no longer quite so predictable and with funds tight after so large a purchase, it was deemed appropriate not to expend further money on roof reconstructions of the kind now being engaged in by the company. These would be reserved for established makes.

Acquired from Thames Valley Traction Co Ltd, Reading, April 1932

490	MO 9313	Tilling-Stevens B9B	Park Royal	C22R	1927
491	MO 9314	Tilling-Stevens B9B	Park Royal	C26	1927
492-3	RX 1398-9	Tilling-Stevens B9B	Park Royal	C22R	1928
494	MO 9312	Tilling-Stevens B9B	Park Royal	C22R	1927
495	MO 9315	Tilling-Stevens B9B	Park Royal	C22R	1927

With a goodly stock of Tilling-Stevens spares available at Portslade this second-hand purchase made good sense. Only the chassis were acquired from Thames Valley and they were fitted with bodies from the early withdrawals from the Chapman fleet, thus giving up to six years extra service with Southdown.

Although no longer being ordered from new, Tilling-Stevens coaches were still an established force in the Southdown fleet when, in 1932, half a dozen B9B chassis were made available to the company by Thames Valley Traction of Reading. Their existing Park Royal bodies discarded, these short wheelbase models were rebodied with 22-seat 'sunsaloon' bodies from withdrawn ex-Chapman vehicles. Numbers 490, left, (MO 9313) and 495, below, (MO 9315) demonstrate various detail differences in both wet and dry weather configurations.

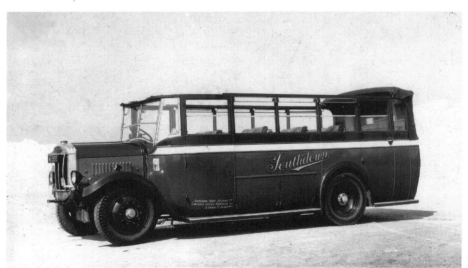

Leyland Cub KP2, 1933

1-2	ACD 101-2	Leyland KP2	Harrington	C14F	1933

Leyland's Cub range of passenger chassis was built at Kingston-upon-Thames. The first model produced (from 1931 onwards) was the KP2 which had a 14ft-wheelbase and was designed to seat up to twenty. Its engine was a new Leyland 6-cylinder side valve petrol unit of 4.4 litres. Intended initially for intermediate 'coach cruise' work, Southdown's pair of KP2s were re-seated to the full capacity of twenty places in 1949 and served a further four years.

TSM B39A6, 1933

1216-21	ACD 116-21	TSM B39A6	Short	B26R	1933

These six saloon buses were specially ordered by Southdown to cope with the then weight restrictions on the road bridge to Hayling Island. Each was fitted with Short Brothers' all-metal lightweight coachwork. Such matters do not appear to have concerned the War Department, who took them all away in September 1940.

Above: Leyland's contribution to the small-bus market was the highly-regarded Cub range. Southdown was cautious at first and bought just two, and to be on the safe side had them bodied in 'sunsaloon' style by Harringtons of Hove. To start with, the pair were allotted to up-market coach-cruise duties – they provided only 14 seats of comfortable proportion in those days. In the early 'fifties and with six extra seats, No. 1 (ACD 101) served on South Coast Express relief duty and is about to call in at Worthing.

Right: Photographer Alan Bell, looking considerably younger than he does nowadays, poses at South Parade Pier, Southsea in front of a saloon bus whose particular significance could not have meant much to him at the time. Number 1216 (ACD 116) was the first of a batch of six TSM B39A6 saloons purchased specially to cope with the severe weight restrictions on Langstone Bridge, Hayling Island. They had special lightweight metal bodies by Short and proved to be the last TSMs purchased.

Acquired from Fairway Coaches, London SW4, December 1933

342	UL 1509	Maudslay ML3	?	C24	1929
343-4	UL 8823-4	Maudslay ML3	Dodson	C24	1929
345-6	GU 8930-1	Maudslay ML4	?	C26	1929
397-9	GX 2618-20	Dennis Lancet	Strachan	C30	1932

Eight coaches were transferred to Southdown by Fairway when it relinquished its Worthing-London express route. All were offered for sale soon after, despite receiving fleet numbers, and – surprisingly – that included the practically new Dennis Lancets. Southdown's interest in the make had come to an end for the time being.

Leyland Titan TD3 and TD3c, 1934

960-3	AUF 660-3	Leyland TD3c	Short	H26/24R	1934
964-9	AUF 664-9	Leyland TD3	Short	H26/24R	1934
970-5	AUF 670-5	Leyland TD3	Short	H26/24R	1934

The Titan TD3 model differed from the TD2 mainly in the redesign of the vehicle's front-end. The engine, gearbox and radiator were now placed farther forward above the front axle, and the latter had been redesigned. It now had parallel sides and a larger but well-proportioned overall area, and would become the standard T type radiator for double and single-decked buses and for coaches. Southdown's first four TD3s were fitted with the Leyland torque converter – an attempt to eliminate constant gear changing in town traffic – thus becoming TD3c type, identified by a seemingly larger autovac and a 'Gearless Bus' badge upon the radiator. Southdown may have been inspired by Eastbourne Corporation's earlier order for six. Eight of the remaining TD3s had oil engines – the first in the Southdown fleet. At £1,000 per chassis, an oil-engined Titan cost £150 more than the petrol version; the saving would come in the relative fuel costs. The Short Brothers' bodywork also had an updated appearance and originally all had folding sunshine roofs: the seating capacity remained at Short's standard 50.

Considered on at least two counts to be the first truly modern double-decker, the Leyland TD3 came on to the Southdown scene in 1934. First, the moving forward of mechanical units permitted more passenger room and comfort in the lower saloon. Secondly, with Southdown's examples, Short Brothers gained a little more space upstairs by doing away with their precious 'vee-shape' front. Both that and the cab front could have come even further forward but the profile was in keeping with the times: No. 967 (AUF 667) post-WWII at Hilsea.

Leyland Tiger TS6 1934

| 1086-8 | AUF 786-8 | Leyland TS6 | Harrington | C32R | 1934 |

Only three new coaches joined the fleet in 1934, but they were to establish the typical Southdown coach outline that would remain virtually unchanged until 1939 deliveries – and remain dominant on Southdown express services until well after World War II. Harrington built the bodies on the Leyland Tiger TS6 chassis which, like the Titan TD3 model, had the more compact front end introduced soon after the 1933 deliveries of TS4 and TD2 models. All three vehicles were fitted with Leyland 8.6 oil engines in 1950-1 and the last retired from Southdown service in 1954.

The pre-World War II outline for the Southdown express coach was set by a trio of Leyland Tiger TS6 units with Harrington bodywork purchased in 1934. Whilst there was still a ladder and hand grips at the rear, passengers' luggage was now carried in an air-smoothed pannier, which replaced the previous barred cage on the rear roof. Heavier items now went into a boot at the rear. All three, like No. 1088 (AUF 788), provided seats for 32 passengers who entered through a rear door and enjoyed new levels of comfort.

Acquired from W. G. Waugh (Regal Coaches) Brighton, January 1934

| 26 | UF 5985 | AEC Regal 662 | Harrington | C32 | 1930 |

Despite being allotted fleet and body number, this vehicle was sold almost immediately to Bath Tramways.

Leyland Tiger TS6T, 1934

| 50-1 | AUF 850-1 | Leyland TS6T | Short | B40C | 1934 |

The route to Beachy Head from Eastbourne having been declared by the Traffic Commissioners 'unsuitable for double-deckers', Southdown sought a saloon bus which could carry a greater number of passengers than the standard single-decker. Leyland came up with its 30ft 3-axle version of the Tiger TS6 and Southdown purchased two – the suffix 'T' disclosing that the extreme rear axle was 'trailing' or undriven. Doug Jack records that the Southdown examples featured regularly in the *Leyland Journal* and company publicity.

Built to look as much as possible like company coaches, the three-axle Tiger TS6T saloons purchased for duty at Eastbourne were the first of their kind to enter Southdown service. Ordered by the Traffic Commissioners to use only saloons on the run to the top of Beachy Head on route 97, Southdown came up with this pair. Even the route-boards at the sides of the roof echoed express usage. The extra axle permitted the length to go up to 30ft (another first) and provided 40 seats in a cavernous saloon body entered from a central door. Number 50 (AUF 850) shows off its length before the Belle Vue Hotel, Eastbourne, whilst the interior view is a Short Brothers' official record by the manufacturer.

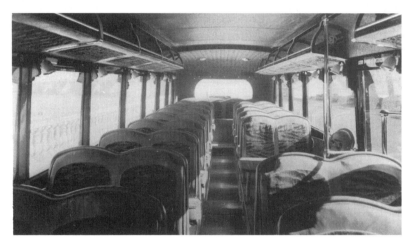

Leyland Titan TD4 and TD4c, 1935-36

100-11	BUF 200-11	Leyland TD4	Short	L26/26R	1935
112-21	BUF 212-21	Leyland TD4c	Short	H26/24R	1935
122-38	BUF 222-38	Leyland TD4c	Short	H26/24R	1935
139-44	CCD 939-44	Leyland TD4	Beadle	L26/26R	1936
145-50	CCD 945-50	Leyland TD4c	Beadle	H26/26R	1936

A Lockheed vacuum hydraulic braking system, a larger clutch and a further redesigned front end which permitted more space in the lower saloon were all features of the Titan TD4 model. Short Brothers were again the favoured bodybuilder for the 1935 intake which were all petrol-engined, the TD4c's being of course fitted with torque converters, and 122-38 were originally fitted with folding roofs. Numbers 139-44 were to prove the last petrol-engined double-deckers ordered by Southdown. The rest of the 1936 intake, TD4cs, were oil-engined and thus helped establish two things; first, the gutsy deep thrum of the Leyland 8.6-litre unit throughout the Southdown area and secondly, the concept of oil engines for double-decks and petrol engines for saloons and coaches – which didn't quite work out, because of the onset of World War II.

Further design improvement led to the production of the Titan TD4 which entered service with Southdown in 1935. Examples bodied by Short and by Beadle were purchased, the latter the first from that manufacturer since 1915. Both provided some lowbridge examples of which one was No. 107 (BUF 207), built by Short Brothers. The designs were similar but close inspection revealed some subtle differences – rounded corner panels, wider window frames and the outward flare of the skirt-panelling of the Beadle product won on points for style.

The bus version of the Tiger TS7 was something special. Harrington designed for these vehicles a special 31-seat body quite different from the current coaches, but with a specification more than adequate to permit them to perform in that role if called upon to do so. The panoramic window layout brought about by the curved glass at the rear quarters was immediately appreciated by passengers on the more scenic routes upon which they were employed. The seats too were luxurious by stage-carriage standards and looked particularly well in the new pattern of Southdown moquette – in brown, orange and fawn. Number 1402 (BUF 982) was one of a batch of 24 launched at Brighton amid great praise in 1935.

Leyland Tiger TS7 coaches and saloons, 1935-37

1089-1100	BCD 889-900	Leyland TS7	Harrington	C32R	1935
1101-6	BUF 401-6	Leyland TS7	Park Royal	C32R	1935
1107-12	BUF 407-12	Leyland TS7	Harrington	C32R	1935
1400-19	BUF 980-99	Leyland TS7	Harrington	B31R	1935
1420-23	CCD 30-3	Leyland TS7	Harrington	B31R	1935
1113-24	CCD 713-24	Leyland TS7	Harrington	C32R	1936
1125-30	CCD 725-30	Leyland TS7	Harrington	C32R	1936
1131	CCD 731	Leyland TS7	Beadle	C32R	1936
1132-33	CCD 732-3	Leyland TS7	Harrington	C32R	1936
1134-44	CCD 734-44	Leyland TS7	Beadle	C32R	1936
1145-50	CCD 745-50	Leyland TS7	Harrington	C32R	1936
1151-9	CUF 151-9	Leyland TS7	Burlingham	C32R	1936
1160-76	DUF 160-76	Leyland TS7	Harrington	C32R	1937
1177-78	DUF 177-8	Leyland TS7	Harrington	C26R	1937
1179	DUF 179	Leyland TS7	Harrington	C32R	1937
1424-9	DCD 324-9	Leyland TS7	Harrington	B32R	1936

The Tiger TS7 featured the same mechanical and spatial improvements found in the Titan TD4. Some interesting variations of bodywork were featured in the examples ordered by Southdown. Thirty-two of the coaches were fitted with roll-back centre sections to the roof for touring and excursion duties. Beadle and Park Royal shared some of the work with Harrington; whilst nine coaches were bodied by the Blackpool firm Burlingham, not previously represented in the fleet. The saloon-bodied examples, by Harrington, were built to a new design quite distinct from the contemporary coach styles. This incorporated the same three-window destination and route number arrangement featured on the 'tween-decks side panels of the TD4 double-deckers being delivered at that time.

The equivalent of the Titan TD4 in the saloon range was the Tiger TS7, purchased in both coach and bus form by Southdown. Number 1109 (BUF 409) pauses in the midst of its relief express run from Worthing to London after an already eventful life. A now-standard Harrington 32-seater, it had been new in 1935 and seen four years on the roads to London when it was commandeered for service as a World War II ambulance; survived attacks which destroyed two of its fellows, and gone back into express service with Southdown in 1946.

Leyland Tiger TS7T, 1935

| 52-3 | BUF 552-3 | Leyland Tiger TS7T | Short | B40C | 1935 |

The Tiger TS7T had been updated in the same way as the TS7, but as with the TS6T again featured three axles and a resultant seating capacity in excess of the standard saloon bus. Increased traffic on the Beachy Head-Eastbourne route caused Southdown to purchase this pair, which joined the Tiger TS6Ts on the service.

Two additional Tigers with three axles joined the activity on the Beachy Head route in 1935. Since they incorporated the same improvements as the TS7 model, they were designated TS7T. Number 52 (BUF 552) is at the Eastbourne Pier terminus of route 97, where a special bus stop was established for the company's use. It is fascinating to note that, having denied Eastbourne Corporation the right to run the service, Southdown had adopted the municipality's style of clock whose hands the conductor altered to show the departure time of the next bus. 'It's fast' the helpful would intone.

Acquired from W. H. Rayner & Sons, Horsham, January 1935

| 538 | PX 5776 | Dennis 30 cwt | Harrington | B18F | 1927 |

But for a disastrous fire which destroyed his Barns Green garage – and came close to engulfing his home as well – Rayner would not have sold his business when he did. This vehicle was one which escaped the conflagration to join the Southdown fleet.

Acquired from F. G. Tanner (Denmead Queen), Hambledon, March 1935

39	TP 4760	Thornycroft UB	Wadham	B26F	1927
40	TP 6601	Thornycroft A6	Wadham	B20F	1928
41	TP 7951	Thornycroft A2	Wadham	B20	1929
42	TP 8693	Thornycroft A2	Wadham	B20	1930
43	TP 9164	Thornycroft A2	Wadham	B20F	1930
44	TP 9645	Thornycroft A6	Wadham	S20R	1930
45	OU 7856	Thornycroft BC	Ransomes	B32R	1931
46	CG 7119	Thornycroft CD	Brush	B32F	1933
47	RV 1844	Thornycroft CD	Wadham	B32R	1929

Clearing the decks in the Portsmouth area, Southdown acquired the once familiar red buses of Tanner's Denmead Queen service to Hambledon (Hants) where some stalwart lads devised a game called cricket. Eleven of Tanner's vehicles joined the company fleet – and all of them were Thornycrofts built 'just up the road' at Basingstoke. The oldest was eight years old, the youngest two – and No. 543 (43 when it first joined: TP 9164) was five; a rather nice little vehicle with bodywork built even closer to home by Wadham Brothers at Waterlooville. It was stationed on Hayling Island.

Youngest and smartest of the Tanner fleet was a Thornycroft CD saloon with 35-seater bodywork by Brush. Numbered 46 by Southdown, CG 7119 was of half-cab configuration and by some appropriate fluke had bodywork built to BET-associated British Electric Federation design, despite having been originally a Thornycroft demonstrator. Otherwise known by the chassis-builder as a 'Cygnet' (but a baby it was not), this bus had been the pride of the Denmead Queen fleet and the one which drivers had been happiest to get their hands upon.

| 48 | JK 88 | Thornycroft A6 | Strachan & Brown | B22R | 1929 |
| 49 | HC 9159 | Thornycroft A2 | ? | B20 | 1928 |

Tanner had achieved the ultimate in standardisation so far as choice of manufacturer was concerned. Being somewhat unfamiliar with Thornycrofts, Southdown got rid of most fairly quickly, but retained the three 32-seaters until 1939 when they were passed on to sister company Wilts & Dorset Motor Services Ltd, then desperately in need of additional vehicles because of military work contracts. Numbers 48-9 had previously been Nos. 382-3 in the Southdown fleet (1929). No. 257 is illustrated in Colour Section 1.

Leyland Cub KP3A, 1936

| 30-5 | CCD 700-5 | Leyland KP3A | Harrington | C20F | 1936 |
| 13-5 | CUF 313-5 | Leyland KP3A | Park Royal | B20F | 1936 |

The Cub KP3 type was built with a wheelbase 1ft 6in longer than the KP2 and was 25 inches longer overall, thus permitting a more spacious layout of twenty seats. Southdown's examples were petrol-engined (hence the A suffix in 1936), but No. 13 was converted to oil in 1947.

Small private parties hiring a coach at last got a fully-enclosed weatherproof vehicle for the job in 1936, with the first half dozen Cub coaches delivered that year. Harrington provided the 20 seat bodywork, which looks rather more central than forward entrance, and the seats were of the high-backed, quality type. Car 30 (CCD 700), to use the name which was still current at the time in Southdown parlance, and its five companions granted passengers a more spacious layout by virtue of being just over two feet longer than previous Leyland Cub models.

Like No. 30, also a Cub KP3A model of 1936, No. 15 (CUF 315) was, in contrast, a small-capacity saloon service-bus. The sum total of its features and the fact that the 20-seat bodywork was built by Park Royal give the vehicle a decidedly municipal look, closely resembling those used in Southampton and elsewhere. Together with its two companions, it was originally dressed in a half-and-half livery of apple green and primrose (much later considered a dual-purpose scheme), and served on local bus routes in the Horsham area prior to World War II.

Leyland Tigress LTB3, 1936

318-23	CUF 318-23	Leyland LTB3	Burlingham	C32R	1936

The Tigress was an updated version of the earlier Lioness and although still of normal-control configuration had several features in common with the Tiger. Southdown's six were referred to in the registration records as RLTB3, which simply meant 'right-hand-drive', since the great majority produced went overseas with left-hand drive. In the UK it was therefore an unusual vehicle, thus adding a new dimension to Southdown's 'something-special' image. The six were, together with Tigers 1151-9 also delivered that year, bodied by Burlingham for the long-distance luxury 'coach-cruise programme.

The beautiful and eye-catching Leyland Tigress LTB3 model purred into service with Southdown for the first time in 1936. Unusually, the coachwork was built by the Blackpool firm Burlingham. Since they were well-used to providing good views of the Tower they have in that resort, the coachwork incorporated some very generous curved roof quarterlights and some at the rear quarters also. The net result was a very special coach for a special purpose – long distance coach cruises. They were still at their task well after World War II, when No. 319 (CUF 319) is being prepared at Portslade for a saunter to Mid Wales. A glance inside would have disclosed the ultimate in luxury seats and the leg room between them.

Leyland Cub KPZ1 and KPZ2, 1936-37

3-5	CUF 403-5	Leyland KPZ1	Harrington	C14F	1936
36-7	CUF 436-7	Leyland KPZ2	Harrington	C20F	1936
16-8	CUF 516-8	Leyland KPZ2	Park Royal	B20F	1936
38-54	DUF 38-54	Leyland KPZ2	Harrington	C20F	1937
19-26	ECD 519-26	Leyland KPZ2	Park Royal	B20F	1937

The Cub 'Z' range was fitted with a 4.7 rather than a 4.4-litre engine. The KPZ1, with a total length of 21ft 8in was the shortest of the Cubs and, in Southdown's case, was fitted with only 14 seats as delivered. The KPZ2 was mechanically the same, but 2ft 3in longer and thus suitable for twenty. When built, 3-5 were equipped with folding canvas roofs for excursion work. Number 4, rebuilt with glass quarter lights and reseated to C20F, survived for preservation.

Leyland Cub SKPZ2, 1936

10-12	CUF 410-2	Leyland SKPZ2	Park Royal	B26R	1936
7-9	DUF 7-9	Leyland SKPZ2	Park Royal	B26R	1936

These six vehicles were specially ordered for Hayling Island services and spent their entire Southdown working lives in the Havant area. The Cub SKPZ2 was a forward-control half-cab model capable of seating 26 passengers.

Two further types of Cub were purchased in 1936. First, the KPZ1 and 2 type with normal-control, of which Car 5 (CUF 405) is of the former sub-variant. The bodywork by Harrington for this batch of three featured only 14 seats as befitted its shorter length, and was intended for excursion work. The remainder were of the KPZ2 sub-type and, being longer, sat 20 passengers.

The second type was the forward-control Cub SKPZ2, with bodywork by Park Royal, and purchased simply because they could seat up to 26 passengers on their comparatively light frames on journeys over the still-restricted Langstone Bridge to Hayling Island.

Leyland Titan TD5, 1937-39

151-4	DUF 151-4	Leyland TD5	Park Royal	H26/26R	1937
155-80	EUF 155-80	Leyland TD5	Park Royal	L26/26R	1938
181-200	EUF 181-200	Leyland TD5	Beadle	L26/26R	1938
201-5	EUF 201-5	Leyland TD5	Park Royal	L26/26R	1938
206-11	FCD 506-11	Leyland TD5	Park Royal	H26/26R	1939
212-7	FCD 512-7	Leyland TD5	Park Royal	L26/26R	1939
218-27	FUF 218-27	Leyland TD5	Park Royal	H26/26R	1939
229-39	FUF 228-39	Leyland TD5	Beadle	H26/26R	1939
240-9	GCD 40-9	Leyland TD5	Park Royal	H26/26R	1939
250-61	GCD 350-61	Leyland TD5	Park Royal	H26/26R	1939
262-65	GCD 362-5	Leyland TD5	Park Royal	L26/26R	1939

Identifiable by their square dumb irons, rather than rounded ones, the TD5s included several minor mechanical advances. Oil engines became standard for full-sized Southdown stage-carriage vehicles from 1937, so all 115 Titan TD5s roared deeply from new. Characteristically however, the Leyland 8.6-litre engine did not shake the bodywork when ticking over – unlike numerous oil engines which followed. Number 205 achieved notoriety in December 1948 when a severe gust of wind blew it through the railings of Old Shoreham Toll Bridge – featured on the cover of Volume 1 – and into the River Adur.

Sharing the flared skirts of the Beadle-bodied representatives, No. 151 (DUF 151) was a Park Royal-bodied example of the new Leyland Titan TD5 which entered service from 1937. It was the first of a batch whose deliveries continued until the onset of World War II. Although still fitted with the rather fussy midriff destination screens, the growing cleanliness of line is evident in this view, but the upright front profile was still some way off. This was the era of the well-oiled thrum of the Leyland 8.6-litre diesel engine which reverberated pleasantly through both saloons giving a reassuring note of 'getting there' to all aboard. Evident in the lower saloon are all those handles and spy-holes which enabled the conductor to change the six side screens at cantrail level.

Leyland Tiger TS8, 1938-39

1182-205	EUF 82-105	Leyland TS8	Harrington	C32R	1938
1206-10	EUF 106-10	Leyland TS8	Park Royal	C32R	1938
1211-2	EUF 511-12	Leyland TS8	Harrington	C32R	1938
1430-41	FCD 30-41	Leyland TS8	Harrington	B32R	1938
1442-65	FCD 242-65	Leyland TS8	Harrington	B32R	1938
1466-71	FCD 366-71	Leyland TS8	Harrington	B34R	1938
1213-26	FUF 313-26	Leyland TS8	Harrington	C32R	1939
1472-85	GCD 372-85	Leyland TS8	Harrington	B32R	1939

The coaches in this batch were the first with oil-engines in the Southdown fleet. As with the TD4 and TD5, frame differences were considered by Leyland sufficient to merit designating this model the Tiger TS8. The last fourteen coaches had Harrington bodywork of a new subtly-modernised style which ushered in the curved waist and roof outline; and – as Alan Townsin has pointed out – it was a subtlety not quite achieved thereafter. Saloon bus No. 1443 was severely damaged by a German bomb on 2nd November 1940. The chassis was re-straightened, a petrol engine installed and an unusual 32-seat centre-entrance coach body lying spare at Harrington's was fitted. It featured a three-fifths canopy, but full-size front indicator over the cab.

The ultimate in pre-war resolve was activated by the appearance of the Leyland Tiger TS8 express coaches which came on-stream in 1938. They looked rugged and purposeful and, by virtue of their oil engines, sounded the part also. Not dissimilar from the majority built by Harrington, No. 1207 (EUF 107) with 32-seat coachwork by Park Royal was a fine example of the five built by the London concern. The 1938 deliveries proved to be the last designed with horizontal lines for decades to come.

Leyland Cheetah LZ3 and LZ4, 1938-39

500-4	EUF 500-4	Leyland LZ3	Park Royal	C24C	1938
505-10	FUF 505-10	Leyland LZ4	Park Royal	C24C	1939

Once again the then fragile Hayling bridge was responsible for a specialised Southdown purchase. Lightweight Leyland Cheetah LZ3/4 coaches with Park Royal centre-entrance bodywork were built for the Hayling Island express route to London and for excursion work from the island. Their entire working lives with Southdown was spent in the area, so much so that when the notorious bridge was about to be replaced with a more substantial one, they were promptly withdrawn from service. There were no outwardly visible differences between the LZ3 and LZ4.

Another special effort to overcome the difficulty imposed by Langstone Bridge between the mainland and Hayling Island: five Leyland Cheetah LZ3 coaches and six LZ4 models delivered in 1938 and 39 respectively in order to provide the good folk of that island with an express route direct to London and a local excursion provision. They were larger than Cubs, but considerably lighter than the conventional Tigers used on other express services. No. 502 (EUF 502), an LZ3 is at Victoria Coach Station.

Leyland Cub KPZ4, 1938

55-8	EUF 555-8	Leyland KPZ4	Harrington	C20F	1938

The last four of Southdown's Cubs were designated KPZ4 by Leyland, which indicated improvements to the braking system. Intended for excursion and private hire work, they were nevertheless roped in for the occasional London express relief working after World War II. They were much liked little work-horses and as most other Southdown Cubs lasted in the company's service until the end of the 1956 season.

Southdown rounded off its Leyland Cub purchases in 1938 with a quartet of KPZ4 models. These gave a foretaste of things to come in that their Harrington bodywork displayed a distinct downward curve of bodyline toward the rear of the vehicle, echoing the line of the cream flash which, in turn, had developed from the simple horizontal waistband of a few years before. Number 55 (EUF 555) has set up stall for an excursion to Penshurst Place and Chiddingstone Castle, near Tonbridge, for the princely sum of 7/6 (37½p).

Acquired from Tramocars Ltd, Worthing, August 1938

T3	PX 886	Shelvoke & Drewry Freighter	Hickman	B20R	1924
T4	PX1593	Shelvoke & Drewry Freighter	Hickman	B20R	1925
T5	PX 6872	Shelvoke & Drewry Freighter	Hickman	B20R	1927
T6	PO 1626	Shelvoke & Drewry Freighter	?	B20R	1930
T7	PO 1748	Shelvoke & Drewry Freighter	?	B20R	1930
T8	PO 1780	Shelvoke & Drewry Freighter	?	B20R	1930
T9	PO 7706	Shelvoke & Drewry Freighter	Harrington	B26R	1933
T10	PO 8014	Shelvoke & Drewry Freighter	Harrington	B26R	1933

T11	PO 9665	Shelvoke & Drewry Freighter	Harrington	B26R	1934
T12	PO 9890	Shelvoke & Drewry Freighter	Harrington	B26R	1934
T15	APX 237	Shelvoke & Drewry Freighter	Harrington	B26R	1935

What might be described as the first full-fronted vehicles in the Southdown fleet, the little red 'Tramocars' of Walter Gates and his colleagues had become very much part of the Worthing scene (under the nose of Mackenzie and Cannon) before the firm at last agreed to sell out to the company. The 'Tramocar', although by no means unique to Worthing, does seem to have been Gates' idea, and was based for him by S&D upon their well-tried 'Freighter' refuse cart. It had tram-type tiller controls and extremely small solid-tyred wheels. So too did the earlier 'Tramocars', but those bodied later by Harrington introduced slightly larger wheels with pneumatic tyres.

Not unique, but highly unusual, the eleven-strong fleet of Tramocars Ltd, operator of Shelvoke & Drewry 'Freighters' fitted with passenger-carrying bodywork and designed to make access easy for the elderly at Worthing, was purchased by Southdown in August 1938. Thought to have been the first on pneumatic tyres and the first bodied by Harrington, PO 7706 became No. T9 in the Southdown fleet where, together with its fellows, it retained the Tramocar logo at the front until dispensed with.

Apart from the green paint, the Tramocar image remained strong after 1938. Number T17 (FCD 17), the last of the Shelvoke & Drewry Freighters, wears the Tramocar fleetname at the front, the route number T1 – and the crew are still in Tramocar uniforms. Southdown could not claim credit for the advanced design of the last two vehicles for they were already on order when the purchase of Tramocar was agreed. They were rear-engined, and bodied by Harrington in a style highly reminiscent of the much larger AEC Q coaches which had passed through their hands.

Shelvoke & Drewry 'Freighter', 1938

| T16-7 | FCD 16-7 | Shelvoke & Drewry Freighter | Harrington | B26C | 1938 |

Ordered by Walter Gates, but delivered direct to Southdown in the company's green livery. These broke new ground in being of a new rear-engined type of very modern coach-like appearance, not unlike Harrington's earlier work on AEC 'Q' chassis. Southdown continued to operate the fleet as a separate entity, with the prefix 'T' for the fleet and service numbers, until the Tramocar Freighters were sold off *en bloc* in 1942.

Dennis Falcon, 1939

80-1	FUF 180-1	Dennis Falcon	Harrington	B30C	1939

Rather than order further 'Freighters' for service in Worthing, Southdown instead turned once again to Dennis for a pair of that manufacturer's Falcons. Specially-built with low-loading configuration and bodywork by Harrington, the two vehicles were initially labelled 'Tramocar' also. In addition, the *Southdown* fleetnames were in Mackenzie script. As late as the 'fifties, the residents of West Worthing still referred to their local buses as 'Tramocars'.

Late evening sun on Worthing seafront as No. 80 (FUF 180) operates route T1 dressed in Tramocar logo and original style route boards at roof level. The vehicle is one of a pair of special low-loading Falcons specially ordered for the task from Dennis of Guildford, the bodywork produced with appropriate knowledge by Harringtons. The vehicles were immediately more productive than the Shelvoke & Drewry Freighters, whose maximum of 26 seats was now exceeded by four. Nevertheless, the crews quickly learned to shuffle between stops like the real thing, whilst passengers found the centre-exit interiors to be a cross between a Tramocar and a scaled-down Southdown bus.

Leyland Titan TD7, 1940

266-88	GCD 666-88	Leyland TD7	Park Royal	H26/26R	1940
289-92	GCD 689-92	Leyland TD7	Park Royal	L26/26R	1940

The restrictions upon travel on the south coast, imposed by the Ministry of War Transport in 1940 because of the fear of invasion by the German army, were thought at the time likely to have a serious effect upon the revenue-earning capacity of Southdown. So firmly was this view held that the company's already-ordered, fleet-numbered and Brighton-registered Titan TD7 models were diverted to three other operators well outside the perceived danger area where the production of war materials had gone into overdrive. Accordingly, these vehicles saw no service with Southdown: instead they served with Crosville (16), Western Welsh (7) and Cumberland (4) – the latter vehicles, which were lowbridge models, being re-registered before entry into service; and the numbers GCD 689-92 were made available for further use by Southdown (see below).

What should have been a Southdown bus. Number 286 (GCD 286), a Leyland Titan TD7 with Park Royal 52-seat bodywork, was one of 27 TD7s diverted away from the south coast by Ministry of War Transport directive in 1940, thus seeing no service in Southdown colours., Number 286 was one of sixteen diverted instead to Crosville Motor Services Ltd in whose post-war livery it has been photographed., The flush front had arrived – but not at Southdown.

Replacement Leyland Titans on loan, 1940

301-10	AJG 31-40	Leyland TD5	Park Royal	L27/26R	1939
321-30	AJG 21-30	Leyland TD5	Park Royal	L27/26R	1939
400	JK 2337	Leyland TD2	Leyland	H24/24R	1932
401	JK 2334	Leyland TD2	Leyland	H24/24R	1932
402	JK 1808	Leyland TD1	Leyland	H24/24R	1931
403	JK 1237	Leyland TD1	Leyland	H24/24R	1930
404	JK 5062	Leyland TD4c	Leyland	H24/24R	1935
405	JK 5604	Leyland TD4c	Leyland	H24/24R	1936

Diverting the Leyland TD7s from Southdown had not been such a good idea. It overlooked the fact that there would be a considerable demand for transport in the vicinity of the naval base at Portsmouth and around the military airfields also – and that the company required further vehicles following its transfer of rolling stock to Wilts & Dorset Motor Services Ltd the previous year. With eastern Kent and the seaside town of Eastbourne particularly vulnerable, the company was able to negotiate the loan of almost an equivalent number of replacement vehicles from East Kent Road Car Co Ltd (20) and Eastbourne Corporation (6) for delivery in August and December of that year respectively. The East Kent vehicles were operated with Southdown fleetnames on cherry red panelling to the waistrail, medium grey above overall – and this was the livery still borne by 301-5 inclusive when, in November 1941, they went in convoy from Portsmouth farther west to Devon General. The remainder of the batch stayed with Southdown and were returned piecemeal to East Kent throughout the victorious year of 1945. The Eastbourne buses had gone home much earlier (see below).

Leyland Titan TD3c and 4c on loan from Eastbourne Corporation, January 1941

400	JK 3720	Leyland TD3c	Leyland	H24/24R	1934
401	JK 5063	Leyland TD4c	Leyland	H24/24R	1935
402	JK 3724	Leyland TD3c	Leyland	H24/24R	1934
403	JK 5606	Leyland TD4c	Leyland	H24/24R	1936

In January 1941, Southdown sent home the four Titan TD1/2 models, and Eastbourne replaced them with a like number of TD3c/4c double-deckers which were promptly given the same fleet numbers carried by their predecessors. Number 400 went back to Eastbourne later that year but the remainder were returned, together with 404-5, in 1943 as Southdown began to take delivery of its first Guy utility vehicles.

East Kent Road Car and Eastbourne Corporation to the rescue. The over-hasty diversion of the TD7s to Crosville, Western Welsh and Cumberland necessitated a replacement scheme for a Southdown company predictably hard-pressed to cope with a sudden increase in wartime traffic movements. Eastbourne Corporation's JK 5063, a Leyland TD4c, was one of four vehicles loaned in a second wave in January 1941 to replace a like number of older borrowed buses which went home to Eastbourne. Until 1943, this one was Southdown No. 401.

Guy Arab I 5LW and II 5LW/6LW, 1943-46

400-1	GCD 974-5	Guy Arab I 5LW	NCME	L27/28R	1943
402	GCD 976	Guy Arab II 5LW	Strachan	L27/28R	1943
403-4	GCD 689-90	Guy Arab II 5LW	Strachan	L27/28R	1943
405-6	GCD 691-2	Guy Arab II 6LW	Strachan	H30/26R	1944
407	GUF 37	Guy Arab II 6LW	Strachan	H30/26R	1944
408-9	GUF 68-9	Guy Arab II 6LW	Park Royal	H30/26R	1944
410-3	GUF 70-3	Guy Arab II 5LW	Park Royal	H30/26R	1944
414-5	GUF 74-5	Guy Arab II 5LW	Weymann	L27/28R	1944
416-26	GUF 116-26	Guy Arab II 6LW	NCME	H30/26R	1944
427-41	GUF 127-41	Guy Arab II 5LW	NCME	H30/26R	1944
442-3	GUF 142-3	Guy Arab II 6LW	Park Royal	H30/26R	1944
444-5	GUF 144-5	Guy Arab II 5LW	Park Royal	H30/26R	1944
446-7	GUF 146-7	Guy Arab II 6LW	Park Royal	H30/26R	1945
448-51	GUF 188-91	Guy Arab II 5LW	NCME	H30/26R	1945
452-62	GUF 152-62	Guy Arab II 5LW	NCME	H30/26R	1945
463-5	GUF 163-5	Guy Arab II 6LW	NCME	H30/26R	1945
466-72	GUF 166-72	Guy Arab II 5LW	NCME	H30/26R	1945
473-86	GUF 173-86	Guy Arab II 5LW	Weymann	H30/26R	1945
487-94	GUF 387-94	Guy Arab II 5LW	Weymann	H30/26R	1945
495-99	GUF 395-99	Guy Arab II 5LW	Park Royal	H30/26R	1946

During World War II, Leyland was one of the manufacturers heavily committed to the production of military vehicles and few of its bus chassis were released onto the market – and none of those to Southdown. Bristol, Daimler and Guy were the three firms selected to re-supply British bus fleets with double-deckers and following a more realistic assessment of Southdown's contribution to the war effort, a total of 100 of the latter make were earmarked for delivery to the company – although 37 of them were actually available only after victory had been achieved. Nevertheless, the first pair were accepted (at Brighton) in May 1943 and deliveries continued in irregular batches thereafter. Four bodybuilding firms were involved in the construction of austerity designs laid down strictly by the Ministry of Supply – elevations flat, corners angular, rear domes of the 'lobster-back' shape, and in many instances headlamps of small diameter. Some 40 of Southdown's 'Arabs' delivered in this very large batch were fitted with wooden slatted seats, rather than cushioned ones, from new. By special dispensation, those constructed by Northern Counties (NCME) were metal-framed: the rest were of composite build and displayed yards of clear varnished timber inside the saloons. Because of extensive war damage to stockpiles, much of this wood proved unseasoned, thus contributing to early withdrawal (1955) or body replacement (1951) in some cases. The Arab II had a chassis lengthened beyond the previous legal limit to 26ft 9in to permit the instillation of Gardner's 8.4-litre 6LW 6-cylinder engine. During the 'fifties however, a series of engine-swaps put 5LW units into some of these chassis. In August 1950 No. 409 was converted by Southdown to permanent open-top form. Between then and May 1959 a further 32 were similarly treated, thus creating a minor classic, seven examples of which were to continue as very popular seasonal vehicles with Southdown as late as 1964.

Cheap and cheerful – and well-liked after a while, the whistling, Guy Arab utilities with their gear-crashing drivers presented themselves to an astonished but resigned public in 1943; the wooden-seated ones presenting one more indignity to go with existing austerity measures like food-rationing. At least it was no longer obligatory to carry a gas-mask. Number 404 (GCD 690) was delivered in December of that year in a green and grey livery but at least offered its passengers cushioned seats from new. It was a Strachan-bodied lowbridge model.

Taken on strength in March 1944 whilst tip-and-run Luftwaffe raiders were still on the prowl, number 409 (GUF 69) was a sorry sight during its first few weeks in service. It was painted grey overall and only a small transfer on the lower saloon bulkhead informed the public that it was the property of Southdown. Furthermore it was one of those with wooden slatted seats on both decks. It got its seat cushions before the end of hostilities however together with proper Southdown livery plus 'war surplus' dark green roof.

Courtesy of Alan Bell who took the picture, we can see what the rear-end of a Guy Arab utility really looked like. Whereas No. 409 was bodied by Park Royal, this one, No. 484 (GUF 184) was constructed by Weymann, but whichever manufacturer was responsible, the framework pattern – whether wood or metal – was structurally similar. The Guys were by no means hidden in odd corners – on the contrary, they were sent out to bustle along on virtually all routes including the distinguished No. 31.

Leyland Titan PD1, 1946-47

| 266-90 | GUF 666-90 | Leyland PD1 | Park Royal | H28/26R | 1946 |
| 291-315 | HCD 891-915 | Leyland PD1 | Leyland | H28/26R | 1947 |

A welcome return to peacetime standards was ushered in with the delivery to Southdown of its first Titan PD1 chassis, a model which featured a new Leyland 7.4-litre engine, the E181. Though not the most powerful built by the Leyland company to that date, it nevertheless featured improvements incorporated as a result of the firm's wartime construction experience with military contracts. The first 25 delivered had composite bodywork by Park Royal. Although based upon that firm's utility-style framework, it was acclaimed as its most glamorous direct derivative. The 1947 batch of 25 had Leyland metal-framed bodywork, now acceptable to Southdown following its comparative experience with both methods of construction in World War II. No. 315 is illustrated in Colour Section 1, No. 280 on p9.

Rebodying programme for double-deckers 1943-50

Southdown had much the same problems during World War II and its aftermath as most other operators. Principally they encountered the difficulties associated with trying to maintain an ageing fleet, almost all over the life-span of about eight years intended when each vehicle was built. The structural condition of double-decked timber-framed buses (always put under greater stress on corners than the contemporary saloon bodywork) gave particular cause for alarm. On a comparatively small scale, a solution presented itself when selected bodybuilders not fully committed to the military were given sanction to provide the bodies for such vehicles as the Guy Arab double-deckers which came on stream for Southdown in 1943.

Following its considerable support for Wilts & Dorset Motor Services Ltd in its hour of need (see Vol. 1 p55ff), Southdown was left in a rather unusual position. All 23 of its first Leyland Titan TD1 open-toppers survived – and from October 1941 had been fitted with dark green canvas tops to permit them all-year use. But of the rest of the TD1 fleet, only eight survived. It was these, and thirteen remaining Titan TD2 models which were the subject of a utility-specification rebodying programme undertaken between 1943-45 for Southdown by three firms, two of which had been given the task specifically of building upon reconditioned rather than new chassis – Willowbrook and East Lancs.

Park Royal was the exception. As well as providing the bodywork for seventeen new utility Guys, it produced six H28/24R bodies for Titan TD1s 871/4/6 and 937/8/9 in 1943. To Willowbrook went the task of building five lowbridge bodies (L27/24R) for Titan TD2s 946/9 in 1943 and 951/3/7 in 1944. Back in the H28/24R mode, East Lancs rebodied TD1s 940/2 in 1943 and TD2s 954/5/9 in 1944 and 947/50/2/6/8 in 1945. Whereas some operators specified a long 'Covrad' replacement radiator as part of the overhaul exercise, Southdown retained the original squat Titan early-'thirties version on these vehicles.

In late 1944 Willowbrook commenced rebuilding four Titan TD3 and TD4 models, whilst others were later refurbished by Portsmouth Aviation, Beadle, Saunders and West Nor, this time on TD4 and TD5 chassis. The condition of some of the vehicles, however, demanded more radical treatment. A major re-bodying campaign was put in hand for Titan TD3; 4 and 5 type double-deckers new between 1934-39. Work commenced in 1946 and continued until 1950. Ultimately, 152 out of the company's 182 chassis of these types had been rebodied and they then continued in service until 1958-62, some chassis thus completing 25 years' service.

Continued on page 91

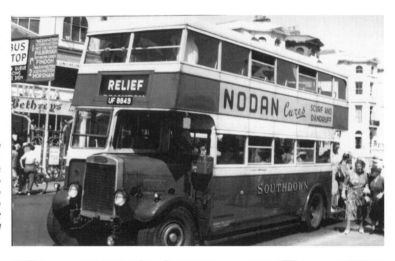

Twenty-one Titan TD1 and TD2 chassis were rebodied during the latter years of the war. According to the maker involved, the degree of utility of construction varied. The five examples to lowbridge format rebodied by Willowbrook represented the most austere. For some unknown reason, whether at Warsash or Worthing, drivers of this variant felt inspired to drive it with considerable panache and usually a grin. Each scurried about like a motorised matchbox. Number 949 (UF 8849), rebodied in 1943 unloads at Worthing in 1947.

Looking far less constrained by the exigencies of wartime control is the East Lancs bodywork applied to No. 940 (UF 8380), a Titan TD1 in that same year of 1943. This is one of the few occasions where the bodywork on a Southdown bus looked too modern for the chassis which bore it. The company chose not to specify the longer Covrad replacement radiator at the time of these wartime rebuilds and that gave such flush-fronted rejuvenations a rather button-nosed appearance. When photographed, 940 was nearing the end of its service.

Top left: Number 113 (BUF 213), Titan TD4c of 1935 with East Lancs body of 1947.

Top right: Number 117 (BUF 217), a Titan TD4c of 1935 with Saunders bodywork of 1947.

Centre left: Number 110 (BUF 210), a Titan TD4 of 1935 with Beadle 6-bay bodywork of 1947.

Centre right: Number 156 (EUF 156), a Titan TD5 of 1938 with Beadle 5-bay bodywork of 1949.

Lower left: Number 159 (EUF 159), a Titan TD5 of 1938 with Park Royal bodywork of 1950.

Lower right: Number 260 (GCD 360), a Titan TD5 of 1939 with Northern Counties bodywork of 1950.

Facing page left:Creating quite a stir when they appeared, the first post-war coaches seemed, to Southdown eyes at least, to incorporate many of the utilitarian lines of the double-decked austerity vehicles. Yet these were examples of a very new Leyland product, the Tiger PS1/1, bodied, in that firm's usual straight lines, by Eastern Coach Works (ECW) – the first products of that manufacturer to be employed by Southdown. Number 1227 (GUF 727) and its companions were built for the restarting express coach trade and were delivered in 1947.

Facing page right: Whilst in this immediate post-war period a hissing vintage Tiger with enamelled feline face on its radiator might turn up on relief duty somewhere – curtains at the windows and all – it had not been company policy to rebuild coaches as service buses as they matured. The straight lines of the ECW bodywork made these 31-seat coaches a different proposition. From November 1954 onwards, most of them were fitted with bus seats, had their route boards removed from the roofline, received full-size bus-screen boxes and were renumbered. GUF 733 was now No. 679.

Such was the pressure on the bodybuilding industry that the work was shared between five concerns, each using their own design details and – save those built by East Lancs between 1946-48 – the main proviso being that each vehicle should seat 54 in H28/26R configuration. Between-decks triple side-screens on many of the previous bodies were to disappear, but drivers' sun visors were to remain *de rigeur*. Production was as follows per vehicle fleet number:

East Lancs H28/24R   in 1946 – 119/22/3/4/5/7/31/3 and 969/70
                             in 1947 – 113/6/30/4/6/7/66/71 and 963/8
                             in 1948 – 114/68/70/3 and 203

Thereafter all rebodied vehicles under this heading were H28/26R

East Lancs   in 1949 – 102/8/29/51 and 202/6/7/8/13/20/5/8/39/44
                            in 1950 – 118/40/9/57/61/2/77/93 and 201/10/2/5/21/9/20/7/46/9/61/5

Saunders   in 1947 – 115/7/28/35/45/83/6/89 and 960/1

Beadle   in 1947 – 110/2/6/20/6/38 and 965
                            in 1948 – 153/5/8/63/72

These twelve bodies were unusual for post-war construction in that they were of the old fashioned' 6-bay format. The following Beadle bodywork was of a revised design based on 5-bay structure.

Beadle   in 1949 – 141/6/56/87/214/27/36/47 and 964/6
                            in 1950 – 121/60/216/22/6/43 and 962/71/3/5

Park Royal   in 1949 – 152/64/5/7/8/74/5/8/9/80/94 and 204/5/17/8/9/23/4/35/9/42/9/50/6/64
                            in 1950 159/76 and 231/2/3/40/8/51/8/62

Northern Counties   in 1950 – 139/47/54/90 and 209/11/34/41/52/3/4/5/7/9/60/3

Leyland Tiger PS1 and PS1/1, 1947-49

1227-46	GUF 727-46	Leyland PS1/1	ECW	C31R	1947
1227-51	HCD 447-51	Leyland PS1/1	ECW	C31R	1947
1252-54	HCD 852-4	Leyland PS1/1	Park Royal	C32R	1947
1255	HUF 285	Leyland PS1/1	Park Royal	C32R	1947
1256-63	HCD 856-63	Leyland PS1/1	Park Royal	C32R	1947
1264-9	HUF 4-9	Leyland PS1	Harrington	C32F	1947
1270-5	HUF 270-5	Leyland PS1	Windover	C32F	1947
1276-84	HUF 276-84	Leyland PS1	Beadle	C32R	1948
1285	HCD 855	Leyland PS1	Beadle	C32R	1948
1286-9	HUF 286-9	Leyland PS1	Beadle	C32R	1948
1290-8	HUF 290-8	Leyland PS1	Beadle	C32R	1949
1299-311	HUF 299-311	Leyland PS1	Park Royal	C32R	1948
1312-26	HUF 312-26	Leyland PS1	Duple	C32R	1947
1327-31	HUF 927-31	Leyland PS1	Duple	C32R	1947
1332-7	HUF 932-7	Leyland PS1	Duple	C32R	1948
1338-51	HUF 938-51	Leyland PS1	Duple	C32R	1949

Peacetime conditions returned in earnest for Southdown from 1947, when deliveries of the new Tiger PS1 type commenced. It incorporated the same mechanical features as the PD1 double-decker and the 125 delivered went a long way toward satisfying Southdown's urgent need for coaches to replace those requisitioned by the War Department in World War II. At a time when the industry was hard-pressed with orders for coachwork, Southdown spread the work among five firms, with varying results upon delivery dates. Eastern Coach Works, Duple and Windover were the three which received first-time orders from the company, and all the vehicles, save the six each from Harrington and Windover featured the rear-entrance layout favoured on the company's pre-war Tiger coaches. The ECW product, used initially solely for express work, was, in outline, not much removed from that firm's post-war standard for single-deck bodywork; whilst Park Royal's contribution had been designed originally to East Kent Road Car express coach specification, but looked 'near-enough' in Southdown livery. In contrast, Duple moved

Top left: Harrington's contribution to the PS1 fleet was a toned-down version of its post-war flight of fancy – a curvaceous coach with a fin-tail over the rear window. 'We don't want the tail' said Southdown, but kept the strakes on the pirate's hat over the rear wheel. Rather unkindly, Harrington seem to have pinched the rear window design from Beadle, but all-in-all this bravura post-war effort by the normally restrained coachbuilder from Hove added up to an impressive if somewhat showmanlike vehicle to suit the resurgent spirit of the times.

More restrained bodywork for the post-war Tigers was provided by three traditional supplies to Southdown. First, top right, No. 1282 (HUF 282) was an example of a continuing gentle evolution by Beadle. Secondly, centre left, Park Royal came up with thirteen built to the slightly slab-sided design they'd already produced to East Kent specification – like No. 1397 (HUF 307) and, thirdly, above right, back to more subtle curves where only the upper edges of the window frames remain straight – as produced by Duple on No. 1315 (HUF 315); going to Arundel Castle for 4/9 (23.75p).

Above: As new underfloor-engined coaches came on stream in the early 'fifties, a mild panic overcame many operators, Southdown included. A coach with an exposed radiator was suddenly old-fashioned, unlikely to attract customers anymore. It was a time when private motorcars were getting transatlantic grilles rather than radiators whose shape identified the make. Southdown joined the rush to take the perceived sow's ear in hand and, in 1954, all the post-war Tigers bodied by Duple and Beadle were converted to full-front by the latter. The new silk purse is No. 1280 (HUF 280). A Windover-bodied example may be seen in Vol 1, p78.

away from its usual product of the time toward a much closer approximation of the Southdown express coach; whereas Harrington and Windover's contributions to the private hire, excursion and coach-cruise sector closely followed both firms' separate concepts in production at that time – with the result that, few in number, they looked a little odd in the Southdown fleet. Number 1351, by Duple, was to prove the last of a long line of full-size, half-cab, front-engined Southdown coaches. All the Beadle and Duple examples were converted to full-front arrangements in 1954. This work, carried out by Beadle, also involved the removal of the front-bulkhead, which increased the noise level inside the coach.

Leyland Titan PD2/1, 1948

| 316-95 | JCD 16-95 | Leyland PD2/1 | Leyland | H28/26R | 1948 |

The introduction of a synchromesh gearbox and the new Leyland E600 9.8-litre engine, together with other refinements, were the usual identifying mechanical features of the Titan PD2 model. Not so with Southdown, however; only a few of this batch had synchromesh gearboxes. If, like Southdown's examples, the type was fitted with Leyland's standard bodywork, at-a-glance recognition was possible from the shorter front panel to the cab, which left an area of mudguard exposed – although for Southdown enthusiasts, the registration letters did the trick. The model was to prove extremely durable, many lasting in the Southdown fleet until 1967.

Guy Arab III, 1948-49

| 500-5 | JCD 500-5 | Guy Arab III | NCME | H28/26R | 1948 |
| 506-11 | JCD 506-11 | Guy Arab III | NCME | H28/26R | 1949 |

Subject of a 'free-choice' order from Southdown, as a result of its satisfactory experience with the wartime Mark II model, were a dozen Guy Arab III double-deckers. The robust Northern Counties product was the favoured bodywork, again as a result of experience with earlier Guys.

The batch were all fitted with Gardner 6LW engines, but the bodywork of one (No. 502), which was exhibited at the 1948 Commercial Motor Show, had a more elaborate finish than the rest and featured a patented NCME ventilation system.

It may have been one of the most widely employed buses of its time, particularly by municipalities and BET companies, but this all-Leyland standard took some beating for looks – and the slightly bulbous waistrail in the midst of all that flush panelling was a masterstroke. The only problem with the now metal-framed bodywork was that it tended to pick up the vibration of that big 9.8-litre Leyland engine on tickover. However, this was a bus that, in the early days at least, tended to be reserved for the more distinguished routes – as No. 324 (JCD 24) shows.

As though to show its gratitude to Guy Motors Ltd for its World War II rescue act, Southdown placed an order for a dozen of its new Arab Mark III chassis. The bodywork was carried out by Northern Counties of Wigan, the front elevations immediately recognisable as products of that manufacturer. For such a small batch, however, there were some interesting variations. Number 502 (JCD 502) for instance, the bodybuilders exhibit at the 1948 Commercial Motor Show, was the test bed for the company's new ventilation system. The quarterlights probably acted also as a prototype for those used in a double-decker coach, on a Leyland chassis, built by NCME for Southdown (see next page). Number 503 (JCD 503), meanwhile, employed a more orthodox window arrangement with a less-obvious ventilation system.

Bedford OB, 1948

70-1	JCD 370-1	Bedford OB	Duple	C27F	1948

In order to help out the Leyland Cheetah coaches on the Hayling Island to London express service, Southdown made what was, for the company, a most unusual purchase – a pair of new Bedford OB/Duple coaches. The chassis/coachwork combination was thoroughly standard, although the usual seating capacity for the Duple Vista bodywork was 29. The type prolonged the use of petrol in the fleet, being fitted with Bedford's 3.5-litre 6-cylinder engine. The whining but not unpleasant rise and fall of the gearbox noise, common elsewhere, was peculiar in vehicles bearing Southdown colours. The opening of the replacement Hayling Bridge in 1956, doomed them to just two years further service with Southdown, downgraded for bus work at other locations.

More like the local garage-proprietor's bus than a Southdown – but there were two of them delivered in 1948. Frequently depicted on film and TV as a typical World War II vehicle – which of course, it was not – the Bedford OB with Duple coachwork was Britain's favourite country-lane coach of the early 'fifties. Southdown had other plans for theirs; they were purchased specifically for the relief of those Leyland Cheetah coaches providing Hayling Island with an express route to London. Number 70 (JCD 370) catches the evening sun during a well-earned rest from such duties.

Dennis Falcon P4, 1949

82-91	JUF 82-91	Dennis Falcon P4	Dennis	B30R	1949

Southdown's first post-war saloon buses, and that after a ten-year gap, were somewhat unexpected in choice of manufacturer. Supportive purchases by sister BET company Aldershot & District for the local Guildford firm of Dennis had been long-established practice, but in Southdown's case a resumption of orders from Leyland was generally expected. Instead the honour to provide the company with its last half-cab, front-engined saloons fell to the Guildford company. The Falcon, with 4-cylinder engine, was almost identic1al to those purchased by Southdown in 1939, although this batch of ten were now fitted with rear-entrance bodywork by Dennis. They went to work on Hayling Island, where they were joined by the 1939-vintage Falcons, transferred there from Worthing in 1950.

'That bridge' was also the reason for the purchase of Southdown's last vehicles of Dennis manufacture – in 1949. There were ten of them; the Falcon P4 model, each featuring Dennis's peculiarity of the time, an asymmetrically-mounted engine – giving the buses a somewhat thoughtful expression. The lightweight Dennis bodywork sat 30, and the rather cavernous interior came as a surprise in what appeared outwardly to be a small bus. Number 84 (JUF 84) makes one of its last crossings of the bridge.

Leyland Titan PD2/12, 1950

700	KUF 700	Leyland PD2/12	NCME	FCH28/16RD	1950

Since Northern Counties had been chosen to provide the bodywork for the Guy Arab III double-deckers that firm was also approached to design and construct an experimental one-off double-deck express coach. This was built on Southdown's first PD2/12 version of the Leyland Titan chassis which took advantage of the 27ft by 8ft dimensions first permitted for double-deck two-axle vehicles in general operation that year. As built, it seated 44 and was tried out on the Eastbourne-London service. Several difficulties surfaced, however; it was more than a ton overweight, which made it sluggish on hills, and rolled, disconcertingly for the top-deck passengers, on every bend. Reseating to 58 places in 1952 did not help and it was reconverted to 50 seats for private hire duties that same year. In that capacity the vehicle survived until 1966, although it remained in Southdown ownership until 1973 after some half-hearted attempts to turn it into a breakdown lorry. The main contribution made by the vehicle, however, is that the ancestry of the later and highly successful NCME bodywork on PD3 series chassis may be traced to it. No. 700 is illustrated in Colour Section 1.

Left, and facing page top: An innovation which led to a great deal of interest in the trade press in 1950 was the launch of Southdown's new double-decker coach for express working on the London-Eastbourne service. Number 700 (KUF 700) was the first Leyland Titan PD2/12 model for Southdown – the concept being both to carry more passengers per trip and to give over half of them a railway-standard view of the countryside en route. It incorporated that special NCME ventilation, had glass roof-coving and padded coach seats throughout; looked good and sounded good. Unfortunately, it was overweight, rolled in a way which made even the downstairs passengers queasy and proved underpowered – all factors which even an official trip by the top brass of Southdown couldn't put right. The vehicle was repainted in standard stage-carriage pattern, up-seated to 50 and down-graded for private-hire duties, which penance it performed until 1966.

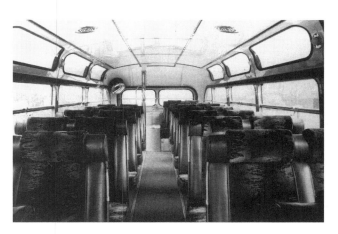

Acquisitions from various operators for oil-engines, 1950-51

As part of its considerable refurbishment of pre-war Titan vehicles, then on-going, Southdown purchased 55 Tiger and Titan buses second-hand, solely for the re-use of their oil-engines. They were not given fleet numbers and did not enter service with Southdown. Acquisitions were as follows; from Yorkshire Woollen District, Dewsbury: eighteen Tiger TS8 saloons and ten Titan TD5 double-deckers; from East Midland Motor Services, Chesterfield: three Tiger TS6 saloons; eight Tiger TS7 saloons; one Tiger TS8 saloon (and two Cub KPZ2 saloons for exchange with Cub petrol units already in the fleet); from County Motors, Lepton: two Tiger TS8 saloons; from Yorkshire Traction, Barnsley: one Tiger TS7 saloon; from East Yorkshire Motor Services, Hull: seven Tiger TS7; and five further oil-engined units from Sunderland District, Philadelphia, Co Durham. These vehicles were variously scrapped or, in most cases, re-engined with discarded petrol units before re-sale. The engines were to be employed in the drive to establish an all-compression ignition-engined fleet.

The remains of the open Paddock at Portslade Works with a sea of Leyland Tiger saloons, including three lobster-backed utilities, from East Midland Motor Services Ltd and other operators. The mildly sinister scenario was that they were wanted solely for their diesel engines which were about to be removed and placed in the 'Unit Store' or 'Fridge', as it was nicknamed, in the background. Southdown was about to embark upon a drive toward the establishment of a completely diesel-engined fleet. The Short-bodied Titan with covered top awaited a different fate.

Leyland Titan PD2/12 1951-57

701-24	KUF 701-24	Leyland PD2/12	Leyland	H32/26R	1951	
725-32	LUF 225-32	Leyland PD2/12	Leyland	H32/26R	1951	
733-44	LUF 233-44	Leyland PD2/12	Leyland	H32/26RD	1952	
745-54	MCD 745-54	Leyland PD2/12	Leyland	H30/26RD	1953	
755-64	MUF 455-64	Leyland PD2/12	NCME	H30/26RD	1953	
765-76	OCD 765-76	Leyland PD2/12	Park Royal	H31/26RD	1955	

Continuous evolution of the post-war Leyland double-decked body is evident on No. 704 (KUF 704), a Titan PD2/12 from the 1951 delivery showing off its lines at Hilsea coach station. As originally built it featured the now old-fashioned open platform. Farther down the line at South Parade Pier, Southsea, No. 760 (MUF 460) collects passengers for Worthing. This was Northern Counties' solution to the bodybuilding task for this model and was fitted with platform doors from new. The sliding driver's door was a new feature for Southdown.

777-88	RUF 177-88	Leyland PD2/12	Beadle	H33/26RD	1956
789-804	RUF 189-204	Leyland PD2/12	East Lancs	H33/26RD	1956
805-12	RUF 205-12	Leyland PD2/12	East Lancs	H33/26R	1957

Even as late as 1951, Nos. 701-24 were delivered with crash gearboxes, but the long-running production life of the Titan PD2/12 type provided Southdown with 112 vehicles in addition to the ill-starred No. 700. The more prosaic stage-carriage vehicles got off to a famous start, when No. 701 was on show at the Festival of Britain exhibition in 1951 as an example of the wonders of all-Leyland construction. Number 725-32 had enclosed platforms without doors initially, but the latter were fitted at Portslade Works in 1952. The following year, 701-24 began entering the works to be brought up to the same standard. All future deliveries, with five different makes of bodywork, were so fitted from new. The type was represented in the Southdown fleet until 1971.

Beadle's dozen ! John C. Beadle of Dartford produced bodywork for twelve of the 1956 delivery of Leyland Titan PD2/12s. What was not realised at the time was that these would be the last double-deckers produced for Southdown by this firm. In just over two years hence this designer and manufacturer of a long series of stylish and sought-after public service vehicles would begin to wind down that side of the business to concentrate upon private car sales. That the firm made the decision to withdraw from the field on a high note was evidenced by the simple clean lines, both outside and in, up and down, of No. 777 (RUF 177). It was a fine example of what amounted to the ultimate half-cab conventional double-decker, which although based on Park Royal frames, and using a number of that builder's parts, nevertheless retained an essential Beadle characteristic.

Leyland Royal Tiger PSU1/15, 1951-53

800-9	LCD 200-9	Leyland PSU1/15	Duple	C26C	1951
810-29	LUF 810-29	Leyland PSU1/15	Harrington	C26C	1952
1600-19	LUF 600-19	Leyland PSU1/15	Duple	C41C	1952
1620-44	LUF 620-44	Leyland PSU1/15	Leyland	C41C	1952
1645-9	MCD 45-9	Leyland PSU1/15	Duple	C41C	1953

Wheras previous Titan types had been marketed with a corresponding Tiger single-decked counterpart, the PD2/12 was the first to find itself without such a similar UK stablemate. A 30ft-long underfloor-engined single-deck chassis was now considered a more promising line of development; it was called the Royal Tiger and was fitted with basically the same O.600 9.8-litre engine as the PD2 with many other mechanical features in common – even if the overall appearance was radically different. Southdown's first coaches of this type were modest in carrying capacity, seating a mere 26 in 'two and one' formation as they were intended as touring coaches. Those for express service duties were numbered in a separate series and seated 41 within the same dimensions. Duple's coachwork for the first twenty of these was the same 'Ambassador' shell provided for numbers 800-9, but the five from that firm in 1953 were built to a very different design called the 'Coronation Ambassador'. The Leyland bodywork on the 25 examples delivered in 1952 was the manufacturer's own coachwork design for this model – and consequently as 'unusual' as the ECW bodies had been in the Tiger PS1 era. Nos. 1641/5 are illustrated in Colour Section 2.

The radical change in coach design which ushered in the 'fifties was the removal of the engine from the front of the chassis and placing it underfloor. This provided clear floor-space at the front and permitted the front axle to be placed much farther rearwards to improve manoeuvrability whatever the length of the vehicle.

Leading experts in the field were Leyland with their Royal Tiger PSU1/15 model which, in 1951, attracted Southdown as an early buyer. The first ten were bodied by Duple to its 'Ambassador' design (seen upper right) and were fitted out, like No. 801(LCD 201), with cove lights and only 26 seats for 'coach-cruise' duties. Deliveries commenced in May of that year. Secondly, a contract for 20 was placed with Harrington who constructed them to a design (below left) which was at once similar but different. The Harrington example offered higher ground clearance at the front for instance, the advantage of which still dawns late over forty years later. The most avante garde design for the chassis was Leyland's own 41-seater express coach. Number 1620 (LUF 620) is en route for Bournemouth in June 1957 on the famous South Coast Express run jointly with Royal Blue, and East Kent.

Leyland Royal Tiger PSU1/13, 1952-53

1500-9	LUF 500-9	Leyland PSU1/13	East Lancs	B40R	1952
1510-39	MCD 510-39	Leyland PSU1/13	East Lancs	B40C	1953

The stage-carriage saloon-bus form of the Royal Tiger was designated PSU1/13. Southdown ordered 40, all bodied by East Lancashire in a very purposeful design incorporating Southdown specification details. Since there was at that time no thought of one-man-operation of such a vehicle, the traditional rear entrance was retained on the first ten, and a centre one on the remainder – the latter type being electrically operated. Nos. 1525/8 are illustrated in Colour Section 1.

Waste-not-want not'. Prior to putting the flat faces on the post-war Leyland Tigers, Beadle had already taken to task numerous pre-war Tiger and Titan running units and used them for the basis of some revamped Leyland-Beadle integral coaches. The first twenty, with original identities removed from the registration plate, were 30ft models providing seats for 35 passengers. Number 851 (LCD 851) and its companions entered service in 1952. Clearly, one needed a flat front to attract customers to the races.

Leyland-Beadle integral 30ft coaches, 1952

850-69	LCD 850-69	Leyland-Beadle	Beadle	FC35C	1952

Although the arrival of underfloor-engined Royal Tigers began to signal the end of the pre-war Tiger bus and coach fleets, major parts of the chassis of 50 of them were to see a further decade's use with the company. Like several BET companies, Southdown took delivery of Beadle integral coaches using pre-World War II Leyland units, the first batch of twenty delivered in 1952 having chassis extended to 30ft and seating 35 passengers.

Leyland-Beadle integral 26ft coaches, 1953-54

870-84	MCD 870-84	Leyland-Beadle	Beadle	FC26F	1953
885-92	MUF 485-92	Leyland-Beadle	Beadle	FC26F	1953
893-6	NCD 93-6	Leyland-Beadle	Beadle	FC26F	1953
897-7	NCD 97-9	Leyland-Beadle	Beadle	FC26F	1954

The remaining thirty integral units were more unusual among those delivered to BET companies in that they were 26ft, 26-seater vehicles. The running gear of both types was from Tiger TS8 saloons and coaches, the chassis being cut to form front and rear sub-frames. Coming in the midst of deliveries of underfloor-engined coaches, however, and despite the best efforts of the makers, they looked dated from the outset. Car 876 was built upon the chassis frame of 1443, latterly a one-off half-canopied Harrington coach, but earlier the unfortunate saloon blown over the hedge by a German bomb whilst on the road between Rushlake Green and Punnett's Town on 2nd November 1940. No. 885 is illustrated in Colour Section 2.

Duple continued to employ their straightforward 'Ambassador' design for the Leyland Royal Tiger PSU1/16 variants which they bodied for the company in 1953-4. Number 1676 (NUF 76) was a 41-seater primarily intended for middle-range coach tours, but capable also of being made ready at short notice for express work. Some detail differences from earlier examples are evident at both front and rear ends and there is a different treatment of the vehicles' high waistline, but the same basic jigs appear to have been used.

Leyland Royal Tiger PSU1/16, 1953-55

830-1	MUF 430-1	Leyland PSU1/16	Harrington	C26C	1953
832-4	OUF 832-4	Leyland PSU1/16	Harrington	C26C	1955
1650-9	MUF 650-9	Leyland PSU1/16	Duple	C41C	1953
1661-8	NCD 661-8	Leyland PSU1/16	Duple	C41C	1954
1669-80	NUF 69-80	Leyland PSU1/16	Duple	C41C	1954

The inclusion of refinements such as air pressure braking identified the Royal Tiger PSU1/16 model. The gentle evolution of their first underfloor-engined coach design was commenced by Harrington on the five touring examples, whilst Southdown evidently favoured the earlier 'Ambassador', rather than the arguably more modern 'Coronation Ambassador', for the next batch of express coaches from Duple. No. 831 is illustrated in Colour Section 2.

Leyland Tiger Cub PSUC1/1, 1954-62

After a considerable time lapse, and the legislation in 1961 which permitted the legal length of a saloon bus or coach to be increased to 36ft (11 metres), Southdown took the opportunity to purchase ten further Tiger Cubs. These were stretched PSUC1/1 models however and the Marshall bodies fitted to them could seat 45 in their front-entrance bodies. All entered service in 1962, and No. 660 (7660 CD) is about to reach the Pool Valley, Brighton terminus of service 36 from East Grinstead in June 1964.

The Leyland Tiger Cub PSUC1/1 saloon bus bodied by the Duple associate Nudd Brothers & Lockyer offered one seat fewer (at 39) than the heavier Royal Tiger saloons delivered two years previously. And there's the reason why: a central emergency door instead of an upholstered bench for five across the rear of the gangway. The standard Southdown moquette is retained, but the entrance has gone to the front. This is the highly functional interior of No. 626 (MUF 626), delivered in 1954.

620-39	MUF 620-39	Leyland PSUC1/1	Nudd Bros & Lockyer	B39F	1954
640-3	OUF 640-3	Leyland PSUC1/1	Park Royal	B39F	1955
644	PUF 844	Leyland PSUC1/1	Park Royal	B39F	1955
655-64	7655-64 CD	Leyland PSUC1/1	Marshall	B45F	1962

Reaction against the sharp increase in weight of most early underfloor-engined models as compared to their predecessors led to the development of lighter chassis, among which the Leyland Tiger Cub was to form a considerable part of Southdown's fleet from the mid-'fifties. It employed a horizontal 5.76-litre 6-cylinder engine known as the O.350, and with the reduced weight gave better economy than the Royal Tiger, though at the cost of more noise. The PSUC1/1 was the saloon bus version of the type. Nudd Bros & Lockyer, the builder of the first twenty delivered, was a Duple offshoot. Nos. 620/41 are illustrated in Colour Section 1.

Leyland Tiger Cub PSUC1/2 and PSUC1/2T, 1955-62

1000-3	OUF 100-3	Leyland PSUC1/2	Beadle	C37C	1955
1004-8	OUF 104-8	Leyland PSUC1/2	Beadle	C41C	1955
1009-14	OUF 112-4	Leyland PSUC1/2	Beadle	C37C	1955
1015-39	OUF 115-39	Leyland PSUC1/2	Beadle	C41C	1955
1040-74	RUF 40-74	Leyland PSUC1/2	Beadle	C41C	1956
1075-90	SUF 875-90	Leyland PSUC1/2	Beadle	C41C	1957
1091-3	SUF 891-3	Leyland PSUC1/2	Beadle	C37C	1957
1094-6	SUF 894-6	Leyland PSUC1/2	Beadle	C41C	1957
T1097-102	SUF 897-902	Leyland PSUC1/2	Beadle	C41C	1957
1103-14	SUF 903-14	Leyland PSUC1/2	Beadle	C41C	1957
115-9	UCD 115-9	Leyland PSUC1/2	Beadle	C41F	1958
1220-5	UCD 120-5	Leyland PSUC1/2	Beadle	C37F	1958
T1126-7	UCD 126-7	Leyland PSUC1/2	Beadle	C41F	1958
1128-9	UCD 128-9	Leyland PSUC1/2	Beadle	C32F	1958
1130-44	XUF 130-44	Leyland PSUC1/2	Weymann	C37F	1960
1145-50	8145-50 CD	Leyland PSUC1/2T	Weymann	C37F	1962
1151-4	8151-54 CD	Leyland PSUC1/2T	Weymann	C41F	1962

The coach version of Leyland's Tiger Cub model was the PSUC1/2. Southdown's first examples arrived in 1955, starting a renewed 1000-up fleet number series. Between 1955 and 1958, Beadle provided the coachwork for 130 of the type, which batch included two interesting departures from the usual Southdown colours. Numbers T1097-102 and T1126-7 entered service in the blue and cream livery of Triumph Coaches, Portsmouth, whose excursion and forces leave programme Southdown acquired in May 1957. Although the T prefix was dropped in 1960, Nos. 1091/2/106/8/15/7/45-8 were repainted into Triumph livery also at various times in the 'sixties, whilst the Triumph excursion programme continued to be operated as a separate entity until 1968. Meanwhile No. 1129, dating from January 1958, was painted in the blue livery of Linjebuss and used exclusively for that Swedish operator's tours of Britain. It wore its fleet number for the first time in 1964 when it was repainted into Southdown livery. The last fifteen were fitted with Weymann Fanfare coachwork, supplied by that firm to several BET companies at that time. The Beadle-bodied examples served until 1970, the Weymann 1973. The 37-seaters were allocated mainly to the Beacon Tours programme which was a new venture aimed at the cheaper end of the 'centred-tour' market – Southdown's version of a fantail. In the manufacturer's designation, the suffix T meant two-speed back axle. Nos. 1067, 1100/39 are illustrated in Colour Section 2.

One final order for Guy chassis was placed by Southdown in 1955. Forty-eight Arab IV units with Gardner 6LW engines were delivered in two batches, all with bodywork by Park Royal. Number 528 (PUF 628) was a member of the second (1956) group of vehicles. The twelve which arrived in the previous year differed only in such details as wind-down ventilation on alternate windows rather than sliding units on all, and the provision of an indicator box over the rear entrance. They served Southdown until the start of the NBC era.

Guy Arab IV 6LW, 1955-56

| 512-23 | OUF 512-23 | Guy Arab IV 6LW | Park Royal | H31/26RD | 1955 |
| 524-59 | PUF 624-59 | Guy Arab IV 6LW | Park Royal | H33/26RD | 1966 |

The Guy Arab with 6LW Gardner engine, this time the Mark IV, was again in favour in 1955-56, when 48 were delivered with Park Royal bodywork. Southdown was among those operators who rejected the now standard 'tin front' version in favour of the traditional Guy radiator. The projecting bonnet of Marks II and III had now gone. Number 547 was fitted with a sliding door instead of the usual folding type. Several of the 1966 batch lasted in Southdown service until 1971.

Southdown No. 1 (RUF 101), a generous honour for a rather noisy coach. The bodywork by Beadle – their 'Rochester' type – owed much to the current Southdown idea of what a coach should look like, particularly one which could seat 41 passengers; but the running units were Beadle-Commer integral composites fitted with the TS3 diesel engine. Delivered in 1956, No. 1 departs from Brighton with a day-tripper excursion: the following day it could have had its boards attached and be off on a London express.

Beadle-Commer TS3, 1956-57

1-5	RUF 101-5	Beadle-Commer TS3	Beadle	C41C	1956
6-15	TCD 6-15	Beadle-Commer TS3	Beadle	C41F	1957
16-25	TUF 16-25	Beadle-Commer TS3	Beadle	C41F	1957

The choice of Commer units for the Southdown fleet must go down as another company 'surprise'. Twenty-five of these lightweight integral coaches entered service over two seasons, fitted with the snarling TS3 two-stroke diesel engine made at the old Tilling-Stevens factory in Maidstone, whence in earlier times had come so many of Southdown's vehicles. The coachwork on these Beadle-Commers was known as the 'Rochester' type. It looked like a Southdown coach, even if it didn't quite sound like one. No. 15 is illustrated in Colour Section 2.

Leyland Titan PD3/4 and 3/5, 1958-67

813-27	TCD 813-27	Leyland PD3/4	NCME	FH39/30F	1958
828-42	VUF 828-42	Leyland PD3/4	NCME	FH39/30F	1959
843-53	XUF 843-53	Leyland PD3/4	NCME	FH39/30F	1959
854-62	XUF 854-62	Leyland PD3/4	NCME	FH39/30F	1960
863	2863 CD	Leyland PD3/4	NCME	FH39/30F	1960
864-912	2864-912CD	Leyland PD3/4	NCME	FH39/30F	1961
913-31	6913-31CD	Leyland PD3/5	NCME	FH39/30F	1962
932-52	6932-52CD	Leyland PD3/5	NCME	FH39/30F	1961
953-77	953-77 CUF	Leyland PD3/4	NCME	FH39/30F	1964
400-24	400-24 DCD	Leyland PD3/4	NCME	FCO39/30F	1964
250-56	BUF 250-56C	Leyland PD3/4	NCME	FH39/30F	1965
257	BUF 257C	Leyland PD3/4	NCME	FH39/28F	1965
258-84	BUF 258-84C	Leyland PD3/4	NCME	FH39/30F	1965
425-9	BUF 425-9C	Leyland PD3/4	NCME	FCO39/30F	1965
285-314	FCD 285-314D	Leyland PD3/4	NCME	FH39/30F	1966
315	GUF 250D	Leyland PD3/4	NCME	FH39/30F	1966
346-69	HCD 346-69E	Leyland PD3/4	NCME	FH39/30F	1967

There are many parallels between Ribble Motor Services Ltd and Southdown, as fellow members sequentially of Tilling & British Automobile Traction, BET and NBC with a strong affinity for Leylands; as may be judged from a comparison between these volumes and the corresponding ones on Ribble. Both companies turned to the Titan PD3/4 with full-fronted forward-entrance bodywork for their first 30ft-long double-deck buses in 1956 but the first Southdown example to arrive was No. 827 of May 1958, although numerically the last of the first batch of fifteen. Few could have realised then that the all-time classic Southdown bus had joined the fleet – the vanguard of the company's largest single group of vehicles, comprising 285 units eventually. Northern Counties of Wigan obtained the body contract for all of them, the seating capacity, save No. 257, being a restrained 69. Unladen weight was 8 tons 3 qtrs, rather less than some of the Royal Tiger coaches of the early 'fifties. There was, nevertheless, a certain irony in the use of what was clearly a modified 27ft structure, with resultant short bay amidships. By mid-1961, Southdown had exactly 100 of them in service. A 1961-62 batch of 40 differed in an important respect in being on PD3/5 chassis with pneumocyclic semi-automatic rather than synchromesh gearbox – Southdown's first departure from conventional transmission since the torque-converter Titans of the 'thirties. None were delivered in 1963, but in 1964 came 50 more, including 25 of a new 'convertible' version with detachable top cover. For these Southdown decided to revert to synchromesh gearbox, so they were PD3/4 models once again. The open-top buses were given a new series of fleet numbers commencing at 400, thus replacing the last survivors, themselves converted to open-top, of the wartime Guy Arabs which had been the previous occupants of this series. This batch would become a source of 'cherished number' plates for later Southdown vehicles in the far-off 'eighties. Further PD3/4 double-deckers of basically similar design were delivered until 1967. Numbers 257 of 1965 and 315 of the following year, however, were two 'special' versions of the body with experimental heating and ventilating systems. Number 315 was a Northern Counties exhibit at the Earls Court Show in 1966. With other operators beginning to go rear-engined, the very wide side windows and curved-glass front screens of this pair provided a sub-type which was at one and the same time both futuristic and anachronistic. Clearly, Southdown thought so too. The PD3s proved reliable, long-lived and

Same Commer Avenger IV chassis, same moquette, but considerably different interior design concepts are evident between the products of Blackpool and Hove. In No. 35 (VUF 935) (left) the Burlingham notion of togetherness on the seat prevails. The Harrington version (right) No. 41 (XUF 41) seems more concerned with keeping the trippers firmly in their places and keeping the headrests clean. Neither type reached the usual high standards of their builders on the outside either. Add to that the clatter of the TS3 engine and . . .

liked by their crews. Nos 8125/32, 942, 257 and 286 are illustrated in Colour Section 1; 356 and 424 in Section 3.

Numbers 409 and 424 survived to serve in traditional livery with Stagecoach South, primarily for publicity reasons – but it is not unknown for them to be called out on service when needs must. That they continue to perform without fuss surprises only those unfamiliar with the type.

Although nominally a new chassis make to Southdown, apart from acquired vehicles, the fifteen Commer coaches of 1959 were effectively a continuation of the Beadle-Commer of 1956-57, the Avenger IV chassis having the TS3 engine and other mechanical units in common. More noteworthy was a return to Burlingham after some 23 years. The second batch had Harrington bodywork, again seating 35. Neither reached the standard of elegance achieved by their builder in earlier designs for Southdown. Nos. 38 and 46 are illustrated in Colour Section 2.

Thomas Harrington's masterpiece – the light and airy interior of the Cavalier in touring coach form with glass quarterlights. To keep all round and upward vision as clear as possible, a fabric-masked lightweight luggage rack for small possessions was restricted to the right hand side of the vehicle only. In long-established 'coach-cruise' format the comfortable armchair seats were arranged two-and-one beside the gangway and a generous collection of 'coach rugs' was supplied from the stores at Portslade Works.

Leyland Leopard L2T, 1961-63

1700-29	2700-29 CD	Leyland L2T	Harrington	C28F	1961
1730-9	8730-9 CD	Leyland L2T	Harrington	C28F	1961
1740-2	8740-2 CD	Leyland L2T	Harrington	C28F	1962
1745-8	545-8 BUF	Leyland L2T	Harrington	C28F	1963
1749-53	749-53 DCD	Leyland L2T	Harrington	C28F	1963

Harrington's most successful and elegant design of the underfloor-engine era was the now-famous 'Cavalier'. Southdown took delivery of a new touring fleet in the spring and summer of 1961 consisting of 30 coaches with 28-seat bodywork of this type on the recently introduced Leyland Leopard L2T chassis. The initial version of this model was very like the Tiger Cub, with the important difference of having the O.600 engine and synchromesh gearbox, but Southdown's had the added distinction of air suspension, a rare feature at that date. A further 22 L2T coaches, again bodied by Harrington followed, the last five to the prototype 'Grenadier' pattern. No. 1745 is illustrated in Colour Section 2.

Leyland Leopard PSU3/3RT and 3R, 1962-68

1155-9	8155-9 CD	Leyland PSU3/3RT	Weymann	C49F	1962
I743-4	8743-4 CD	Leyland PSU3/3RT	Harrington	C49F	1962
1160	160 AUF	Leyland PSU3/3RT	Weymann	C45F	1962
1161-5	161-5 AUF	Leyland PSU3/3RT	Weymann	C45F	1963
1166-74	166-74 AUF	Leyland PSU3/3RT	Weymann	C49F	1963

Number 1180 (480 DUF) was a one-off downseated 36ft Leyland Leopard PSU3/3R coach delivered in 1965 and put at the disposal of the Swedish touring concern Linje-Tours International. Dressed in that firm's logo, the vehicle was bodied with Plaxton's Panorama model with exceptionally wide windows and 35 seats gained from a front-entrance and intended for long distance 'coach-cruise' operations throughout the British mainland. Its career was launched with a successful appearance at the 10th British Coach Rally.

1175-9	175-9 DCD	Leyland PSU3/3R	Plaxton	C49F	1964
1180	480 DUF	Leyland PSU3/3R	Plaxton	C35F	1964
1181-90	BUF 81-90C	Leyland PSU3/3RT	Plaxton	C49F	1964
1754-63	BUF 154-63C	Leyland PSU3/3RT	Harrington	C41F	1965
1191-224	EUF 191-224D	Leyland PSU3/3RT	Plaxton	C49F	1966
1774-98	HCD 374-98E	Leyland PSU3/3RT	Duple Northern	C41F	1967

1225-49	LCD 225-49F	Leyland PSU3/3RT	Plaxton	C49F	1968

The Leyland PSU3/3 range was the 36ft-long version of the Leopard introduced in 1962. Deliveries commenced with Weymann's 'Castilian' bodied examples, being a development of that firm's shorter 'Fanfare' design. Number 1160 had been the coachbuilder's Earls Court Show exhibit before arrival. The deliveries also represented a first and, sadly, a last. A 'new' bodybuilder to Southdown was Plaxton, who introduced their 'Panorama' design to good effect whilst, in October 1964, Harrington of Hove prepared to deliver their last ten coaches to Southdown prior to closing their coachbuilding section after virtually half a century's association with the company. These included Harrington's 'Grenadier' design reduced to 33ft for Beacon Continental Tours work. Thus the firm departed the scene on a high aesthetic note, winning prizes at the British Coach Rally, as of old. Weymann-bodied Nos. 1157-9 were in Triumph livery. Nos. 1158/78, 1796/7 are illustrated in Colour Section 2.

Leyland Leopard PSU3/1RT and 1R, 1963-69

665-89	265-89 AUF	Leyland PSU3/1RT	Marshall	B51F	1963
100-19	100-19 CUF	Leyland PSU3/1RT	Marshall	B51F	1963

The 1961 legislation on the permissible length of buses of course led to the production of specially-designed 36ft (11 metre) saloon buses, the Leyland Leopard PSU3/1R range among them. Between 1963-68, 135 of the marque would be bodied to a basic BET Federation design. The first, like No. 681 (281 AUF) were by Marshall, a firm which had reinforced its Southdown order book of late. Detail differences from those bodied by Weymann – No. 144 (EUF 144D) was an example – are only evident to the sharp-eyed. Those constructed in 1968 by Willowbrook, however, were much easier to identify at a glance by virtue of obvious structural differences, but which still complied with the BET pattern, like No. 204 (KUF 204F).

120-39	BUF 120-39C	Leyland PSU3/1RT	Marshall	B45F	1965
140-59	EUF 140-59D	Leyland PSU3/1R	Weymann	B45F	1966
160-9	HUF 760-9E	Leyland PSU3/1R	Marshall	B45F	1967
170-94	KCD 170-94F	Leyland PSU3/1R	Marshall	B45F	1967
195-209	KUF 195-209F	Leyland PSU3/1RT	Willowbrook	B45F	1968
450-459	NUF 450-9G	Leyland PSU3/1RT	NCME	DP49F	1969
460-79	PUF 160-79H	Leyland PSU3/1RT	NCME	DP49F	1969

PSU3/1R was the designation for the saloon bus version of the 36ft-long Leyland Leopard. Fitted with synchromesh gearbox, this was Southdown's choice of single-decker from 1963 to 1968. A total of 135 were delivered, all having bodywork to the BET Federation design, though the construction was split between Marshall (100), Weymann (20) and Willowbrook (15). The Weymann batch were among the last bodies built before that firm's Addlestone works was closed. The 1963 deliveries seated 51, but from 1965 the capacity was reduced to 45, this being the maximum under which one-man-operation was possible under the terms of a national trade union agreement then in force. Delivered towards the end of 1969 were 30 dual-purpose vehicles on the same chassis. These were bodied by Northern Counties to an unusual design having the front end basically to BET outline but with the main structure built to a considerably higher level; the rear end being of a style evolved by the bodybuilder. The original livery of this batch was two-tone green, the darker colour being, unusually, in the form of a continuous waistband. No. 477 is illustrated in Colour Section 1.

Acquired from A. W. Buckingham (Bucks Coaches), Worthing, May 1963

-	JBP 856	Bedford OB	Duple	C29F	1947
-	JPX 523	Bedford OB	Duple	C29F	1948
-	LPX 150	Bedford OB	Duple	C29F	1950

These three vehicles were not allotted fleet numbers and JBP 856 was not operated by Southdown. The other two ran in their original blue and cream Bucks livery until August of that year, when JPX 523 became a temporary left luggage office for the company at Eastbourne. The Bucks trading name was sufficiently highly thought of in Worthing for Southdown to keep it in being for a further couple of seasons, actually going so far as to repaint two Royal Tiger Coaches (OUF 832-3), recently returned from long-term tour duties for Southdown in Northern Ireland, into the blue Bucks livery until their withdrawal in 1966. LPX 150 is illustrated in Colour Section 2.

The availability on the open market for the first time in two decades of buses of Bristol manufacture led to some BET companies, Southdown among them, to jump the gun and purchase that manufacturer's RE saloon model before such matters were decided for the subsidiaries by the emergent National Bus Company. Original examples to reach Southdown in 1968 were an interesting amalgam of Tilling and BET-style interests – Bristol RE chassis and Marshall bodywork. Nevertheless the Bristol/Eastern Coach Works combination, already standard among Transport Holding Company subsidiaries such as Hants & Dorset, was not neglected. The National Bus Company was an established fact, however, before the first examples of those arrived at Portslade Works in 1970. Number 602 (UCD 602J) was an RELL6L – a Leyland-engined, long-bodied 50-seater of 1971. No-one seems to have warned Eastern Coach Works that if a Mackenzie-style transfer were put on horizontally it would look as though it was falling to the right: the whole batch were the same – the missing ha'p'orth of tar.

Bristol RESL6G, RELL5G, RESL6L, RELL6L saloons, 1968-71

210-249	KUF 210-249F	Bristol RESL6G	Marshall	B43F	1968
430-449	NUF 430-449G	Bristol RELL6G	Marshall	B49F	1969
481-490	TCD 481-490J	Bristol RESL6L	Marshall	B45F	1970
600 (2213)	TCD 600J	Bristol RESL6G	ECW	B37+28D	1970
2211-2212	TCD 611-612J	Bristol RESL6G	ECW	B37+28D	1970
601-603	UCD 601-630J	Bristol RELL6L	ECW	B50F	1971

The Bristol era began at Southdown early in 1968, just after BET had agreed to sell its British bus-operating interests to the State and thence leading to Southdown's incorporation within the National Bus Company from 1st January 1969. However, the first order, for 40 RESL6G single-deckers, was one of quite a number placed by BET companies after Bristol chassis came back on to the open market (they had previously been restricted to fully-nationalised operating companies), when it was widely agreed that the RE series represented the best available among rear-engined single-deckers. For the first batch, Southdown chose the shorter-length RESL model with Gardner 6HLW horizontal engine; the Marshall bodywork remaining very much BET-flavoured on that and two subsequent deliveries. In 1970-71, thirteen of those purchased were fitted with Leyland O.680 engines (RESL and RELL6L types), and by a combination of chassis-length and engine make managed to purchase four differing sub types of the model – or five if the bodywork is taken into account, for the last six vehicles represented the start of the company's first-hand purchases of the classic Bristol/Eastern Coach Works combination. Number 600 was delivered in Southdown apple green and primrose but did not enter service until it had been repainted red and deep cream and renumbered into the BH&D fleet, thus placing all thirteen dual-door REs into the same livery, for duties as BH&D one-man-operated vehicles. Nos. 231/5 are illustrated in Colour Section 1.

Acquired from the Brighton Hove & District Omnibus Co Ltd, Hove, January 1969

426	FNJ 108	Bristol KS5G	ECW	H32/28R	1951
2442	GPM 902	Bristol KSW6G	ECW	H32/28R	1952
443	GPN 991	Bristol KSW6G	ECW	H32/28R	1953
444	GPN 992	Bristol KSW6G	ECW	H32/28R	1952
445	GPN 993	Bristol KSW6G	ECW	H32/28R	1953
447-9	HAP 985-7	Bristol KSW6G	ECW	H32/28R	1953
2450	HAP 988	Bristol KSW6G	ECW	H32/28R	1953
451	HAP 989	Bristol KSW6G	ECW	H32/28R	1953
2452-7	HAP 990-5	Bristol KSW6G	ECW	H32/28R	1953
2458-61	HAP 996-9	Bristol KSW6G	ECW	H32/28R	1954
462	JAP 500	Bristol KSW6G	ECW	H32/28R	1954
2463-71	JAP 501-9	Bristol KSW6G	ECW	H32/28R	1954
2472-6	JAP 510-4	Bristol KSW6G	ECW	H32/28R	1955
2477-80	KAP 551-4	Bristol KSW6G	ECW	H32/28R	1955
2481-3	KNJ 556-8	Bristol KSW6G	ECW	H32/28R	1955

2485-92	LNJ 485-92	Bristol KSW6G	ECW	H32/28R	1956
2493-500	MPM 493-500	Bristol KS6G	ECW	H32/28R	1957
2001-3	OPN 801-3	Bristol LDS6B	ECW	CO33/27R	1959
2004-8	OPN 804-8	Bristol LDS6B	ECW	H33/27R	1959
2009-11	RPN 9-11	Bristol FS6B	ECW	CO33/27R	1960
2012-20	RPN 12-20	Bristol FS6B	ECW	H33/27R	1960
2021-2	SPM 21-2	Bristol FS6B	ECW	CO33/27R	1960
2023-5	SPM 23-5	Bristol FS6B	ECW	H33/27R	1960
2026-7	TPN 26-7	Bristol FSF6B	ECW	H34/26F	1961
2028-30	UAP 28-30	Bristol FSF6B	ECW	H34/26F	1961
2031-5	VAP 31-5	Bristol FSF6G	ECW	H34/26F	1961
2036-40	WNJ 36-40	Bristol FSF6B	ECW	H34/26F	1962
2041-4	XPM 41-4	Bristol FS6G	ECW	CO33/27R	1962
2045	XPM 45	Bristol FS6G	ECW	H33/27R	1962
2046-50	XPM 46-50	Bristol FS6B	ECW	H33/27R	1962
2051-2	AAP 51-2B	Bristol FS6B	ECW	CO33/27R	1963
2053-4	AAP 53-4B	Bristol FS6B	ECW	CO33/27R	1964
2055-7	4655-7 AP	Bristol FS6G	ECW	H33/27R	1963
2058-9	BPM 58-9B	Bristol FS6G	ECW	H33/27RD	1964
2060-1	CNJ 60-1B	Bristol FS6G	ECW	H33/27RD	1964
2062-4	DAP 62-4C	Bristol FS6B	ECW	H33/27RD	1964
2065-7	DPM 65-7C	Bristol FS6G	ECW	H33/27RD	1965
2068-70	ENJ 68-70C	Bristol FS6B	ECW	H33/27RD	1965

Of similar proportions, but arranged with folding doors at the front, was the FSF range, better suited to longer cross-town journeys with less stopping and starting. No. 2029 (UAP 29) was also Bristol-engined and was therefore an FSF6B. On 19th August 1973, it was going about its normal duties wearing NBC-style SOUTHDOWN-BH&D stickers, in two layers on the nearside because of the available space between door and wheel-arch. The letters BH&D were eventually dropped as the fleet was drawn further into leaf green anonymity.

The management agreement of 1st January 1969 which entitled Southdown to use the assets of the Brighton Hove & District Omnibus Company placed that company's vehicles under Southdown control. They were of 100 per cent Bristol/ECW construction. Most numerous and important were the double-decked Lodekka variants, the backbone of the BH&D fleet. Of those variants, the most useful workhorse for heavily trafficked in-town working was the FS model. Number 11 (with 2000 added to avoid confusion: RPN 11) was a Bristol-engined example.

Yet another livery evident within the joint Southdown-BH&D fleet for some years was the latter's 'open-top' dress of overall cream with black wings. The fleetname in this instance was the interim gold block style which was briefly adopted prior to the standard NBC white adhesive type. Number 2042 (XPM 42) was a Gardner-engined FS Lodekka, a convertible open-topper. Number 2011 was also capable of conversion but was repainted in traditional Southdown colours. Both were photographed in winter.

2071-2	FAP 71-2C	Bristol FS6G	ECW	H33/27RD	1965
2073-5	FPM 73-5C	Bristol FLF6G	ECW	H38/32F	1965
2076-7	GPN 76-7D	Bristol FLF6G	ECW	H38/32F	1966
2078-9	HPN 78-9D	Bristol FLF6G	ECW	H38/32F	1966

Southdown, of course, picked up those orders already placed by BH&D. Among them were the first local examples of Bristol's rear-engined VRT – and few could have foreseen just how many of those there would be in the long run. Number 2011 (OCD 771G), on a town service at Old Steine, was in the first batch of ten delivered in 1969. They provided Portslade Works with their first experience of rear-engined double-deckers – and were given full marks for accessibility to the Gardner engines fitted.

2080-2	JPM 80-2D	Bristol FLF6G	ECW	H38/32F	1966
2083-6	KPM 83-6E	Bristol FLF6G	ECW	H38/32F	1967
2087-92	KPM 87-92E	Bristol FLF6G	ECW	H38/32F	1967
2201-10	PPM 201-10G	Bristol RESL6G	ECW	B35+27D	1968

* see note on fleet numbers below.

The formation of the National Bus Company and the automatic transfer to it of both the Southdown and Brighton Hove & District companies was marked by an agreement which placed responsibility for the day-to-day running of the latter with Southdown, taking effect on 1st January 1969, the same day as NBC itself became operative. Thus the entire extant Bristol/ECW fleet of BH&D came under Southdown control. At first, BH&D was operated as a separate section within Southdown, the fleet retaining its own red and deep cream livery, which had been the subject of an agreement with Brighton Corporation who had also been using the same colours. *In order to avoid confusion, 2000 was added to the fleet numbers of the BH&D vehicles in June 1969, the nine vehicles remaining in the 400 series in the above list having been withdrawn before that date. The BH&D livery and fleetname remained in being for the best part of three years, during which time Southdown purchased new vehicles

Whilst the Daimler CR double-deckers delivered in 1970-71 had bodywork by Northern Counties, those of 1972 were completed by Eastern Coach Works, with prominent engine-bustle at the back. Even at this late stage of the 'honeymoon' period with NBC, these vehicles were painted initially in Southdown apple green and primrose. Number 389 (XUF 389K) is one of several allocated to Chichester depot, where they became a familiar sight and sound. Like virtually all other double-deckers they were eventually repainted leaf green and white.

which it added to the still separate fleet. A start was made in September 1971 on a repainting programme into Southdown apple green and primrose, the fleetname applied to such vehicles being a gold *SOUTHDOWN-BH&D* in the initial NBC universal style, although the larger white NBC standard lettering which supplemented it was for a brief period to be found on vehicles still in red and deep cream livery. The latter style was applied to appropriate vehicles in NBC leaf green and white – until the summer of 1974, when all reference to BH&D was removed from the buses. Thought by many to have ceased to exist, the Brighton Hove & District Omnibus Co Ltd had merely gone into hibernation, and would re-emerge eleven years later. Nos. 2058 and 2206 are illustrated in Colour Section 1.

Number 1840 (UUF 340J) was one of the coaches in the 1971 10-metre batch of Leyland Leopards delivered to Southdown for use on extended 'coach-cruise' duties. To that end, they were fitted with only 32 luxurious seats apiece and dressed in apple and BET dark green with Mackenzie script fleetnames. The bodywork was by Plaxton appropriately named for its wide windows, the 'Panorama Elite'. Some did find their way on to National Express workings eventually but that was not their purpose.

Two 36ft (11 metre) Leopards with Duple Dominant coachwork meet at Chichester Cross on 8th April 1975 and give us an opportunity to view the after end of one of the first Southdown coaches to be delivered in National livery. Number 1258 (CUF 258L) displays its fleetname in red with red and blue double-N National logo beneath. It also gives a clue as to the geographical range of its activities because it was wearing a GB plate also.

Bristol VRT/SL6G double-deckers 1969-70

2093-2012	OCD 763-772G	Bristol VRT/SL6G	ECW	H39/31F	1969
500-505	SCD 500-505H	Bristol VRT/SL6G	ECW	H39/31F	1970
506-509	TCD 506-509J	Bristol VRT/SL6G	ECW	H39/31F	1970

Ordered by Brighton Hove & District, but delivered after the transfer of legal ownerhsip to Southdown, the first ten Bristol VRT double-deckers followed on numerically in the BH&D double-decker sequence, again with 2000 added to avoid duplication. These were Southdown's first rear-engined double-deckers, and compared with other operators, the company had proved late to go front-to-back. With the 1970 deliveries, a new series starting at 500 was commenced for Bristol VRTs. The sequence would go on to reach 699 in 1980 – with more still to come, as the Bristol VRT became NBC's standard double-decker ordered for its subsidiaries. All those delivered to Southdown in 1969-70 were fitted with 6-cylinder Gardner engines. No. 2095 is illustrated in Colour Section 1.

The 'management of BH&D by Southdown' in action. BH&D route 46B being operated on 12th May 1973 by a one-year-old vehicle in full Southdown livery. Number 530 (WUF 530K) was one of a batch of Bristol VRTs with dual-doors specially purchased for keeping the ebb and flow of passengers going in congested in-town situations. This was in contrast to all other VRT batches delivered in 1971-75 which were front-door only and thus better suited to Southdown's long-ranging routes between towns and across the countryside.

Daimler CRG6LX and CRL6 double-deckers, 1970-72

| 2103-2112 | PUF 203-212H | Daimler CRG6LX | NCME | H41/30F | 1970 |
| 370-384 | TCD 370-384J | Daimler CRG6LX-30 | NCME | H40/31F | 1970 |

In overall silver with grey-blue band and SOUTHDOWN fleetname, Bristol VRT No. 566 (GNJ 566N) was one of the vehicles 'dressed overall' by the company to celebrate the Queen's Silver Jubilee in 1977. The vehicle is picking up passengers en route to Portsmouth on the 700 'Coastliner' limited-stop service – and a young lady about to board is unsure whether to proceed or pause eloquently before the camera. The non-reflective BET style windscreen was now to become standard for all future VRT deliveries.

| 2113-2127 | VUF 313-327K | Daimler CRL6L | NCME | H41/30D | 1971 |
| 385-399 | XUF 385-399K | Daimler CRL6L | ECW | H43/31F | 1972 |

In addition to the Bristol VRTs which joined the main Southdown fleet from 1970, the number of rear-engined double-deckers was expanded by the arrival of Daimler Fleetline models. The first delivery was again allocated by Southdown to the BH&D fleet, and was powered by Gardner engines. A further batch of fifteen for BH&D the following year had Leyland units. Green and cream Southdown examples arrived in 1970 and 1972, the latter, Leyland engined Fleetlines, having Eastern Coach Works bodies, basically similar to the contemporary VRT style but built to conventional highbridge dimensions rather than the VRT's lower overall height. They also had 'bustle-type' engine compartments, radically altering the rear-end appearance. No. 2118 is illustrated in Colour Section 1.

Leyland Leopard PSU3A/4RT, PSU3B/4RT coaches, 1970-73

1800-1819	RUF 800-819H	Leyland PSU3A/4RT	Duple	C32F	1970
1820-1844	UUF 320-344J	Leyland PSU3B/4R	Plaxton	C32F	1971
1250-1264	CUF 250-264L	Leyland PSU3B/4RT	Duple	C49F	1973

The suffix letters for these batches of Leyland Leopards indicated further design refinements; PSU3A signified the 'nationalised' pneumo-cyclic gearbox, and PSU3B, redesigned axle units. The first two batches, with Duple Commander IV and Plaxton Panorama Elite bodywork respectively, were 10-metre models, purchased largely for coach-cruising and excursion duties. The 1973 delivery comprised fifteen 11-metre express service vehicles with Duple Dominant coachwork. Numbers 1250-64 were the first Southdown coaches to be delivered in NATIONAL white livery, although all sixty eventually plied their respective trades in the same fashion. Nos. 1816 and 1252 are illustrated in Colour Section 2.

Bristol VRT SL/6LX and VRT SL2/6LX double-deckers, 1971-75

510-518	UUF 110-118J	Bristol VRTSL/6LX	ECW	H39/31F	1971
519-526	WCD 519-526K	Bristol VRTSL2/6LX	ECW	H39/31F	1971
527-541	WUF 527-541K	Bristol VRTSL2/6LX	ECW	H43/27D	1972
550-559	NCD 550-559M	Bristol VRTSL2/6LX	ECW	H43/31F	1973
560-563	NCD 560-563M	Bristol VRTSL2/6LX	ECW	H43/31F	1974
564-574	GNJ 564-574N	Bristol VRTSL2/6LX	ECW	H43/31F	1974
575-577	GNJ 575-577N	Bristol VRTSL2/6LX	ECW	H43/31F	1975

Fitted with Gardner 6LX engines, the 1971-72 intake retained the original ECW body styling with flat-glass windscreens. They also entered service in the traditional Southdown apple green and primrose livery, albeit with white NBC style fleetname and double-N logo: later examples incorporated the BET-style windscreen which, apart from its admirable non-reflective qualities, considerably smartened-up the design of the type, despite its now being painted in NBC's bland leaf green and white. Number 564-77 introduced the former East Sussex 'NJ' registration mark to the company's first-hand purchases following the national revision of registration indices.

One of eight Scottish Omnibus Bristol VRTs swapped for Bristol FLFs from the BH&D fleet in 1973, No. 548 (LFS 300F) and its companions were immediately recognisable by virtue of their destination screens – a shape familiar to Scots and Lancastrians but not in Sussex. In the main, the vehicles were put to work on the routes previously served by the vehicles they displaced, repainted in NBC leaf green with corporate grey wheels so that they could be changed in some other subsidiary's garage should the need arise. These stayed inside their new territory, however.

Leyland National saloons, 1973-79

1-25	BCD 801-825L	Leyland National 115/1R/0102	B49+22F	1973
26	PCD 126M	Leyland National 115/1R/3302	B49+24F	1974
27-36	PCD 73-82R	Leyland National 11351A/1R	B49+24F	1976
37-46	RUF 37-46R	Leyland National 11351A/2R	B44+25D	1977
47-62	UFG 47-62S	Leyland National 11351A/2R	B44+25D	1977
63-71	WYJ 163-171S	Leyland National 11351A/2R	B44+25D	1978
72-88	YCD 72-88T	Leyland National 11351A/2R	B44+25D	1978
89-108	AYJ 89-108T	Leyland National 113510A/1R	B52+23F	1979
109-118	ENJ 909-918V	Leyland National 113510A/1R	B52+23F	1979

In 1972, a joint project between Leyland and the National Bus Company came on stream. Providing as a start-point its plans for a new single-deck bus, Leyland contributed toward the construction of an assembly plant at Workington, Cumbria, initially designed for its exclusive mass-production. Thus *the* NBC bus, the Leyland National, came into being. It comprised an integral structure of pressed-steel components, featured air suspension and was powered with the horizontal Leyland 510 turbocharged 8.2-litre engine mounted under the rear floor.

Southdown's first examples arrived in February 1973 in overall and unrelieved leaf green livery of the kind which would have come in handy during World War II. The first 36 were of the single-doorway type but, in 1977-78, deliveries of a 44-seat two-doorway version were received. Once again, the national revision of index marks resulted in another unfamiliar registration; 'FG' having hitherto being issued by Fife, but from 1974 reallocated to Brighton Local Vehicle Licensing Office. Number 6 of the 1973 intake lead a curious existence – it was sent to Maidstone & District Motor Services Ltd in May 1974 in exchange for what became Southdown's No. 26, acquired to gain experience with its automatic gearbox, which in the event was replaced by conventional equipment. After the best part of seven years with M&D as that firm's No. 3500, No. 6 was re-acquired by Southdown and restored to its former fleet number. Six years later it passed to Eastbourne Buses (1987) and then to jointly-owned Hastings Top Line (1988) before becoming nominally Southdown's property once again at Silverhill Depot, Hastings.

Number 20, meanwhile, lives in honourable retirement, having been repainted in NBC livery and acquired, as an example of the Leyland National, by the Science Museum and stored at its Wroughton, Wiltshire annexe. No. 9 is illustrated in Colour Section 1 and 117 in Section 3.

Acquired from Scottish Omnibuses Ltd, Edinburgh, February and March 1973

542	LFS 282F	Bristol VRT/LL6G	ECW	H47/36F	1968
543	LFS 289F	Bristol VRT/LL6G	ECW	H47/36F	1968
544-548	LFS 296-300F	Bristol VRT/LL6G	ECW	H47/36F	1968
549	LFS 288F	Bristol VRT/LL6G	ECW	H47/36F	1968

The Bristol VR fleet was enlarged in 1968 when these eight vehicles were received in exchange for Bristol FLF double-deckers from the Brighton Hove & District fleet. They had been members of an early batch of 25 and were unusual in being of the rare 33ft-long VRT LL6G type. Number 549 came south by way of the United Counties Omnibus Company, Northampton. The seating capacity of the batch was reduced to H43/31F before entering service with Southdown, but the vehicles remained easily identifiable because the typical Scottish Bus Group shape of the destination box was retained. Despite trade union concern, No. 547 was refitted as an 83-seater in June 1974 and the whole batch bought up to Mark 2 standard, served until 1980.

Leyland Atlantean AN68/1R double-deckers, 1974-75

701-714	PUF 131-144M	Leyland AN68/1R	Park Royal	H43/30F	1974
715-727	PUF 715-727M	Leyland AN68/1R	Park Royal	H43/30F	1974
728-737	SCD 728-737N	Leyland AN68/1R	Park Royal	H43/30F	1974
738-741	SUF 138-141N	Leyland AN68/1R	Park Royal	H43/30F	1974
742-747	LCD 42-47P	Leyland AN68/1R	Park Royal	H43/30F	1975

The National Bus Company decided to depart from its general policy of standardisation upon Bristol/ECW double-deckers to allow expansion of the 1974 programme, and orders were placed for a total of 174 Leyland Atlantean AN68/1R buses with Park Royal bodywork, all being allotted to former BET companies. Southdown received 41 that year, and a further six the next, all with 73-seat single-door bodywork. The company thus received its first Atlantean models, after rather pointedly avoiding the type in the 'sixties, but the then recently introduced AN68 version was a much more reliable machine than the previous PDR series and was possibly the best of its generation. The body was of a style that had been developed for London County Bus Services in 1972, though the basic design was Park Royal's standard of the time. The 701-up series of fleet numbers previously occupied by PD2/12 buses was an appropriate choice for a new batch of Leyland double-deckers. Numbers 742-were initially allocated to Portsmouth, where they carried publicity displays for the new 'Solenteer' X71 service to Southampton.

By 1974, the National Bus Company, anxious to fulfil its targets, permitted the purchase of vehicles other than the standard Bristol/ECW product. Thus Southdown got its hands on what it would most likely have purchased anyway if NBC hadn't come along – the Leyland Atlantean AN68. This was a greatly revised rather than altered version of the earlier Atlantean PDR1/1, which Southdown had eschewed, and was considerably more reliable. Number 736 (SCD 736N) wears the grey glazing-gaskets employed by NBC in the mid 'seventies to match wheels and fleet numbers of the same colour.

Ford R1114 general purpose coaches 1974-1977

1401-1427	PUF 241-267M	Ford URC-R1114	Duple	C49F	1974
1428	SCD 28N	Ford URC-R1114	Duple	C49F	1974
1429	PUF 269M	Ford URC-R1114	Duple	C49F	1974
1430-1437	SCD 30-37N	Ford URC-R1114	Duple	C49F	1974
1438-1440	RNJ 538-540R	Ford URC-R1114	Duple	C47F	1977

Another new chassis type delivered to Southdown in 1974 was the Ford R1114. Production difficulties elsewhere led to an unexpected departure from the NBC standardisation programme in the saloon and coach sector also. NBC subsidiaries were thus given access to Ford chassis: according to their needs; ex-Tilling group companies tended to use them for service buses, ex-BET companies for coaches. Accordingly, Southdown took delivery of 37 with Duple 'Dominant' 49-seat coachwork in 1974 and a further batch of three 47-seaters three years later, all of which were intended for general coaching duties in white *NATIONAL* livery and logos. Rather like the Commer coaches of the 'fifties, the Fords were not overpopular and tended to be left about odd corners of the depots to which they were allotted. The future East & Mid Sussex Division of Southdown sold the last three in 1987.

The 1974 'window of opportunity' was seized upon by Ford, who supplied several NBC subsidiaries with its URC-R1114 chassis for saloon bus or coach bodywork. Southdown utilised forty of them as coaches which were bodied by Duple with 'Dominant' 49-seat units. Number 1401 (PUF 241M) was the first of a batch which received somewhat mixed reviews, and was not going anywhere when photographed on 5th November 1974. The Duple bodywork was constructed at Blackpool in a factory which had been Burlingham's – now departed like Harrington and Beadle.

Bristol VRT SL3/510 double-deckers, 1975

578-583	GNJ 578-583N	Bristol VRTSL3/510	ECW	H43/31F	1975

The chassis of these fully-automatic VRTs were built before those of the 564-577 batch, but the process of getting them fitted with Leyland 510 turbocharged engines seem to have been the reason for their later registration and entry into service in February 1975.

Ford A 0609/Alexander midibus, 1976

650-651	LWV 650-651P	Ford A	Alexander	B27F	1976

Fully automatic they well may have been, but these two midibuses were added to the Southdown rolling stock solely upon the insistence of the National Bus Company. After a few months trial and error with them, Southdown discreetly placed them in store and then felt sufficiently bold to transfer them to the Western National Omnibus Co Ltd, Exeter. Number 651 is illustrated in Vol 1, p97.

Bristol VRT SL3/6LXB double-deckers, 1976

584-593	PUF 584-593R	Bristol VRTSL3/6LXB	ECW	H43/31F	1976

These Gardner-engined VRTs were despatched to Southdown in December 1976, but almost immediately Nos. 584/90-3 were diverted to United Automobile Services, then in urgent need of vehicles; only No. 584 being used on service by Southdown before removal to Darlington where, still with their Brighton registration numbers, they became Nos. 708-12 in the United fleet.

Replacement Bristol VRT SL3/6LXB double-deckers, 1977

584	SNJ 684R	Bristol VRTSL3/6LXB	ECW	H43/31F	1977
590-593	SNJ 590-593R	Bristol VRTSL3/6LXB	ECW	H43/31F	1977

Delivered in May and June 1977 as direct replacements ex-factory for those redirected to United Automobile Services Ltd, and mechanically identical to the originals.

Leyland Leopard PSU3C/4R, PSU3E/4R and PSU3F/4R coaches, 1976-1981

1265-1270	LWV 265-270P	Leyland PSU3C/4R	Plaxton	C47F	1976
1271-1272	LWV 271-272P	Leyland PSU3C/4R	Plaxton	C44F	1976
1273-1280	OWV 273-280R	Leyland PSU3E/4R	Plaxton	C44F	1976
1281-1289	RYJ 881-889R	Leyland PSU3E/4R	Duple	GC49F	1977

As delivered in 1978, No. 1293 (VCD 293S) a Leyland Leopard PSU3E/4R was one the Standard New Bus Grant vehicles subsidised following government legislation provided it spent half of its time on stage-carriage work. Now dressed in independent Southdown's apple green and primrose and sporting the 'Hissing Sid' logo, with West Sussex Division titles as well, it is still fulfilling its long spent obligation on just such a service to Ovingdean on 1st January 1987, just the time of year the original ruling envisaged for what became known as 'grant coaches'.

Also a 'grant coach' is No. 1343 (MAP 343W), a Leopard PSU3F/4R on National Express service 075 London-Portsmouth on 18th December 1985. First delivered to Southdown in 1981, the coach has Plaxton bodywork with forced ventilation rather than windows which the passengers could open for themselves – a sticking point with many customers for several years. Fully appreciated in contrast were the two-piece folding doors which were obligatory on such coaches for use when they were on stage-carriage work around the country lanes and villages.

1290-1297	VCD 290-297S	Leyland PSU3E/4R	Duple	GC47F	1978
1304-1316	ANJ 304-316T	Leyland PSU3E/4R	Plaxton	GC49F	1978-79
1317-1320	BYJ 917-920T	Leyland PSU3E/4R	Plaxton	GC48F	1979
1321	EAP 921V	Leyland PSU3E/4R	Plaxton	GC48F	1979
1322	BWV 922T	Leyland PSU3E/4R	Plaxton	GC48F	1979
1323	ENJ 923V	Leyland PSU3E/4R	Plaxton	GC48F	1979
1324-1335	GWV 924-935V	Leyland PSU3E/4R	Plaxton	GC48F	1980
1340-1353	MAP 340-353W	Leyland PSU3F/4R	Plaxton	GC48F	1981

Southdown continued to order even more Leyland Leopards, the descriptive type suffix letters changing from time to time to denote continuing refinements. The 1976 deliveries with Plaxton coachwork were fitted with the firm's 'Supreme' body, the 1978-81 batches the 'Supreme IV Express'. Duple-bodied coaches of 1977-78 were that firm's 'Dominant' type. All these designs could have their ancestry traced to Plaxton's Panorama Elite of 1968, in Duple's case by virtue of an ex-Plaxton designer who transferred his services to the former. Numbers 1281-97/1304-35/1340-53 were 'grant coaches' – built to full coach specification, but fitted with two-piece doors in laminated glass to facilitate one-man-operation on stage-carriage services, mainly in the low season; their seating reduced by two places to allow for the fitment of a luggage pen. Such vehicles permitted the operator to qualify for the Standard New Bus Grant, then 50 per cent of their original cost, set up by the Labour government before its demise, provided they spent at least half their operating mileage on such stage-carriage work. Thus Nos. 1281-89 were delivered in dual-purpose NBC leaf green below the window line, white above, although the remainder were initially in white overall. Numbers 1265-70 were originally in a sea green, orange and white livery for 'Continental Mini Breaks' operated in conjunction with the ferry operator Townsend Thoresen. In an unusual exercise, Nos. 1276/7/8 were rebuilt in 1985, including the fitment of more modern Plaxton fronts to attract National Holidays clientele. At the same time they were re-registered 406-408 DCD, thereby setting in motion the fashion whereby Titan PD3/4s were raided for their registration numbers to hide the ages of selected coaches. Nos. 1282 and 1316 are illustrated in Colour Section 2.

Bristol VRT SL3/6LXB convertible open-topped double-deckers, 1977-78

594-599	TNJ 994-999S	Bristol VRTSL3/6LXB	ECW	CO43/27D	1977
600-603	TPN 100-103S	Bristol VRTSL3/6LXB	ECW	CO43/27D	1977
604-614	UWV 604-614S	Bristol VRTSL3/6LXB	ECW	CO43/31F	1977
615-623	UWV 615-623S	Bristol VRTSL3/6LXB	ECW	CO43/31F	1978

Within the standard double-deck design regime NBC recognised the need for convertible open-topped buses for seaside use. Southdown's vehicles were part of a group batch of 50 such buses. With its top in place during winter season duties, the type was distinguishable from a normal fixed-top ECW-bodied VRT only by the slightly different moulding layout at upper-deck level and the lifting eyes on the first and fifth frames of the roof edges. Nos. 598 and 620 are illustrated in Colour Section 3.

Bristol VRT SL3/6LXB and 680 double-deckers 1977-81

624-633	UFG 624-633S	Bristol VRTSL3/6LXB	ECW	H43/27D	1977
634-645	XAP 634-645S	Bristol VRTSL3/6LXB	ECW	H43/31F	1978
646-652	AAP 646-652T	Bristol VRTSL3/6LXB	ECW	H43/31F	1978
653-661	AAP 653-661T	Bristol VRTSL3/6LXB	ECW	H43/27D	1978
662-672	AAP 662-672T	Bristol VRTSL3/6LXB	ECW	H43/27D	1979
673-682	EAP 973-982V	Bristol VRTSL3/6LXB	ECW	H43/31F	1979
683-699	EAP 983-999V	Bristol VRTSL3/6LXB	ECW	H43/31F	1980
250-258	JWV 250-258W	Bristol VRTSL3/6LXB	ECW	H43/31F	1980
259-265	JWV 259-265W	Bristol VRTSL3/6LXB	ECW	H43/31F	1981
266-275	JWV 266-275W	Bristol VRTSL3/680	ECW	H43/31F	1981
276	JWV 976W	Bristol VRTSL3/680	ECW	H43/31F	1981

This large intake of Bristol VRs brought the numbers in the Southdown ranks to over 200. With retirements of Leyland PD3s under way, the model thus became the most numerous single type in the fleet. Those with two doors were intended largely for high density in-town working whilst the single entrance type was more suited to inter-urban and long-distance working. Nevertheless, Nos. 259-264, specially painted for service with the East Sussex CC, Brighton Borough Transport and Southdown 'Mile Oak Shuttle' exercise (see Vol 1 pp 102-3), were of the single-front-entrance type. From No. 673 onwards (including 250-76) a rear route number box was incorporated in the ECW designs. The three Leyland 680-engined VRTs would prove to be the last new double-deckers purchased by Southdown until 1989 – and its last new Bristol VRTs also. Nos. 673 and 252/76 are illustrated in Colour Section 3.

Leyland Leopard PSU5C/4R, PSU5D/4R and PSU5E/4R coaches 1978-82

1298-1303	YYJ 298-303T	Leyland PSU5C/4R	Plaxton	C53F	1978
1336-1339	EAP 936-939V	Leyland PSU5C/4R	Duple	C53F	1979
1354-1360	LPN 354-360W	Leyland PSU5D/4R	Plaxton	C53F	1981
1361-1363	TFG 221-223X	Leyland PSU5E/4R	Plaxton	C50F	1982
1364-1367	HHC 344-367Y	Leyland PSU5E/4R	Plaxton	C50F	1982

An important part of NBC's policy had been to provide 12-metre Leopard PSU5 coaches for its National Travel subsidiaries from 1976, thus providing seating for 50 or more passengers per vehicle. Southdown were allotted 24 of the type in three variations between 1978 and 1982. The 1978 batch of six were fitted with Plaxton 'Supreme' coachwork, as were the seven delivered in 1981, whilst the 50-seaters of 1982 received 'Supreme V' bodies. The four vehicles taken into stock in 1979 featured Duple 'Dominant II' bodywork. So far as the Southdown fleet-numbering system was concerned, these vehicles were considered primarily as general purpose coaches and they were fitted into the same series as the smaller 11-metre Leopards delivered between 1976-81 (qv); although the 1978 batch were all in *National Holidays* livery. In 1984, following a fire, No. 1358 re-emerged with Plaxton 'Paramount 3200' coachwork and in 'Southdown Express' livery of green, white, yellow and black.

Not a 'grant coach', but painted with dual-purpose livery anyway and at rest on 11th April 1987, No. 1303 (YYJ 303T) is a Leopard PSU5C/4R with Plaxton 'Supreme' coachwork first delivered in 1978. At that time it was one of the first 12-metre coaches in the Southdown fleet and the first to provide seats for 53 passengers. One planned their itineraries carefully and avoided hump-backed bridges and those too-picturesque villages with impossible corners. Probably Alfred Cannon would not have been too impressed – rather too many people in one place at a time.

Acquired from National Travel (London) Ltd, March 1979

1200	VYM 506M	Leyland PSU3B/4R	Plaxton	C49F	1974
1201	OLL 479L	Leyland PSU5/4R	Plaxton	C42FT	1973
1202	OLL 480L	Leyland PSU5/4R	Plaxton	C44F	1973

Received in National white livery, Nos. 1201-2 were re-seated to C53F in February 1980. All three were operated upon express work and other duties.

Leyland National '2' NL116L11/1R, 1980-81

119-122	GYJ 919-922V	Leyland National NL116L11/1R		B52+23F	1980
123-124	HFG 923-924V	Leyland National NL116L11/1R		B52+23F	1980
125-128	JWV 125-128W	Leyland National NL116L11/1R		B52+23F	1980
129-138	RUF 429-438X	Leyland National NL116L11/1R		B49+24F	1981

First launched in prototype form at the Commercial Motor Show in 1978, the Leyland National 2 underwent further refinement until it emerged from the production line at the start of 1980 with, most noticeably, a front-mounted radiator and a more rounded windscreen of DAB origin.

In the late 'seventies there was what turned out to be a late flurry in coaching activity of most kinds, although the National Express work remained steady rather than spectacular. In order to maintain its rate of commitment to the latter, Southdown found it necessary to seek the transfer from National Travel (London) Ltd of three further Leopards with Plaxton coachwork. Despite their common origin, each had differing seating capacity and equipment. Number 1200 (VYM 506M) wears the 'Chairman's Award' logo.

Even at that late stage painted in unrelieved NBC leaf green, Leyland National '2' No. 123 (HFG 923V) wears the celebratory '70 years of Southdown' logo (of 1985) on 2nd May 1987. It was on service in Portsmouth for restructured Southdown's Hampshire Division. The National '2' was a considerably improved model with more powerful engine and increased length and carrying capacity. They could lawfully shift up to 75 passengers at a time when that was thought to be the best way to move people about a city the size of Portsmouth.

Southdown's first National (No. 120) arrived at Haywards Heath in April 1980, the first of 20 which were of 11.6-metre length and fitted with a new-generation 11.1-litre engine, the L11. Numbers 125-26 still in unrelieved leaf green were considerably brightened up in their earlier years by the addition of logos for Stage Coach service 728, on which they served between Lewes, where they were based, and Brighton.

Acquired from Maidstone & District Motor Services Ltd, September 1980 and March 1981

139-141	OKJ 506-508M	Leyland National 1151/1R/0102	B49+23F	1973
142	OKJ 511M	Leyland National 1151/1R/0102	B49+23F	1973
143-144	GKE 501-502L	Leyland National 1151/1R/0102	B49+23F	1973

Six additional Leyland Nationals, of the earlier 1151/1R pattern, new in 1973 to Maidstone & District, were transferred to Southdown in 1980 (139-142) and 1981 (143-144), and based at four different locations across the company area – thus curtailing the need for further Leyland National '2' models.

Leyland Tiger TRCTL11/3R coaches, 1983-85

1001-1005	XUF 531-535Y	Leyland TRCTL11/3R	Plaxton	C50F	1983
1006-1011	A806-811 CCD	Leyland TRCTL11/3R	Duple	C50F	1984
1012-1015	B812-815 JPN	Leyland TRCTL11/3R	Duple	C50F	1985
1184	A184 EWV	Leyland TRCTL11/3RH	Duple	C21F	1984

After consultations with the National Bus Company, Leyland produced an extensively updated replacement for the Leopard coach which came on to the market bearing the respected old name 'Tiger'. The TRCTL11/3R was a chassis for a 12-metre coach, powered with a turbocharged TL11 engine and had air suspension as standard. Southdown's first five had Plaxton Paramount 3200 coachwork in dark green and gold livery, going one each to the five main depots. Numbers 1006-11 were fitted with Duple Laser bodies in white with *NATIONAL HOLIDAYS* fleetnames, and the 1985 intake with Duple Caribbean II for 'Flightline Gatwick' service 777 based in Brighton. Number 1184 was the one-off executive-hire coach 'The Statesman', fitted with 21 arm chairs, tables, kitchenette and toilet, based at Brighton and on offer with driver and courier. Curiously, it was painted in two tones of brown until it lost its name and was painted in National Holidays livery after two seasons. Nos. 1012 and 1184 are illustrated in Colour Section 2.

At Chichester garage on 27th August 1985 is No. 1004 (XUF 534Y), a Leyland Tiger TRCTL11/3R, then some two years old. It wears the green, gold and white 'universal' livery in the pattern which NBC permitted its subsidiaries to adopt as it relaxed its grip prior to compulsory dismemberment and demise. One of five 12-metre coaches with Plaxton Paramount 3200 body111work dispersed by Southdown to its main depots, this was Chichester's and they looked after it and used it for 'Sussexlink' services.

Also a Tiger, but not looking remotely like the Plaxton-bodied version, was No. 1008 (A808 CCD). Illustrated by way of contrast, this was one of six with Duple Laser coachwork initially intended for 'National Holidays' work but, as Southdown withdrew from that in early 1987, finding their way instead onto National Express duties. Number 1008 is collecting passengers for London express service 065 at Portsmouth on 15th August 1987. With its black window surrounds and accessories the design was impressive – even more so with windscreen wipers going.

Leyland Redline Cub CU335 and CU435 special saloons, 1983-84

800	KJK 800Y	Leyland CU335	Reeve Burgess	B24F	1983
801-803	B801-803 GFG	Leyland CU435	Reeve Burgess	B30F	1984

'County Rider' was a joint Southdown/East Sussex County Council project in which the duties of a country bus were extended to include the ability to carry disabled passengers, thus providing the functions of a Social Services vehicle. The chosen combination was a Leyland chassis which revived another old name, the 'Cub' CU335, and bodywork by Reeve Burgess fitted with rear wheelchair lift and 'Transign' electronic destination screen at the front. Number 800 was a 24-seater delivered to Lewes in July 1983. Its success was such that three additional and 30-seat Cub 435s were added the following year to serve on additional routes based on Seaford and Uckfield (see Vol. 1, p103).

Initial Divisional Re-allocation of vehicles, 1st March 1985

In line with government plans for the demise of the National Bus Company, the partition of most of its subsidiaries and the eventual privatisation of their several parts, the operating activities of Southdown were divided into four 'divisions' from 1st March 1985. Based at the Central Workshops in Portslade, Southdown Engineering Services had already been created as a separately accountable unit the previous year. The allocation of vehicles to the divisions was as follows:

Hampshire Division:

Leyland National 11351A/2R	Nos 68-71/76/86-7
Leyland National 113510A/1R	No. 92
Leyland National '2' NL116L11/1R	Nos. 121-4
Bristol VRTSL3/6LXB	No. 251
Bristol VRTSL3/680	Nos. 266-9
Bristol RESL6L	Nos. 483/90
Bristol VRTSL6LX	Nos. 511/24/26/556/569
Bristol VRTSL3/6LXB	Nos. 605/8-12/634/47-9/660-2/668-72/685-8
Leyland Atlantean AN68/1R	Nos. 701-21/742-7
Leyland Tiger TRCTL11/3R	Nos. 1005-7
Leyland Leopard PSU5/4R	No. 1201
Leyland Leopard PSU3B/4R	Nos. 1257/59/61-2
Leyland Leopard PSU3C/4R	No. 1270
Leyland Leopard PSU3E/4R	Nos. 1284/90/95-7
Leyland Leopard PSU5C/4R	Nos. 1300/03
Leyland Leopard PSU3E/4R	Nos. 1318-21/24/30-3
Leyland Leopard PSU3F/4R	Nos. 1343-5/52
Leyland Leopard PSU5D/4R	Nos. 1357/60
Leyland Leopard PSU5E/4R	No. 1367
Leyland Leopard PSU3B/4R	Nos. 1830/2/4/6/41/3
Bristol VRTSL6LX	Nos. 2093/5
Leyland Titan PD3/4	Nos. 3202/11-2/21-3 (renumbered from 402/11-2/22-4 in 1978)

West Sussex Division:

Leyland National 1151/1R/0102	Nos. 6/13-25
Leyland National 11351A/1R	No. 28
Leyland National 11351A/2R	Nos. 37/61-2/64-5/81-4/88
Leyland National 113510A/1R	Nos. 89-91/93/96-105
Leyland National '2' NL116AL11/1R	Nos. 129-38
Leyland National 1151/1R/0102	Nos. 139-42
Bristol VRTSL3/6LXB	Nos. 252-6/8
Bristol VRTSL3/680	Nos. 274-6
Bristol RESL6L	Nos. 481-2/4-5/9
Bristol RELL6L	No. 491
Bristol VRTSL6LX	Nos. 518-9/21/538-40/557-60
Bristol VRTSL3/6LXB	Nos. 604/7/13-4//16-7/22/36-7/43//77-8/80-4/96
Leyland Tiger TRCTL11/3R	Nos. 1003-4/8-9
Leyland Leopard PSU3B/4R	No. 1200
Leyland Leopard PSU5/4R	No. 1202
Leyland Leopard PSU3B/4R	No. 1250-4/60
Leyland Leopard PSU3C/4R	Nos. 1268/72/5
Leyland Leopard PSU3E/4R	Nos. 1281/91-3
Leyland Leopard PSU5C/4R	Nos. 1299/302
Leyland Leopard PSU3E/4R	Nos. 1307-8/10-3/22-3
Leyland Leopard PSU5C/4R	No. 1338
Leyland Leopard PSU3F/4R	Nos. 1346-7/53
Leyland Leopard PSU5D/4R	Nos 1354/8
Leyland Leopard PSU5E/4R	Nos. 1362/4
Leyland Leopard PSU3B/4R	Nos. 1822/8/31/3
Bristol VRTSL6LX	Nos. 2094/6/102
Leyland Titan PD3/4	Nos. 3200/1/3/5/7-8/13-20/24-5 (renumbered from: 400-1/3/5/7-8/13-20/25-6 in 1978)
Leyland G7	No. 0135
Leyland Titan TD1	No. 0813

Brighton & Hove Division:

Leyland National 1151/1R/0102	Nos. 1-4/7-12
Leyland National 11351A/2R	Nos. 38-41/46-7/49-60/63/66-7/79-80
Leyland National 113510A/1R	No. 106
Leyland National '2' NL116L11/R	No. 127-8
Bristol VRTSL3/6LXB	Nos. 250/7/9-65
Bristol VRTSL3/680	Nos. 270-3
Bristol VRTSL6LX	Nos. 510/2/5/22-3/5/41/50-1/4-5/8/61-8/70-7
Bristol VRTSL3/510	Nos. 578-83
Bristol VRTSL3/6LXB	Nos. 584-96/8-603/6/15/9/24-33/5/8-42/5-6/50-1/3-9/63-7/74-6/9/89/93-5/8-9
Leyland Atlantean AN68/1R	Nos. 732-6/8-40
Leyland Tiger TRCTL11/3/R	Nos. 1010-1/12-5
Leyland Leopard PSU5C/4R	No. 1301
Leyland Leopard PSU3E/4R	Nos. 1306/17/25-6/34-5
Leyland Leopard PSU5C/4R	No. 1336-7/9
Leyland Leopard PSU3F/4R	Nos. 1340-2/51
Leyland Leopard PSU5D/4R	Nos. 1361/3/5-6
Leyland Leopard PSU3B/4R	No. 1829 (The Southdown Diplomat)
Bristol VRTSL6LX	Nos. 2097-100
Bristol Lodekka FS6G	No. 3226-9 (renumbered from 2010-1/21-2 in 1979)

East & Mid Sussex Division:

Leyland National 11351A/1R	Nos 27/9/30-6
Leyland National 11351A/2R	Nos. 42-5/8/72-5/7-8/85
Leyland National 113510A/1R	Nos. 94-5/107-18
Leyland National '2' NL116L11/1R	Nos. 119-20/5-6
Leyland National 1151/1R/0102	Nos. 143-4
Bristol RESL6L	No. 486
Bristol VRTSL6LX	No. 514/7/20/52-3
Bristol VRTSL3/6LXB	No. 618/20-1/3/44/52/73/90-2/7
Leyland Redline Cub CU335	No. 800
Leyland Redline Cub CU435	No. 801-3
Leyland Tiger TRCTL11/3R	Nos. 1001-2
Leyland Leopard PSU3B/4R	Nos. 1255-6/8/63-4
Leyland Leopard PSU3C/4R	Nos. 1265-7/76-7
Leyland Leopard PSUE/4R	Nos. 1282-3/7
Leyland Leopard PSU5C/4R	No. 1298
Leyland Leopard PSU3E/4R	Nos. 1304-5/9/14-6/27-9
Leyland Leopard PSU3F/4R	Nos. 1348-50
Leyland Leopard PSU5D/4R	No. 1355
Ford URC-R1114	Nos. 1438-40
Leyland Leopard PSU3B/4R	Nos. 1823/35/42
Bristol VRTSL6LX	No. 2101
Leyland Titan PD3/4	Nos. 3204/6/9-10 (Renumbered from 404/6/9-10 in 1978)

Acquired from Yorkshire Traction Co Ltd, May and June 1985 for Brighton & Hove Division

145	FHE 402L	Leyland National 1151/1R/0401		B49+23F	1973
146	FHE 404L	Leyland National 1151/1R/0401		B49+23F	1973
147	FHE 403L	Leyland National 1151/1R/0401		B49+23F	1973

Three 12 year-old Leyland Nationals, surplus to the requirements of the Yorkshire Traction Co Ltd were acquired for use by the Brighton & Hove Division. Since FHE 403L (403 in the Yorkshire Traction fleet) did not arrive until June, and after the others, it put the allotted fleet numbers out of sequence. The first was allocated to Whitehawk garage, the others to Conway Street. Upon acquisition Nos. 145-6 were repainted in traditional BH&D red and deep cream. Number 147 became the first vehicle to receive the new Brighton & Hove livery.

Leyland National '2' saloons, 1985, for use by Brighton & Hove Division

| 150-157 | C450-457 OAP | Leyland National '2' NL116HLXCT/1R | | B49+24F | 1985 |

The major difference between these vehicles and the four previous batches of Leyland National '2' saloons was that Nos. 150-157 were powered by Gardner engines rather than the Leyland L11. Numbers 150-155 were diverted before registration and delivery from a Blackpool Borough Transport order.

Hestair Duple Integral 425 coach, October 1985, for use by Hampshire Division

| 1016 | C716 NYJ | Hestair Duple 425 | | C57F | 1985 |

Considered the star of the show at the 1984 International Motor Show in Birmingham the Hestair Duple Integral 425 coach could seat up to 63, offered 14 cubic metres of luggage space and a wide entrance with easy-access steps. The bodywork was a stainless steel corrosion-free structure of advanced aerodynamic design, yet was a ton lighter than most contemporary coaches. Southdown was allotted just one, for tours and private hire work – but this was an area on the wane. It was transferred onto National Express work. Technically ahead of its time, in practice too late in a changed world. The vehicle is illustrated in Volume I pp79 and 91 and in Colour Section 2.

Mercedes-Benz L608D minibuses, 1985, for Brighton & Hove Division

| 200-212 | C200-212 PCD | Mercedes-Benz L608D | Alexander | B20+6F | 1985 |

One of the last acts of the National Bus Company was to consider the future of its subsidiaries in the privatised and competitive market place which awaited them. Whereas many of those subsidiaries had already gained experience with 16-seat minibuses converted from panel vans – and privatised successors such as Transit Holdings would continue to utilise them – NBC concluded that competition would be best met by rather larger load-carrying vehicles, well-equipped to deal with a high degree of stopping and starting. Its choice fell upon the Mercedes-Benz panel van with a reliable 4-cylinder engine, good running characteristics and a 5-speed synchromesh gearbox. Whereas those earmarked for the East & Mid Sussex Division of Southdown were to be converted for passenger use by Reeve Burgess and Potteries Motor Traction, the fourteen made available to Brighton & Hove were fitted out by Alexander and delivered in red and deep cream Brighton & Hove livery in keeping with that division's early move towards separate identity, achieved formally on the 1st January 1986. The thirteen L608D minibuses received in December 1985 were therefore: by the thinnest legal thread, Southdown vehicles – and are included in this list as such. The remaining one of the batch, delivered in January 1986, was not.

Mercedes-Benz L608D minibuses on loan from Eastern National Omnibus Co Ltd, February 1986

	C204 HJN	Mercedes-Benz L608D	Reeve Burgess	B20+6F	1985
	C210 HJN	Mercedes-Benz L608D	Reeve Burgess	B20+6F	1985
	C217 HJN	Mercedes-Benz L608D	Reeve Burgess	B20+6F	1985
	C224 HJN	Mercedes-Benz L608D	Reeve Burgess	B20+6F	1985

Planning for its 'Southdown Mini Bus' service from Eastbournee to Polegate having moved ahead of available equipment to run it, East & Mid Sussex Division were obliged to use these four vehicles from Eastern National pending the arrival of its own vehicles of the same model, which started in earnest the following month. The vehicles borrowed from Eastern National did not carry fleet numbers and remained throughout the property of that company.

Mercedes-Benz L608D minibuses, February-June 1986 for East & Mid Sussex Division

| 901-909 | C581-589 SHC | Mercedes-Benz L608D | Reeve Burgess | B20F | 1986 |
| 910-916 | C590-596 SHC | Mercedes-Benz L608D | PMT | B20F | 1986 |

East & Mid Sussex Division's own L608D minibuses relieved the Eastern National vehicles of their temporary duties by April 1986. Mostly, those converted to passenger standards by Reeve Burgess entered service at Eastbourne; those by Potteries Motor Traction at Haywards Heath. A new livery in which apple green and chrome yellow was prominent was devised for them. They remained, however, an imposition upon Southdown by the National Bus Company and did not fit in with the vehicle policy adopted by the management now removed to Lewes. Number 911 is illustrated in Volume I, p116. No. 915 is illustrated in Colour Section 3.

Leyland Tiger TRCTL11/3R coaches, April 1986, for Hampshire Division

1016	YDG 616	Leyland TRCTL11/3R	Plaxton	C51F	1986
1017	YDK 917*	Leyland TRCTL11/3R	Plaxton	C51F	1986
1018	WVT 618	Leyland TRCTL11/3R	Plaxton	C51F	1986

* re-registered JPU 817 upon delivery

These three Tigers were delivered to Portsmouth in National Express livery and, as part of a policy adopted by the Hampshire Division, received cherished registration numbers from new, in order to disguise the delivery year of the vehicles as they aged, and were placed upon their expected later private hire and tours work – especially at a time when deliveries of new vehicles of any kind were extremely thin and likely to remain so for the foreseeable future.

Following the de-regulation of road passenger transport in October 1986, the three remaining divisions which now constituted Southdown Motor Services Ltd each found it necessary to sell off – and in the case of Hampshire and East & Mid Sussex divisions, buy in – vehicles piecemeal as they felt their ways forward in the now competitive marketplace. The need for rapid adjustments in vehicle requirements was felt nationwide at that time, and one of the companies thus affected and which decided to acquire additional second-hand double-deckers to permit the reinforcement of existing services or the establishment of new ones at short notice was Ribble Motor Services Ltd of Preston. Southdown felt able to help out and Ribble took an initial nineteen Leyland Atlantean AN68 double-deckers in exchange for an equal number of that company's surplus Leyland National saloons. However, the Preston company quickly found itself to be still in need of further double-deckers which it began to acquire from several sources; and among them once again was Southdown whose surviving eight Atlanteans together with three Bristol VRTs were exchanged for four VRTs of 1978 and 1980 vintage.

Acquired in exchange deals with Ribble Motor Services Ltd, Preston, October 1986

for the Hampshire Division:

757	UHG 757R	Leyland National 11351A/1R		B49+24F	1977
768	CBV 768S	Leyland National 11351A/1R		B49+24F	1978
770-2	CBV 770-772S	Leyland National 11351A/1R		B49+24F	1978
775-84	CBV 775-784S	Leyland National 11351A/1R		B49+24F	1978
788-90	CBV 788-790S	Leyland National 11351A/1R		B49+24F	1978
798	CBV 798S	Leyland National 11351A/1R		B49+24F	1978

Since they did not clash with those currently employed by Southdown, the existing Ribble fleet numbers of these vehicles continued in use, but new Southdown fleet numbers were allotted to the following VRTs from the same source, which were also allotted to Portsmouth:

225	DBV 25W	Bristol VRTSL3/6LXB	ECW	DPH43/31F	1980
229	DBV 29W	Bristol VRTSL3/6LXB	ECW	DPH43/31F	1980
657-658	LHG 437-438T	Bristol VRTSL3/6LXB	ECW	H43/31F	1978

Number 657-8 were 14ft 6in in height, the increase being immediately recognisable by the higher lower-deck window line and the resultant wider white band at the front, above the windscreen. Virtually all of these ex-Ribble vehicles ran in NBC poppy red livery initially. Number 657 is illustrated in Volume I, p112.

Services gained at both extremities of the Southdown territorial area, however, meant that both the Hampshire and East & Mid Sussex Divisions were in urgent need of additional vehicles of a kind likely to match existing maintenance standards. That meant further Bristol VRT double-deckers and Leyland National saloons. Old acquaintances were not forgotten, and ex-assistant traffic manager of Southdown, Harry Blundred, now managing director of Devon General, made available twelve VRTs and seven Leyland Nationals most of which were delivered whilst the divisional structure of Southdown was still in place.

In 1986 Southdown sent 27 AN68 Atlanteans and three Bristol VRTs north to Ribble Motor Services Ltd of Preston and got 19 Leyland Nationals and four Bristol VRTs – all of them much newer – in return. Whilst there was thought of rapid deployment in Ribble country, other tactics were to be employed in Sussex. Leyland National No. 772 (CBV 772S) was one of the 1978-vintage Ribble saloons which found itself in the south wearing independent Southdown's version of the traditional livery at Waterlooville in May 1989.

Acquired from Devon General Ltd, October and December 1986

for the Hampshire Division:

624	UTO 834S	Bristol VRTSL3/501	ECW	H43/31F	1977
627	UTO 837S	Bristol VRTSL3/501	ECW	H43/31F	1977
630-631	UTO 830-831S	Bristol VRTSL3/501	ECW	H43/31F	1977

| 953 | OUD 4341M | Bristol VRTSL6LX | ECW | H43/34F | 1974 |
| 960 | GUA 379N | Bristol VRTSL6LX | ECW | H43/31F | 1974 |

Number 960 was delivered to Southdown in NBC leaf green. The remainder ran initially in NBC poppy red. Numbers 630-1 were soon repainted in a special livery for the Havant Hypermarket service. Numbers 953/60 used their Devon General fleet numbers in independent Southdown service. No. 953 was an extra-low height type.

For the East & Mid Sussex Division:

160	GTT 394N	Leyland National 11351/1R		B49F	1975
163	SFJ 139R	Leyland National 11351A/1R		B50F	1977
280	GTA 52N	Bristol VRTSL6IX	ECW	H43/32F	1975
281	LOD 721P	Bristol VRTSL3/501	ECW	H43/23F	1975
282	MOD 567P	Bristol VRTSL3/6LXB	ECW	H43/32F	1976
283	MGR 671P	Bristol VRTSL3/6LXB	ECW	H43/31F	1975
284	LOD 726P	Bristol VRTSL3/501	ECW	H43/32F	1975
285	PTT 91R	Bristol VRTSL3/501	ECW	H43/31F	1976

These vehicles entered Southdown service at either Lewes or Eastbourne but in most cases saw service in other areas soon thereafter. Numbers 160 and 284 ran initially in NBC leaf green, the remainder in NBC poppy red.

Acquired from Western National Ltd, October 1986

for the East & Mid Sussex Division:

| 161 | MOD 822P | Leyland National 113510A/1R | | B50F | 1976 |

Never happy with the 'divisional' structure which it had inherited on 1st January 1986, the Southdown management team let it be known in February 1987 that it would be dismantled. Variations in livery, separate divisional identities and the allocation of vehicles to a specific 'division' would cease. The team would form an off-the-shelf company called Sharpton Ltd and in October 1987 this would succeed in purchasing Southdown Motor Services Ltd from the National Bus Company. The intake of further vehicles for the company under this management would be for Southdown *per se*. As it turned out, there would not be very many of them.

Further vehicles acquired from Devon General Ltd, March 1987

162	PTT 89R	Leyland National 113510A/1R		B50F	1977
53-55	VOD 603-605	Leyland National 11351A/1R		B52F	1978
52	VOD 625	Leyland National 11351A/1R		B42F	1978

All five ran initially in the liveries as acquired: Nos. 162, 52, 53 in NBC poppy red, Nos. 54-5 in NBC leaf green.

Acquired from the Provincial Bus Co Ltd, Hoeford, May 1987

| 917* | D115 DRV | Iveco 49-10 | Robin Hood | B19F | 1986 |
| 918-920 | D128-130 DRV | Iveco 49-10 | Robin Hood | B21F | 1986 |

*No. 917 was at first numbered 915 – then someone remembered that there was already a Mercedes-Benz 608D with that fleet number.

These four Iveco 49-10 minibuses came to Southdown from Provincial as part of an exchange deal whereby the Hoeford-based operator received two Southdown Leyland Titan PD3/4 convertible open-toppers. The Ivecos provided the Chichester 'park and ride' facility during the summer of 1987, and did little else until their sale, in October of that same year, to the West Yorkshire Road Car Co Ltd. They had proven a curious acquisition indeed. Iveco was the market name chosen by Fiat for its commercial vehicle range. The 49-10 model was to enjoy considerable success nationwide – even with Southdown when it came under Stagecoach management later. Number 918 is pictured in Vol I, p114.

Largely as a result of the standard set by the Brighton & Hove Bus and Coach Co Ltd with its Scania N11DR/East Lancs double-deckers on the core routes from Brighton to Portsmouth and to Eastbourne, independent Southdown felt the need to upgrade its own contribution to these services in particular. Yet with Horsham, Hailsham and Haywards Heath depots closing as Southdown drew in its horns along its north-eastern fringes, vehicles were being decommissioned rather than new ones purchased. Indeed, during 1988 neither new or second-hand vehicles were added to the fleet and the most recent double-deckers were Bristol VRTs of 1981 vintage. Some of these were refitted with high-back coach-style seats and pressed into service on such 700 series routes. These were hardly a match for Brighton & Hove's Scanias however and independent Southdown decided to deploy its diminished resources and purchase what would prove to be its only new vehicles.

Volvo B10M dual-purpose double-deckers, 1989

| 301-312 | F301-312 MYJ | Volvo B10M Mark III | Northern Counties | DPH43/33+15F | 1989 |

Prior to selecting this chassis and coachwork combination, Southdown employed six different company demonstrators at various times in 1988 – Dennis, Leyland, MCW, Scania and Volvo chassis with body variations by Alexander, MCW and Northern Counties. Deliveries of the Volvos commenced in August 1989 and it was intended that further orders would be placed for the type. The sale of Southdown Motor Services Ltd to Stagecoach Holdings, however, nipped that in the bud, and these twelve double-deckers proved to be the last new Southdown vehicles to be delivered in the traditional colours of apple green and primrose. Northern Counties were delighted to receive an order once again from Southdown after such a long absence and despatched an official to help launch them in Sussex.

Stagecoach Holdings purchased Southdown Motor Services Ltd together with its share of Hastings Top Line Buses Ltd on 16th August 1989. Southdown, now a subsidiary of Stagecoach, continued to be controlled operationally from Lewes, however. The following month, Stagecoach

On tilt-test at Northern Counties, Wigan plant is No. 301 (F301 MYJ), one of an order for twelve on Volvo B10M Mark III chassis and delivered to independent Southdown in 1989. Officially designated for dual-purpose work, they were acquired after much heart-searching to put something more up-to-date and capacious on to the core coast routes west and east of Brighton. But for the sale of Southdown to Stagecoach Holdings that August, there would have been more. In the event they proved the last new buses in traditional colours.

acquired Eastbourne Buses 49 per cent holding in Hastings Top Line; Eastbourne withdrew its contributory vehicles, and Leyland Nationals of Southdown replaced theme on loan; Top Line remaining a separate company. Stagecoach, meanwhile, had inherited the situation at Worthing, where independent Southdown had been operating in competition with local bus service operator C. J. Chatfield.

Acquired from C. J. Chatfield (Cedarbus), Worthing, September 1989

901-904	F561-564 HPP	MCW MF158/9	MCW	B33F	1988
905	F565 HPP	MCW 158/9	MCW	C28F	1988
923	E233 JRF	Iveco 49-10	Robin Hood	B25F	1988
924-925	E64-65 BVS	Iveco 49-10	Robin Hood	B25F	1988

Stagecoach acquired seven of Chatfield's ten routes, together with eight vehicles and the title **Cedarbus** on 24th September 1989 and placed them under the control of Southdown Motor Services Ltd. MCW Metroriders Nos. 901-5 took up the numbers of the smaller Mercedes-Benz/ Reeve Burgess minibuses of 1986, already sold out of service. Of the Iveco Turbo Daily 49-10s, Nos. 923/5 were themselves destined for a short stay, being passed on to Stagecoach subsidiary Hampshire Bus in 1990 – in a sense returning to their home county, for the coachbuilder Robin Hood was a Southampton firm. Number 905, the Metrorider coach became 419 DCD in 1991.

Transferred from East Midland Motor Services Ltd, October 1989

906	F816 CWJ	MCW MF158/10	MCW	B31F	1988
907	F817 DWG	MCW MF 154/1	MCW	DP31F	1988
908	E518 YWF	MCW MF158/3	MCW	B31F	1988

Transferred by Stagecoach from its East Midland subsidiary for use on the Worthing local services – the first two wearing Cedarbus livery – these three Metroriders were each of differing sub-types. In 1991 these vehicles were re-registered 416-8 DCD respectively, taking the numbers from retired Leyland PD3s, as did the Metrorider coach No. 905 (above).

Acquired from United Counties Omnibus Co Ltd, Northampton, October 1989

-	ONH 845P	Bristol VRTSL3/501	ECW	H43/31F	1976
-	OVV 848R	Bristol VRTSL3/501	ECW	H43/31F	1976

No fleet numbers were allotted for these vehicles, nor were they operated; having been acquired solely as a source of spares, primarily for their 6LXB engines (converted to that unit by United Counties in 1982).

Transferred from Top Line, Eastbourne, December 1989

356	YJK 932V	Leyland AN68/2R	East Lancs	H47/35F	1979
355	YJK 933V	Leyland AN68/2R	East Lancs	H47/35F	1979

New in 1979 to Eastbourne Borough Transport, these two Atlanteans had been transferred to Top Line in May 1988. Southdown operated them in the Portsmouth area from December 1989 until divestment came into effect on 19th January 1991 when they were acquired by Thames Transit.

Transferred from Magicbus (Scotland) Ltd, Perth, February and March 1990

926-928	F21-23 PSL	Iveco 49-10	Robin Hood	B23F	1989
929-930	F25-26 PSL	Iveco 49-10	Robin Hood	B23F	1989

The *Coastline* fleet at Chichester was doubled in March 1990 following the delivery of five additional Iveco Turbo Daily Minibuses, transferred by Stagecoach from its *Perth Panther* fleet. These were also employed on a recently re-introduced Chichester 'park and ride' service. No. 930 is illustrated in Colour Section 3.

Iveco Turbo Daily 49-10 Minibuses, 1989

918-922	G418-422 RYJ	Iveco 49-10	Phoenix	B23F	1989

Purchased by Stagecoach and delivered in December 1989, these five minibuses were taken into stock and based at Chichester for the express purpose of running against Westrings Coaches from that city to the Witterings. In order to 'pep-up' that operation, they were the first Stagecoach vehicles to carry the *Coastline* fleetname rather than *Southdown*. Phoenix was previously 'Robin Hood'.

On 20th October 1989, Stagecoach Holdings purchased Southampton City Transport's 75 per cent stake in Portsmouth CityBus Ltd and the following week the PCB employees sold the remainder of the shares. This added a further 126 vehicles to the Stagecoach fleet, several of them survivors of the once-proud City of Portsmouth Passenger Transport Department. Because some of these were not fitted with power-steering, Stagecoach brought six Leyland Atlanteans south from Frontrunner North West to replace them. For some two months, the fleet was operated simply as *Portsmouth*, but on 1st 1990, as Stagecoach searched for a suitable local identity, the Portsea Island subsidiary was given the fleetname *Southdown Portsmouth*. Circumstances explained in Volume 1, p126ff would dictate that this arrangement lasted just over one year only, but the following vehicles came under nominal Southdown control, many of them already renumbered to fit within the Southdown sequence.

Carrying Coastline fleetnames, cleverly underlined with an outline map of the local promontory, Selsey Bill, is No. 919 (G419 RYJ) an Iveco Turbo Daily 49-10 minibus. This 23-seater was one of five specially purchased by Stagecoach to run against Westrings between Chichester and The Witterings – the villages of West and East Wittering. The livery was full Stagecoach – white background, tan, red and blue stripes in descending order and the fleetname in blue – and the bodywork was by Phoenix, previously 'Robin Hood' of Southampton.

Transferred to Southdown control from Stagecoach: *Portsmouth* 1st January 1990; vehicles previously from the fleet of Portsmouth CityBus Ltd

2	LRV 992	Leyland PD2/12	MCCW	033/26R	1956
11	ERV 251D	Leyland PDR1/1 MkII	MCCW	043/33+5F	1966
57	D457 WJH	Freight Rover FR374	Dormobile	B16F	1986
61	D461 WJH	Freight Rover FR374	Dormobile	B16F	1986
140-142	CPO98-100W	Leyland National 2 NL106L11/1R		DP40F	1980
143-146	ERV 115-118W	Leyland National 2 NL106L11/1R		B41+22F	1981
200	THX 187S	Leyland National 10351A/2R		B36+27D	1978

201	THX 172S	Leyland National 10351A/2R		B36+27D	1978
202	THX 211S	Leyland National 10351A/2R		B36+27D	1978
203	BYW 378V	Leyland National 10351A/2R		B36+27D	1979
204	THX 219S	Leyland National 10351A/2R		B36+27D	1978
205	THX 210S	Leyland National 10351A/2R		B36+27D	1978
206	THX 220S	Leyland National 10351A/2R		B36+27D	1978
207	THX 213S	Leyland National 10351A/2R		B36+27D	1978
208	THX 255S	Leyland National 10351A/2R		B36+27D	1978
209	THX 141S	Leyland National 10351A/2R		B36+27D	1978
211	HOR 311N	Leyland AN68/1R	Alexander	H45/30+5D	1975
287	XTP 287L	Leyland AN68/1R	Alexander	H45/30+5D	1973
320-334	UOR 320-334T	Leyland AN68/1R	Alexander	H45/28+5D	1978
335-344	YBK 335-344V	Leyland AN68/1R	Alexander	H45/28+5D	1979
345	CPO 345W	Leyland AN68A/1R	East Lancs	H46/27+5D	1980
346	CPO 346W	Leyland AN68A/1R	East Lancs	DPH46/27F	1980
347-354	CPO 347-354W	Leyland AN68A/1R	East Lancs	H46/27+5D	1980
959-973	E959-973 LPX	Iveco 49-10	Robin Hood	B23F	1989

Also transferred from Portsmouth, but not operated by Southdown were:

3 Leyland Atlantean PDRI/l Mk II – MCCW 043/33+5F double-deckers
48 Leyland Atlantean AN68/1R – Alexander H45/30+5D double-deckers
2 Leyland National 10351A/1R B36 – +27D saloon for spares.

Numbers 2 and 11 had been converted to open-top by CPPTD in 1971 and 1979 respectively; Nos. 57 and 61 were acquired by Portsmouth CityBus from Hampshire Bus – and all four retained their PCB fleet numbers. Numbers 200-9 were purchased by PCB from London Buses Ltd (LS class in 1989. Numbers 287/320-34/335-44/45/6/7-54 carried their original PCB numbers. Numbers 959-73 were Iveco Turbo Dailys of the *Red Admiral* fleet, which had been placed under PCB control by Southampton City Transport in June 1988. Their fleet numbers reflected their previous joint-ownership by SCT and Badgerline. The latter had allotted them Nos. 4959-73, which they never carried. The subtraction of 4000 permitted them to be fitted neatly – more or less – into the existing Southdown minibus sequence.

Transferred to Southdown control from Stagecoach: *Portsmouth* 1st January 1990; vehicles transferred by Stagecoach from the defunct Frontrunner North West fleet of its subsidiary East Midland Motor Services Ltd, December 1989

314	KSA 178P	Leyland AN68/1R	Alexander	H45/29D	1975
315	KSA 180P	Leyland AN68/1R	Alexander	H45/29D	1975
316-317	KSA 182-183P	Leyland AN68/1R	Alexander	H45/29D	1975
318	KSA 186P	Leyland AN68/1R	Alexander	H45/29D	1975
319	KSA 189P	Leyland AN68/1R	Alexander	H45/29D	1975

New to Grampian Regional Transport in 1975, all six came south in East Midland green and cream livery with *Frontrunner* and galloping hare logo between decks. Five of them found their way into Stagecoach livery before transfer to Thames Transit Ltd trading as Portsmouth Transit in January 1991 (qv). No. 315 is illustrated in Colour Section 3.

On loan from East Sussex County Council from January and May 1990

891-892	G91-92 VMM	Leyland Swift	Wadham Stringer	B34F	1989

Long-term loan vehicles in Escort County Rider livery of dark green with yellow band for use on local bus services from Lewes and Seaford. As with other types operated previously on such services, they were fitted with a disabled persons' wheelchair-lift.

Officially on loan to Stagecoach South from East Sussex County Council, but numbered 891-892 in the Southdown fleet anyway, were a pair of Leyland Swifts with Wadham Stringer 34-seat bodies to continue the tradition started locally at Seaford and then Lewes in 1983. They continued to provide a disabled persons capability on rural services otherwise deprived of a local bus service. Wearing the special Escort County Rider livery of dark green and yellow is No. 892 (G92 VMM), one of the pair.

Leyland Olympian double-deckers, 1990-1991

701-710	G701-710 TCD	Leyland ON2R56G13Z4	Alexander	H51/34F		1990
220-222	J720-722 GAP	Leyland ON2R56G13Z4	Alexander	DPH47/27F		1991

The original Leyland Olympian ON had gone into production in 1981 as a replacement for NBC's standard Bristol VRT double-decker, but whilst it became commonplace in Northern fleets such as Ribble and Crosville, it was conspicuous by its absence on the south coast of England. So that model, fitted with ECW 76-seat bodywork – some of the last work undertaken by that respected Lowestoft firm – went unrepresented in the Southdown fleet. Instead, it was the Olympian ON2 10-metre version with Alexander bodywork seating 85 passengers and room for 12 more standing, which belatedly first represented the type in March 1990. The ten delivered that year were the first new double-deckers ordered for Southdown by Stagecoach. Numbers 701-10 were renumbered 231-4/225-30 in 1991-2. The three dual-purpose 74-seaters which arrived in December 1991 were purchased for the core 700 and 729 routes.Nos. 709 and 220 are illustrated in Colour Section 3.

Transferred from Hampshire Bus, January 1992

223-224	J623-624 GCR	Leyland ON2R56G13Z4	Alexander	H47/30+16F		1991

Originally built for delivery to Hampshire Bus, this pair were among five Olympians diverted new to Inverness Traction – another Stagecoach subsidiary. They had barely settled into their originally intended home in Hampshire when they were transferred for use by Southdown at Havant. These three batches of Olympians were both the first and last Stagecoach-ordered double-deckers to carry *Southdown* fleetnames.

Transferred from Hastings & District Transport Ltd, April 1990

799-805	V799-805 SDY	Mercedes-Benz L608D	Alexander	B20+BF		1986
807-812	C807-812 SDY	Mercedes-Benz L608D	Alexander	B20+BF		1986

Originally based at its Silverhill depot, Hastings & District had sent these vehicles over to Eastbourne in March 1989 to counter-attack Eastbourne Buses, and in July to confront Southdown, in retaliation for their joint setting up of Top Line at Hastings. This 'Eastbourne & District' operation was of course acquired by Stagecoach when Hastings & District Transport Ltd was purchased in December 1989. For a transitionary period Stagecoach continued to use the *Eastbourne & District* fleetname. The Eastbourne & District operation, together with these vehicles, was transferred to Southdown upon service reorganisation in the area on 15th April 1990.

Acquired from Southampton City Transport, May 1990

9	ERV 250D	Leyland PDR1/1 Mark II	MCCW	O43/33+5F		1966

One 1966-vintage Leyland Atlantean PDR1 in white livery, exchanged with SCT, for No. 8 (in store) which was still in Southampton's 'Red Ensign' colours. Neither 8 nor 9 were operated by Southdown.

Pictured at Southampton on 23rd April 1989 and still in Southampton City Transport's 'Red Ensign' livery is No. 9 (ERV 250D) a Leyland PDR1/1 open-topper. Somehow or other, whilst still in that operator's ownership, it managed to get itself painted white. 'Southdown Portsmouth' meanwhile had No. 8 in store, still in 'Red Ensign' livery, so Southampton asked for a swop when, once again, they needed a red one. Southdown agreed, took the now white No. 9 in exchange – and promptly put that into store instead. Follow?

Transferred from Magicbus (Scotland) Ltd, Perth, May 1990

931-932	G34-35PSR	Iveco 49-10	Robin Hood	B23F		1989
933	C24 PSL	Iveco 49-10	Robin Hood	B23F		1989
934	G30 PSR	Iveco 49-10	Robin Hood	B23F		1989
957	D936 EBP	Iveco 49-10	Robin Hood	B19F		1987
958	D937 ECR	Iveco 49-10	Robin Hood	B19F		1987

Additional Iveco Turbo Daily minibuses transferred by Stagecoach from its Perth subsidiary: the first two spent a few days with Hampshire Bus before moving on to Chichester. Numbers 957-8 were new to Hampshire Bus in 1987.

Transferred from Ribble Motor Services Ltd, Preston, June to August 1990

935	D618 BCK	Iveco 49-10	Robin Hood	B21F	1987
936	D411 FRV	Iveco 49-10	Robin Hood	B19F	1987
974-987	E634-647 DCK	Renault S46	Dormobile	B25F	1987

Transferred by Stagecoach from its Ribble subsidiary No. 935 was new to Ribble, and No. 936 to United Transport for its Preston-based 'Zippy' fleet, acquired by Ribble in March 1988. Its Portsmouth registration means that the Southampton-based coachbuilder did the paperwork before it was delivered to United Transport. The fourteen Renault S46 minibuses were the entire batch of this type purchased by Ribble in 1987. Delivered in July and August 1990 and intended for a competitive operation against Provincial at Gosport which, in the event, did not materialise. They instead helped compete against that company in Portsmouth, and were placed on loan to Portsmouth Transit upon its commencement of operations in January 1991.

Needless to say, as Stagecoach Holdings' empire grew, so it could transfer vehicles almost at will to the point where they might be needed. Transfers were (and are) many and Southdown too was involved. Into the fold from Ribble in 1990 came fourteen Renault S46 minibuses with 25-seat Dormobile bodywork, all that the Preston-based company possessed. 'Who are you, and are you going anywhere?' a Portsmouth senior citizen asks the driver of a plain No. 986 (E646 DCK) on 12th January 1991, with just one week to go to divestment.

Transferred from Cumberland Motor Services Ltd, Whitehaven, June 1990

| 1014 | WAO 644Y | Leyland TRCTL11/2R | Alexander | DP47F |

Based briefly at the former Citybus garage at Eastney, Portsmouth was this Leyland Tiger with Alexander 'TE' grant-coach bodywork, where it was used on National Express services, in particular the 075 to London. Like all other Portsmouth-based coaches at this time it was in white National Express livery.

In January 1991, following divestment of its Portsmouth depot, Stagecoach's Southdown was left divided into two, rather than three, divisions: 'West Sussex' and 'East Sussex'. Both differed from their counterparts of earlier days. West Sussex incorporated the former Portsmouth CityBus depot at Leigh Park and operations based upon Havant, both locations in Hampshire; whilst East Sussex included the activities of Hastings & District Transport Ltd. The latter remained a separate entity, however and, significantly, it was the former traffic

A one-off transfer into the Southdown fleet from Stagecoach subsidiary Cumberland Motor Services Ltd in June 1990 was Leyland Tiger coach No. 1014 (WAO 644Y). Used to bolster the 075 Portsmouth to London express service as part of Stagecoach's diminished participation in the National Express organisation. It was based by 'Southdown Portsmouth' at its newly-occupied Eastney depot. The vehicle was a 'grant-coach' built by Alexander with 47 seats and was first registered in 1982. It proved to be the last of a long distinguished line of coaches to enter the fleet of Southdown Motor Services Ltd.

manager of that company who became divisional manager (see Volume I, p133). The year 1991 proved to be the last full one in which additions to the fleet would be accredited to Southdown Motor Services Ltd. In that respect, it could hardly be described as a vintage twelve months.

Transferred from Hampshire Bus Co Ltd, July, August, October 1990

939	D939 ECR	Iveco 49-10	Robin Hood	B19F	1987
955	D935 EBP	Iveco 49-10	Robin Hood	B19F	1987
956	D934 EBP	Iveco 49-10	Robin Hood	B19F	1987

Placed under the nominal ownership of Southdown, these three vehicles were transferred by Stagecoach from its Eastleigh-based subsidiary, Hampshire Bus and joined the Chichester minibus operation for varying lengths of service.

Transferred from Hampshire Bus Co Ltd, January 1991

| 925 | E65 BVS | Iveco 49-10 | Robin Hood | B25F | 1988 |

This ex-Cedarbus vehicle was re-acquired by Southdown from Hampshire Bus, whence it had been sent after a short stay in 1989.

Transferred from Hastings & District Transport Ltd, September 1991

| 813-814 | C813-814 SDY | Mercedes-Benz L608D | Alexander | B20+6F | 1986 |

Mechanically identical to earlier members of this batch which came to Southdown in April 1990, this pair came direct from Hastings & District.

Transferred from Hastings & District Transport Ltd, October 1991

| 11 | TRN 811V | Leyland National 'B' LN11351B/IR | | B44+16F | 1979 |

What proved to be the only Mark I 'B' type Leyland National operated by Southdown was a short vehicle needed by Eastbourne depot for the start of a joint operation with Eastbourne Buses of local service 8. It had begun life with Ribble, gone to Cumberland in 1986, to Magicbus (Scotland) in 1989 and to Hastings & District in January 1991. After less than six month's service it returned to Hastings.

Stagecoach had, however, placed an order in 1991 for 80 Dennis Dart saloon buses with bodywork by Alexander for use by its south of England subsidiaries. Just one had arrived by December 1991 and, on the 18th of that month it was the subject of a publicity photo-call at which Brian Souter, the chairman and chief executive of Stagecoach Holdings PLC was present.

Dennis Dart/Alexander Dash saloon, 1991

| 501 | J501 GCD | Dennis Dart | Alexander Dash | B41+18F | 1991 |

The ceremony at Chichester bus station featured the Dart wearing *Southdown* fleetnames for that one day only. It was promptly thereafter despatched to Hastings where it joined its fellows, whose delivery to the Hastings and District company commenced in January 1992 in *Hastings Buses* logos.

Dennis Dart/Alexander Dash saloon, 1992

| 521 | J521 GCD | Dennis Dart | Alexander Dash | B41+18F | 1992 |

Carrying *Southdown* fleetnames and legal owner details, this Dart was the last new vehicle delivered to Southdown Motor Services Ltd. It went into service at Eastbourne on service 8 in March 1992 and displaced TRN 811V (qv). This was an 'odd delivery' for the particular requirement of that route, and was the second of the only two Darts to wear *Southdown* fleetnames. No 521 is illustrated in Colour Section 3.

Transferred from Hastings & District Transport Ltd, March 1992

74	YCD 74T	Leyland National 11351A/1R	B44+25D	1978
90	AYJ 90T	Leyland National 113510A/1R	B52+23F	1979
101	AYJ 101T	Leyland National 113510A/1R	B52+23F	1979

All three were re-acquired by Southdown from Hastings & District to whom they had been transferred in: 74, August 1990; 90/101, September 1990. Together with Dennis Dart 521, they were the last vehicles to join the Southdown fleet.

On 2nd April 1992, Southdown Motor Services Ltd had its name changed formally to Sussex Coastline Buses Ltd, as Stagecoach reorganised its south coast operations into:

Sussex Coastline Buses Ltd, based on the existing West Sussex Division, and trading as *Coastline*.

South Coast Buses Ltd, based on the existing East Sussex Division, trading as *Southdown Buses* from Eastbourne, Lewes an Uckfield, and *Hastings Buses* based on the former Hastings & District operations.
Stagecoach (South) Ltd, renamed from the Hampshire Bus Co Ltd in January 1992 and trading as *Hampshire Bus*.

The *Southdown Buses* and *Hastings Buses* fleetnames had been dropped by the spring of 1993. There had been no additional vehicles for the former.

ACQUISITIONS

During its near 77-year history as Southdown Motor Services Ltd the company was active in acquiring part or the whole of the psv activities of other operators on 92 occasions, involving 88 separate firms. On over 50 of those occasions no property or vehicle was involved in the sale (G0 = goodwill only). Purchase prices have been rounded down to the nearest pound (NK = not known: N/A = not applicable).

Name of operator	Date acquired	Price £	Remarks
A. Davies, Bognor Regis	13.5.15	700	Excursion
Thomas Tilling Ltd, Brighton	28.12.16	4,000	Brighton Excursions
G. Town, Worthing	8.11.18	130	Stage: Broadwater-Elm Grove
W. C. Taylor (T/A White Heather Motor Services) Brighton	8.8.21	500	Excursion
A. F. Trickey, Birdham	23.6.23	850	Stage: West Wittering-Chichester
E. Higgins (t/a De Luxe) Brighton	5.8.23	NK	Excursion
C. G. Shore (t/a Royal Blue Services) Bognor Regis	24.11.23	3,250	Stage: Aldwick-Middleton Excursion
South Coast Tourist Co Ltd, Littlehampton	4.1.24	5,500	Stage: Arundel-Littlehampton Littlehampton-Angmering Excursion
W. G. Dowle (t/a Summersdale Motor Services) Summersdale, Chichester	7.1.24	1,500	Stage: Chichester-East Dean
W. Stretton (t/a Cavendish Coach & Car Company), Eastbourne	9.2.25	3,000	Excursion
Southsea Tourist Co Ltd, Southsea	28.2.25	30,000	Stage: Southsea-Horndean-Petersfield Excursion
Miskin & Strong, Littlehampton	13.5.25	NK	Excursion
W. Hollis & R. N. Fairbanks (t/a Downs Transport Company), Angmering	1.10.25	300	Stage: GO Angmering-Worthing
Holts Motors Ltd, Portsmouth	1.11.26	800	Stage: GO Hayling-Rowlands Castle
W. Stride, Hayling Island	1.12.26	900	Stage: Waterlooville-Hayling Island
S. Foard, Eastbourne	11.12.26	2,875	Excursion
C. R. Shorter, Kemp Town, Brighton	6.5.27	90	Excursion: part only
A. E. Orbell, Brighton	30.9.27	105	Excursion
F. Bevan (t/a Golden Butterfly Motor Coaches) Brighton	1.11.27	NK	Excursion
C. H. Williams (t/a The Pullman Service) Hove	1.11.27	1,000	Excursion
G. E. Noble (t/a Lucille Motor Coaches) Brighton	14.11.27	450	Excursion GO
F. Rhodes (t/a Bonny Doone), Bright	24.10.28	190	Excursion
E. E. Piper (t/a Red Saloon Motor Services) Hellingly	10.4.29	2,000	Stage: Hellingly-Eastbourne
W. E. Pinhorn (t/a Meon Valley Services)Catherington	24.7.29	3,700	Stage: East Meon-Clanfield-Portsmouth
H. J. Twine (t/a Twine's Services Ltd Hailsham	21.9.29	4,012	Stage: Polegate-Eastbourne Eastbourne-Jevington
T. H. Keys (t/a Unic Chars-a-banc), Hove	28.10.29	115	Excursion GO
F. & J. Poole (t/a Royal Red Coaches), Hove	28.3.30	2,250	Excursion
A. Potts (t/a Potts Motor Services), Brighton	5.6.30	9,850	Excursion
Chapman & Sons (Eastbourne) Ltd	25.2.32	28,870	Excursion Express: Eastbourne-London

Southern Glideway Coaches Ltd, Eastbourne	1.3.32	15,000	Express: Eastbourne-London
C. F. Wood & Sons Ltd, Steyning	31.3.32	100	Express GO: Steyning-London
G. B. Motor Tours Ltd, London	1.4.32	1,350	Express GO: London-Worthing and Brighton
G. H. Meaby, Brighton	29.9.32	90	Excursion GO
G. Tate (t/a Red Rover Motor Services) Bognor Regis	-.10.32	NK	Stage GO: Bognor Regis-Pagham
S. S. T. Overington (t/a Blue Bus Service) Horsham	5.11.32	450	Stage: Horsham-Handcross-Balcombe; Horsham-Maplehurst
J. Haffenden, Vines Cross	4.1.33	250	Stage GO: Heathfield-Eastbourne
Keith & Boyle Ltd, proprietors of Pratt & Pearce Ltd (t/a Little Vic Orange Coaches) Eastbourne	14.3.33	1,000	Excursion
London General Country Services	1.7.33	NK	Stage GO and part only: Uckfield-East Grinstead Handcross-Crawley
H. J. Sargent (t/a East Grinstead Motor Coaches)	15.7.33	900	Express GO: East Grinstead-Brighton
G. W. Meekings, Hayling Island	-.7.33	150	Stage: Hayling Island
P. C. Belier, Hayling Island	31.7.33	25	Stage: Hayling Seafront and Excursion GO
Fairway Coaches Ltd, London	18.12.33	5,250	Express: London-Worthing
W. G. Waugh (t/a Regal Coaches), Brighton)	18.12.33	750	Excursion
A. D. Jessett & D. A. Farrence (t/a Jessett's Coaches) Haywards Heath	13.4.34	263	Excursion GO
North End Motor Coaches (Portsmouth) Ltd	3.5.34	850	Express GO: Portsmouth-London
G. A. Cross (t/a Perserverance) Gosport	5.7.34	3,600	Express GO: Gosport-Meon Valley-London
B. R. Roberts, Portslade	1.10.34	300	Excursion
W. H. Rayner & Son (t/a Horsham Bus Services) Barns Green	2.1.35	1,000	Stage: Horsham-Barns Green Horsham-Coolham Horsham-St. Leonards Horsham-The Common
Hampshire Light Railways (Electric) Co Ltd (t/a Portsdown & Horndean Light Railway)	10.1.35	13,500	Tramways GO: Cosham-Horndean replaced by Southdown buses.
T. W. Carter (t/a Carter Brothers), Horsham	10.1.35	450	Stage GO: Horsham-Steyning Excursion
W. F. Alexander (t/a Comfy Coaches), Horsham	15.3.35	200	Excursion GO
F. G. Tanner (ta/ Denmead Queen Motor Services) Hambledon	21.3.35	12,310	Stage:Portsmouth-Hambledon-Worlds End
Aldershot & District Traction Co Ltd	1.4.35	350	Express GO and part only: Hindhead-London
Alexandra Motor Coaches Ltd, Southsea	20.5.35	950	Express: Southsea-London
T. S. Bruce (t/a Imperial Saloon Coaches) Portsmouth	23.5.35	1,000	Express GO: Portsmouth-London
A. Timpson & Sons Ltd, London	-.5.35	1,590	Express, part only: London-Portsmouth
Underwood Express Services Ltd, Portsmouth	6.6.35	400	Express GO: Portsmouth-London
Mrs M. V. Fuger (t/a Fareham & Warsash Coaches, Warsash	-.6.35	300	Express GO: Warsash-Fareham-London
Blue Motor Services (Southwick) Ltd Boarhunt	16.9.35	1,350	Stage, part only: Hambledon-Meonstoke-Portsmouth
W. F. Rowland & G. B. Orr (t/a Silver Queen), Worthing	9.4.36	305	Excursion GO
G. C. Landsall (t/a King of the Road Coaches) Worthing	2.11.36	3,000	Excursion, part only
H. Miller (t/a Miller's Coaches), Portslade	12.11.36	125	Excursion GO
R. J. Smart (t/a Ferring Omnibus Services) Ferring	8.8.37	585	Stage GO: West Ferring-Goring

H. K. Hart (t/a Alpha Coaches) Brighton)	24.8.37	135	Express only and GO Hove and Brighton-Hellingly
H. J. Sargent (t/a East Grinstead Services)	27.9.37	720	Stage: East Grinstead-West Hoathly-Sharpthorne only
F. & H. L. Pownall, Brighton	26.11.37	720	Excursion GO
S. W. Stephens (t/a Sydney Motor Coaches) Eastbourne	1.1.38	1,800	Excursion GO
H. W. Garlick, East Hoathly	24.1.38	135	Stage GO: East Hoathly-Uckfield
H. J. Sargent (t/a East Grinstead Services)	21.1.38	225	Excursion GO
Hartington Motors Ltd, Eastbourne	28.3.38	225	Excursion GO
Tramocars Ltd, Worthing	1.8.38	17,647	Stage: Splash Point -Library Splash Point-West Worthing
L. Cherriman, Hurstpierpoint	15.9.38	540	Stage GO: Hurstpierpoint-Hassocks
C. R. Shorter, Brighton	5.4.39	125	Express GO: Hove-Brighton-Robertsbridge
Harvey's Coaches, Eastbourne	-.9.39	NK	Excursion GO
H. G. Bannister & W. R. Evans, Ditchling	1.2.40	270	Stage GO: Hassocks-Ditchling
C. Walling (t/a Silver Queen Bus Service) Eastergate	21.12.44	10,579	Stage GO: Bognor Regis-Slindon
French & Son, Seaford	3.9.45	1,620	Excursion GO
Mrs M. Hay-Will, Arundel	5.1.47	405	Stage GO: Arundel-Burpham
L. B. Atkins (t/a Beacon Motor Services	24.9.49	(25,305)	Stage: Crowborough local; Crowborough-Jarvis Brook; Crowborough-Tunbridge Wells; Crowborough-Uckfield Express: Rotherfield-London Excursion. Reconstituted as Beacon Motor Services (Crowborough) Ltd, a Southdown subsidiary, with a board comprised of SMS directors and officers. The company continued to run its psv activities under the 'Beacon' brand name until assignment of the goodwill to SMS on 30th March 1954. The 'Beacon Tours' title, however, Southdown continued to utilise for centred tours in Britain and Ireland until the end of the BET era (see Vol 1, p77)
H. J. Sargent (t/a East Grinstead Services)	25.3.51	11,500	Stage: East Grinstead-Ashurst Wood; East Grinstead-Cowden; Edenbridge-Crowborough. These routes passed to Maidstone & District Motor Services Ltd, 30.9.51 (GO).
George Ewen Ltd (t/a Pioneer Coaches) Petersfield	25.10.52	2,000	Excursion GO
Hants & Sussex Motor Services Ltd, Cosham (in receivership)	5.2.55	N/A	The following services awarded to Southdown by the traffic commissioner: Stage: Emsworth-Thorney Island (until 23.7.55); Express: Southsea-Alton Hospitals; Forces Leave Express: Lee-on-the-Solent-Browndown-London

C. F. Wood & Sons, Steyning	-.4.55	NK	Excursion GO
Triumph Coaches Ltd, Portsmouth	28.5.57	(4,000)	Forces Leave Express GO: Portsmouth-Plymouth Portsmouth-Reading, Cardiff, Birmingham, Leeds, Liverpool, etc Excursion GO

Operated as a Southdown subsidiary, with Beddow, Willis and Woodgate as directors, other SMS officers as shareholders and Turner as secretary. As such, Triumph Coaches Ltd purchased as its own subsidiary:

Unity Coaches, Portsmouth	4.1.59	(4,000)	Express GO

Triumph was sold at book value to Southdown on 27.5.59. Southdown utilised the 'Triumph Coach Tours' brand for a programme of eight 'T' tours from points between Bournemouth and Brighton until the end of the BET era.

P. W. Lambert (t/a Little Wonder Coaches) Petersfield	26.10.59	NK	Stage GO: Petersfield-Buriton
G. F. Graves & Sons (Redhill) Ltd	-.7.62	NK	Express GO: Redhill and Reigate-Bournemouth; Folkestone and Ramsgate
Keith & Boyle (London) Ltd, proprietors of Shamrock & Rambler Coaches Ltd, Bournemouth (t/a Brighton Motor Conveyances Ltd), Brighton	19.3.63	15,854	Excursion: Brighton licences only
A. W. Buckingham (t/a Bucks Luxury Coaches), Worthing	-.5.63	NK	Excursion: Southdown retained the 'Bucks' trading name and livery until the end of the 1965 season
Brighton & Hove & District Omnibus Co Ltd, Hove	1.1.69	N/A*	Stage: All services and phsycal wherewithall of this company from the date that it became a dormant subsidiary of NBC until reactivation on 1.1.86
C. J. Chatfield (t/a Cedarbus) Worthing	24.9.89	N/A**	Stage: seven local minibus services in Worthing and district, together with title to the *Cedarbus* fleetname
Portsmouth Citybus Ltd, Portsmouth	(27.10.89)	N/A**	All remaining services and property of this operator placed under Southdown control by Stagecoach 1.1.90 until divestment on 19.1.91

* The £600,000 share capital of BH&D was set aside and upon the shelf by the National Bus Company during the period in which Southdown managed the Hove company's affairs. It was never formally 'the property' of Southdown Motor Services Ltd.

**Purchases made by the Stagecoach Group and placed in the administrative care of Southdown Motor Services Ltd.

This memorial plaque graced 'Southdown House' in Freshfield Road from 1964 until 1985. In 1986 it was removed with the company to Lewes and, in a special ceremony, was re-unveiled by Alfred Cannon's daughter, Phoebe, Mrs Peter Harrison.

Still preserved by Stagecoach for publicity purposes is No. 0135 (CD 7045) with Leyland G7 chassis dating from 1921 and Short bodywork fitted in 1928. The famous apple green and primrose livery sits well upon the vehicle. It had been handed down that the livery was inherited from Worthing Motor Services. During renovation work on the bodywork of a 1914 Tilling Stevens carried out by that stalwart band of preservationists at Amberley Museum (do go and have a look!), a preliminary rubbing down proved that to be true.

Brush-bodied Leyland TD1 No. 0813 (UF 4813) is also retained by Stagecoach for similar reasons. Like its long lost companions, it wore a dark green canvas top during World War II.

About to retire from company service, No. 257 (GCD 357), Leyland TD5 of 1939 awaits collection from Portslade Works. It wears a Northern Counties body fitted in 1950 in a large rebodying programme.

After the receipt of 100 Guy 'Arab' utilities in 1943-6, Leyland deliveries resumed with the PD1 model. Number 315 (HCD 915) is an all-Leyland example of 1947. It is en route to Selsey from Chichester.

Having stepped efficiently into the World War II breach, the Guys survived much longer than expected , particularly those with NCME metal-framed bodies. No. 444 (GUF 144) was converted by Southdown to this open-top form in 1951.

Osborne country ! On a photo-call for members of the Southdown Enthusiasts Club in August 1963, No. 439 (GUF 139) pauses on the way to Devils Dyke atop the Southdown Hills. Whereas No. 444 was a 5LW model with Park Royal frames, No. 439 was a six-cylinder example of the more-usual NCME-based conversion – a more sophisticated job dating from April 1959, with a windscreen for the top deck.

There are flat parts of Sussex ! Pausing near Bognor in September 1962 is No. 700 (KUF 700) of 1950, built as an experimental express coach by NCME. A Leyland PD2/12, it was the forerunner for the PD3/4s which followed.

Deliveries of the classic NCME-bodied PD3/4s commenced in 1958. Number 832 (VUF 832) was delivered the following year. It is at Rottingdean on service for Brighton and followed by a Bristol of BH&D.

One of the originals; No. 815 (TCD 815) of 1958 on Kingsway, Hove in a suitably grand architectural setting. Whereas No. 700 had proved unsatisfactory as an express coach and was downgraded for lighter duties, the PD3/4s were an immediate success, well liked by both crews and passengers and saw service in all company areas.

The deliveries simply went on and on. Number 942 (6942 CD) was a PD3/5 model of 1961 and is seen on service from Littlehampton to Brighton's Pool Valley.

Going in the opposite direction is a rare bird indeed – PD3/4 No. 257 (BUF 257C) of 1965 had its radiator and heating system fitted under the stairs. Note: no filler cap at the front.

Twin headlamp fittings are among the continuing refinements featured on No. 286 (FCD 286D) of 1966. Spotting the variations in each batch called for a practised eye. Like No. 942, this one provided top deck passengers with push-out vents at the front. In common with No. 257 it was also fitted with two spot lamps. Block-type fleetname is carried.

Brighton Hove & District came under Southdown management during the NBC era. Bristols joined the fleet and went into Southdown colours, like No. 2058 (BPM 58B) an FS6G Loddeka parked in Conway Street, Hove.

Other Bristols on order, like VRT No. 2095 (OCD 765G) of 1969, went first into the BH & D fleet. It is leaving South Parade Pier, with NBC-style fleetname and Southdown colours some years later..

Fifteen Daimler CRL6 double-deckers with NCME bodies were delivered in 1971 for service with the then still separately identified BH&D fleet, but wearing NBC-style *Southdown-BH&D* fleetnames soon afterward. Number 2118 (VUF 318K) is collecting passengers for Whitehawk in Churchill Square, Brighton in May 1974.

Meanwhile, the intake of saloons had been based upon a Southdown standard. No. 1528 (MCD 528) was a Leyland Royal Tiger with 40-seat East Lancs bodywork.

Some of these vehicles, like No. 1525, were converted for dual-purpose use and painted accordingly. Both vehicles shown here had been rebuilt from centre to front exit layout.

Number 620 (MUF 620) of 1954 was a Tiger Cub with Nudd Bros & Lockyer bodywork, a Duple subsidiary, fitted with 39-seat front-entrance layout from new. The vehicle is about to pick up a slightly impatient queue on Worthing seafront for a local destination once worked by Worthing's famous 'Tramocars', acquired by Southdown in 1938.

Above: Looking well up to Portslade standards is No. 231 (KUF 231F) one of the first batch of Bristol saloons to serve with Southdown. Delivered in 1968, it was fitted with Marshall 45-seat bodywork.

Left: Also in particularly good condition is No. 641 (OUF 641), a Tiger Cub with Park Royal's version of the standard bodywork. It waits beside Bognor Bus Station in May 1963.

The NBC arrives at Pool Valley, Brighton. Although still in traditional Southdown livery, No. 239, sister vehicle to 231 above, and also a Bristol RESL6G, wears one of those obligatory posters to tell the public how proud all of the subsidiary companies were to be part of the National Bus Company. Unusually, the NBC logo and fleetname are in cream.

Acquired with the BH&D fleet, and still in its colours in January 1975, is No. 2206 (PPM 206G). The vehicle, a Bristol RESLEG with ECW dual-door body, has an NBC style Southdown fleetname.

Thirty dual-purpose Leyland Leopards delivered in 1969 had this unusual two-tone green livery on their NCME bodywork. Number 477 (PUF 177H) is awaiting a wash at the Portslade works.

And then the traditional Southdown days came to an end ! NBC's showpiece Leyland National burst upon the scene with its characteristic clatter and whistling fan. Dressed in an overall leaf green, which looked like an undercoat, NBC claimed they would 'brighten-up' the company's image. Well ! Number 9 (BCD 809L) of 1973.

Compared with what was already in the fleet, the Beadle integrals were 'old-fashioned' from new. Among the more advanced underfloor-engined types was No. 1641 (LUF 641) a Leyland Royal Tiger with Leyland 41-seat body of 1952. Its 'carrot' indicator is out as it leaves Worthing for London.

Since coaching is no longer quite what it used to be, a complete section is here devoted to the memory of some examples utilised by Southdown. Number 885 (646 from 1958: MUF 485) of 1953 was a Beadle integral 26-seater with pre-war running units.

The straight-sided bodywork of the Leyland-bodied Royal Tigers was way ahead of its time in concept. More usual in the 'fifties were the curvaceous lines displayed by No. 1645 (MCD 45) – one of five with Duple's 'Coronation Ambassador' 41-seat express bodywork of 1953. It is seen leaving Steine Street, Brighton on duplicate express duty in July 1963.

The more usual Southdown 'standard' of the period is represented by No. 1067 (RUF 67), a 41-seat coach by Beadle on Leyland 'Royal Tiger' chassis of 1956. The company had no compunction about using such large capacity coaches on seaside 'tripper' excursions when not on express duties. This one awaits custom on Marine Parade, Worthing in September 1963.

The earlier Royal Tiger No. 831 (1691 from 1961; MUF 431, originally a 'coach-cruise' 26-seater was converted for express duties in 1961 and, as such, is here arriving at Manchester Street coach station in October 1962.

Number 1100 (SUF 900) is one of eighteen sister vehicles painted in the subsidiary Triumph coaches livery retained from 1957 to 1963 for forces leave express and for excursion work. These examples are in Cambridge Road, Portsmouth.

Opposite Brighton Aquarium in October 1962 is No. 1139 (XUF 139), a Leyland Tiger Cub with 37-seat Weymann 'Fanfare' Coachwork designed for excursion and tours duties in 1960. Their comparatively 'racy' looks kept them employed for the next thirteen years. No driver would dream of leaning the notice-board against the polished panelling – always against the wheels or beading.

Leaving Hilsea garage for duty on a London express is No. 15 (TCD 15) one of the snarling Beadle-Commer TS3 units of 1957, with Beadle's 'Rochester' version of the standard coach.

'Pretty, but pouting', a Burlingham-bodied Commer Avenger IV leaves Chichester garage in September 1962. New in 1959, it was a 35-seater with central door (No. 38).

Even the grand backdrop of the buildings on Marine Parade, Brighton cannot disguise the fact that this was not one of Harrington's more successful coach designs – maybe it was that 'goldfish' radiator. The somewhat dated wheel-design of the Commer Avenger IV did not help the appearance either. Number 46 (XUF 46) gets an airing in October 1962.

The 'Triumph' brand-name and livery were retained for further coaching activities. No. 1158 (8158 CD), a Leyland Leopard of 1962, with Weymann body, new in Portslade Works.

Garlands and trophies! In contrast, Harrington's beautiful 'Cavalier' on Leyland Leopard L2T chassis was a winner: No. 1745 (545 BUF) after the 1963 British Coach Rally.

Plaxton began to return the bodyline toward the horizontal in 1964 with this coachwork on a Leyland Leopard. Number 1178 (178 DCD) leaves Brighton Aquarium with yet another excursion.

In 1963, Southdown purchased A. W. Buckingham's 'Bucks Coaches' of Worthing. Although not given a fleet number, thirteen-year-old Bedford OB, LPX 150 soldiered on with Southdown during that summer.

The 'Bucks Coaches' trading name was sufficiently well thought of in Worthing for Southdown to keep it on for a further two seasons. On the seafront at Worthing in July 1963 are Southdown coaches 1833 and 1832, repainted at Portslade into Bucks livery. The pair are Leyland Royal Tigers of 1955 vintage; bodies by Harrington.

The fleetname comes forward over the wheel arch on this Duple Northern-bodied Leopard of 1967. The curved side elevation has all but disappeared: No. 1797 (HCD 397E) marked for excursion work from Worthing Pier.

Sister vehicle No. 1796 on National Express duty to London in 1976. The overall white livery with red-blue logo never did look quite appropriate for repainted coaches of the 'sixties.

Arguably, the first of the 'moderns'. Gone are the curves at the side and those fish-mouth grilles. As though to usher in the 'seventies, the Duple bodywork on this 1970 Leyland Leopard coach eschews such frills. Number 1816 (RUF 816H) pauses at Woodstock in 1972 on a lengthy excursion to Blenheim Palace.

Well-suited to its NATIONAL livery, Leyland Leopard No. 1252 (CUF 252L) of 1973 with Duple Dominant coachwork was in a batch of fifteen which were the first to the delivered to Southdown in this colour scheme. Although these 11-metre coaches were designed for express work, this one is soliciting for excursion customers on Brighton seafront.

In Southdown's version of NBC's more relaxed 'universal' or 'venetian blind' livery is Duple-bodied Leopard No. 1282 (RYJ 882R) of 1977 marked for limited-stop duty.

Wearing modified 'Flightline 777' livery in 1985 is No. 1012 (B812 JPN) with Duple Caribbean II coachwork. It is representing the company at the 1985 Coach Rally.

Eye-catching by any standard, Southdown's one-off executive coach 'The Statesman' at rest in Hastings coach park in August 1985. When this 21-seater emerged from the works in 1984 its unique two-tone brown livery caused considerable surprise – but the layout at least was still latterday NBC.

As NBC wound-down (and coaching activities with it) many Leopard coaches were downgraded for dual-purpose work. East & Mid Sussex Division's No. 1316 of 1979 is on duty at Uckfield bus station in 1986.

What might have been if the bottom had not dropped out of the tours business. Hestair Duple Integral 425, once No. 1916 (C716 NYJ) was transferred to express work from Hastings, re-registered 420 DCD.

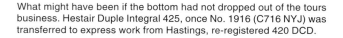

3 | Changing Colours

Far from 'brightening-up' the company's image as NBC promised, the leaf green livery imposed a uniform dullness on all the companies which wore it. After a decade however the Southdown fleet was to enter an era of muti-coloured change. Far too from home is No. 598 (TNJ 998S) in August 1984 – on hire to West Yorks Road Car Co Ltd for a city tour of York. It was a Bristol/ECW dual-door convertible open-topper of 1977.

Making a better show in that livery than most is 'panoramic' Titan PD3/4 No. 356 (HCD 336E) from the 1967 – and last – batch of this popular type.

Number 260 (JWV 260J) a Bristol VRT of 1981 wears 'Mile Oak Shuttle' livery at Brighton in April 1985. It is passing through Castle Square.

Rainbow weather at Uckfield in March 1986, as No. 117 (ENJ 917V) prepares to depart on a limited-stop service to Heathfield. Although still under NBC control and wearing that group's red and blue logo, the vehicle was an early recipient of a restored apple green and primrose livery – with fleetnames and East & Mid Sussex divisional identification in chrome yellow.

Whilst a short search for an appropriate livery took place in 1986, No. 620 (UWV 620S) of East & Mid Sussex wore a white midrif. It is in Terminus Road, Eastbourne in June of that year.

Another version used a very-near-traditional layout of colour – save for the apple green roof. VRT No. 673 (EAP 973V) is at Eastbourne Pier. The chosen final version was all green above the cantrail.

Right: One of several Bristol VRTs acquired from Devon General but originating with Northern General was No. 283 (MGR 671P). Pressed into service in NBC poppy red livery it bears an independent Southdown logo and is on Top Line duty in Warrior Square, St. Leonards in October 1988.

Below: For its Mercedes-Benz L608D minibuses Southdown devised a special green and chrome yellow livery. The logo included the some Mackenzie script. Number 915 (C595 SHC) is on a Sunday service in Tunbridge Wells in 1988.

In a gesture which warmed many a traditionalist heart, when Stagecoach Holdings acquired Southdown they repainted VRT No. 276 (JWV 976W) in full lined-out traditional livery to celebrate 75 years of Southdown service. Pictured at Southsea Rally in June 1990, it displays a Pulborough destination in memory of that first SMRC service.

Stagecoach Holdings purchased Portsmouth CityBus from Southampton City Transport in October 1989 and placed it under nominal Southdown control on 1st January 1990. Among the vehicles transferred was No. 11 (ERV 251D), a Leyland Atlantean PDR1/1 Mark II with MCCW body converted to permanent open-top. It was used on the Southsea seafront service that following summer in its City of Portsmouth Passenger transport livery.

Also used by Southdown in CPPT livery was No. 339 (YBK 339V) an Atlantean AN68/1R with Alexander bodywork. It is in Commercial Road, Portsmouth en route to Eastney, briefly a Southdown depot until divestment.

Many members of the fleet were already in Southampton-style CityBus livery. Number 347 (CPO 347W), going south at London Road, Hilsea, is one such vehicle to join the Southdown ranks. It is an AN68A/!R with East Lancs body.

One of ten Leyland National 36-seaters with places for 27 standing passengers, purchased by PCB from London Buses Ltd, No. 205 (THX 210S) initially operated for Southdown in Portsmouth in its PCB livery. All ten were passed by Southdown to the Transit Holdings Group upon divestment in January 1991.

Right: To help out in Portsmouth, Stagecoach brought six AN68s south from their East Midland subsidiary. Number 318 (KSL 186P) is in that firm's green and cream livery – 'near enough' for some passengers to guess, correctly, that it was a Southdown.

Below: Number 966 (E966 LPX) served Southdown in *Red Admiral* colours in 1990. It had been one of those placed under PCB control by Southampton City Transport in June 1988, and was an Iveco 49-10/Robin Hood minibus.

Stagecoach quickly established its own image throughout the Southdown fleet. Number 930 (F25 PSL) joined the *Coastline* sub-fleet at Chichester in what would become the familiar tan, red and blue stripes.

Stagecoach acquired the 'Eastbourne & District' operation from Hastings & District in December 1990 and placed it under Southdown control the following April. Number 812 (C812 SDV), a Mercedes Benz, ran for Southdown in H&D colours.

Among the vehicles brought in by Stagecoach to boost its 'Eastbourne & District' services was Southdown VRT No. 252 (JWV 252W) of 1980. Stagecoach adapted its stripes for 'true-blue' Eastbourne, but those at destination level still said 'we're Stagecoach really'. Leyland National contributors got mini Stagecoach stripes at that level.

Southdown gained Leyland Olympians – with bodywork by Alexander – bought by Stagecoach in 1990. One of the first batch of ten is at Terminus Road, Eastbourne. It is No. 709 (G709 TCD).

Ex-Portsmouth CityBus No. 140 (CPO 98W) a Leyland National 2 dual-purpose saloon was one of the vehicles from that fleet put into Stagecoach colours and sent east for service in Hastings.

Whilst the Olympians delivered in 1990 could seat 85 passengers apiece, the three received the following year were of dual-purpose configuration with seats for 74. They were purchased specifically for the core 700 and 729 routes. No. 220 (J720 GAP) is on the latter service at Lewes bus station in April 1992.

Unless there's a radical change of heart somewhere, this was positively the last new bus to enter Southdown service – in March 1992. Number 521 (J521 GCD), a Dennis Dart with Alexander Dash 41-seat bodywork, was a one-off delivery to suit the then particular requirement of Service 8 at Eastbourne. Only one other Dart (No. 501) wore *Southdown* fleetnames, and that for one photo-call only. The camber of the road is quite marked at this point.

Right: Stagecoach retain four vehicles in traditional Southdown livery. The two 'twenties veterans and two PD3/4s. 'Worlds End' says the blind on retained 424 DCD. It's not that bad, really.

Below: Released from its duties at Eastbourne, No. 808 (C808 SDY) wears full Stagecoach livery at Lewes in 1992. It is one of the ex-Hastings & District Mercedes.

PERSONNEL

1915
-
1930

1930
-
1970

A 'job for life' is an employment concept currently frowned upon in some circles – an idea redolent of trade-unionism and complacency. Progress means change – and that goes for the staff as well! Yet frequent change and pride make awkward bed-fellows. And pride there was a-plenty among those who worked for Southdown; pride in a job well done, because it was for a company that most of its customers, and the industry generally, considered was something out of the ordinary.

Because the south coast attracts the retired, the elderly and tourists – some not as agile as they used to be, some slow to grasp first time information – the staff, from the beginning, were encoured to be especially patient, careful and courteous. The tone set by Alfred Cannon, the management in its turn tried conscientiously to demonstrate those same qualities in its relationships with the employees. The result – it seems obvious – was a high proportion over the years of dedicated life-long employees.

Thus job-security may be identified as a major factor in the excellent long service record of the company. Furthermore, the directors and officers took pride in the number of long-service employees. In 1955, Arthur Woodgate, the general manager, was 'very pleased that there are still a dozen who were in at the start (and before that with the three constituent companies) and are 'still going strong', and in 1962 Raymond Beddow, the chairman, thought it 'pretty wonderful' that more than 35 per cent of the company's 1936 strength were still working with Southdown. As Woodgate said 'such people laid the foundation of a proud undertaking'.

Those in at the start withMackenzie and Cannon, and still going strong 40 years later, deserve mention: they were drivers G. W. Holland, C. A. Pullen, H. J. Vincent and nightwatchman W. C. Turner of Brighton; drivers W. R. Bennett, C. W. Wye, F. West, greaser E. A. Lee and storekeeper H. J. Henley of Worthing; driver A. E. Weaver of Bolney – and two who secured a kind of immortality: first, George 'Curley' Cowley, an original at Worthing from 1907, but at Portsmouth from 1921, was a driver whom Alfred Cannon always sought-out and reminisced with on his visits to Portsea Island. They enjoyed an 'old-shipmates' relationship not inappropriate to the locality. Cowley left Southdown in 1959 having driven – coaches mostly – for 51 years, and enjoyed a long retirement at Eastney. But it was conductor William Jay, son of a Worthing horse-bus proprietor and the first to collect fares on what would become the famous route 31, who was to outlast them all. Several of the colleagues of these men at the outset are mentioned in Vol 1, pp25-6 and the contribution of numerous other personnel over the years are frequently noted elsewhere.

Several ladies also found a lifetime's work with Southdown, among them Inspector Madge Joslin and telephonist Edna Mathews of Portsmouth, the latter retiring in 1984 with 43 years service. At the Worthing booking office, May Hammond completed almost 45 years in 1966, but the absolute record for a female employee was the 46 years attained by Doris Slater in 1968 as engineering secretary at Central Works, Portslade.

The travelling public seldom met any company employee who did not at least try to brighten their day somewhat. With few exceptions, the management took the same stance in meetings, formal or otherwise, with staff. As befitted its place at the south coast, Southdown was 'a happy ship' – and that spirit had been engendered long before trade unionism got the smallest of toe-holds within the company.

Among company officers, having been a Southdown area manager, did no harm to the prospect of promotion to general manager status; H. E. Hickmott (Ribble), W. A. Budd (Southern Vectis), A. F. R. Carling (Southdown), P. C. Hunt (Hants & Dorset) and J. A. Birks (Southdown and Midland Red) were examples. To have been a Southdown traffic manager, or a deputy traffic manager even, also provided the kind of in-post experience likely to lead to such an appointment. The question has been asked, however, as to whether BET saw Southdown as training ground for senior officers moving on to more distinguished posts; bearing in mind that in their BET heyday, and judged upon the number of vehicles they possessed, the companies could be ranked in the descending order 1: Midland Red, 2: Ribble, 3: Northern General, 4: Southdown, 5: Maidstone & District, 6: Western Welsh, 7: East Kent, etc.

The consensus answer to that question is, no. Southdown certainly did act as a training ground, but that was purely incidental. None of the BET subsidiaries were seen as a training ground at general manager level. The posts were advertised and a successful candidate would be appointed because he had earned it on merit or potential to take a specific task in hand successfully. As one ex-senior officer has said 'to suggest otherwise would be cynical'. For a general manager to move on to a similar post in a larger BET or NBC company would of course be seen as 'a promotion', but that too could only be achieved by competitive interview. More senior posts within BET or NBC were filled by invitation. Those who had served Southdown were well-represented in that quarter also but, 'there was no better job than running a bus company' (anon). And what better place to do that than upon the sunny South Coast?

COMPANY OFFICERS

CHAIRMEN

W. F. French	1915-1925	I. Dalton	1977-1981
S. E. Garcke	1926-1946	D. L. Fytche	1981-1984
R. P. Beddow	1946-1968	J. B. Hargreaves	1984-1986
W. M. Dravers	1968	P. J. Harmer	1986-1987
S. J. B. Skyrme	1968-1970	P. M. Ayers	1987-1989
D. S. Deacon	1971-1972	Brian Souter	1989
F. K. Pointon	1972-1976	Brian Cox	1989-1992

DIRECTORS

A. E. Cannon	1915-1952	F. Paterson	1970-1972
J. J. Clark	1915-1928	I. R. Patey	1971-1972
Sir James Bradford	1915-1924	F. K. Pointon	1972-1976
A. D. Mackenzie	1915-1944	L. S. Higgins	1972-1973
W. S. Wreathall	1915-1918	L. S. Higgins	1975-1977
W. S. Wreathall	1919-1924	G. C. Smith	1972-1975
T. Wolsey	1917-1942	G. C. Smith	1977-1979
C. S. B. Hilton	1918-1919	C. R. Buckley	1973-1975
S. E. Garcke	1924-1948	G. M. Newberry	1975
J. H. Infield	1924-1942	J. A. Birks	1975-1976
A. J. Clark	1928-1954	J. A. Birks	1984-1986
Lt Col G. S. Szlumper	1930-1937	P. H. Wyke-Smith	1976-1981
G. C. Gardner	1930-1931	I. Dalton	1977-1981
R. G. Davidson	1931-1946	A. M. Sedgley	1977-1985
J. C. Chambers	1937-1939	D. W. Glassborrow	1978-1981
J. C. Chambers	1944-1949	R. G. Roberts	1978-1979
C. W. G. Elliff	1939-1944	F. E. Dark	1979-1984
R. P. Beddow	1942-1968	G. R. Brook	1981-1984
H. A. Short	1946-1950	Miss K. H. Mortimer	1981-1983
J. W. Womar	1946-1956	D. L. Fytche	1981-1984
H. E. Osborn	1949-1969	G. Carruthers	1981-1983
W. H. F. Mepstead	1950-1960	B. C. Sellars	1981-1985
E. Infield-Willis	1952-1972	J. B. Hargreaves	1984-1985
Capt The Right Hon		K. M. Bodger	1984-1985
Lord Teynham	1954-1969	P. J. Harmer	1986-1987
R. W. Birch	1956-1967	P. M. Ayers	1986-1989
C. P. Hopkins	1960-1964	M. A. Gooch	1987-1989
G. L. Nicholson	1964-1968	R. M. Higgins	1987-1989
W. M. Dravers	1967-1968	D. Charlton	1987-1989
S. J. B. Skyrme	1968-1970	Brian Souter	1989-1992
F. Harrison	1968-1970	Ann Gloag	1989-1992
D. S. Deacon	1968-1973	Alan Whitnall	1989-1992
G. Duckworth	1969-1972	Brian Cox	1989-1992

GENERAL MANAGERS/MANAGING DIRECTORS

A. E. Cannon	1915	L. S. Higgins	1972
A. D. Mackenzie	1915-1919	G. C. Smith	1972-1975
A. E. Cannon	1919-1947	J. A. Birks	1975-1977
A. F. R. Carling	1947-1954	A. M. Sedgley	1977-1985
A. S. Woodgate	1954-1961	P. M. Ayers	1986-1989
S. J. B. Skyrme	1961-1966	Brian Souter	1989
G. Duckworth	1966-1972	Brian Cox	1989-1992

TRAFFIC MANAGERS

A. D. Mackenzie	1915-1938	E. G. Dravers	1969-1972
A. H. Burman	1938-1946	M. Rourke	1972-1975
F. W. Sellwood	1946-1954	D. J. R. Bending	1975-1980
G. Duckworth	1954-1966	P. M. Ayers	1980-1985
J. C. Clymo	1966-1969	No further appointments	

CHIEF ENGINEERS

A. E. Cannon	1919-1926	W. G. A. Hall	1958-1968
R. G. Porte	1926-1933	C. E. Clubb	1969-1973
R. E. Dunhill	1934-c1936	S. J. Brown	1974-1985
No appointment thereafter until:		M. A. Gooch	1987-1990
H. R. Lane	1954-1958	R. Alexander	1990-1992

COMPANY SECRETARIES

F. Smith	1919-1924	D. H. Wilks	1975-1985
L. G. Hopkinson	1924-1948	Mrs R. Holland	1985
C. A. Sleep	1948-1949	A. J. Ritchie	1986
H. G. Turner	1949-1967	D. Charlton	1986-1989
B. C. Sellars	1967-1972	D Scott	1989
P. J. Harmer	1972-1975	A. Whitnall	1989-1992

AREA MANAGERS*

Portsmouth

F. Bartlett	1923-1929	F. A. Price	1956-1958
W. A. Budd	1929-1932	J. Armstrong	1958-1963
J. B. Chevallier	1932-1940	R. J. Dallimore	1963-1970
A. F. R. Carling	1940-1944	W. Wheeler	1970-1981
S. C. Hollis	1945-1947	M. W. Parkes	1981-1985
G. R. Wakeling	1947-1956		

Bognor Regis

A. Davies	1915-1920	E. H. Cooksey	1920-1948
Combined with Chichester (1948)			

Chichester

W. G. Dowle	1924-1948	Combined with Worthing as Central Division	
E. H. Cooksey	1948-1950	J. H. Green	1970-1975
F. A. Price	1951-1956	M. W. Parkes	1975-1978
F. H. Reeves	1956-1960	A. Bishop	1978-1984
P. C. Hunt	1961-1963	Operating officer for whole company area	
J. H. Green	1963-1970	except Portsmouth and BATS	

Worthing

E. James	1922-1942	E. A. Butcher	1963-1967
W. J. Cooper	1943-1953	P. A. Townley	1968-1970
R. E. Lephard	1954-1962		
Combined with Chichester (1970) as Central Division			

Brighton

H. E. Hickmott	1915	G. B. Dodd	1967-1970
J. Stuart-Smith	1915-1937	A. C. R. Jones	1970-1972
W. A. Stace	1938-1956	P. J. S. Shipp	1972-1976
R. J. Dallimore	1956-1963	A. Bishop	1976-1978
P. C. Hunt	1963-1964	P. S. Williams (BATS)	1978-1985
J. A. Birks	1964-1967		

Eastbourne

S. A. Turner	1919-1927	E. Thompson	1959-1961
S. C. Hollis	1927-1945	J. A. Birks	1961-1964
L. B. Siedle	1945-1959	M. S. Hicks	1964-1966
Combined with Brighton (1966) as Eastern Division			

*some called 'traffic Superintendents' in early years and following reorganisations 'Divisional Managers' and 'District Managers'

Hampshire Division		**West Sussex Division**	
R. M. Higgins	1985-1987	S. L. Noble	1985-1987
Brighton & Hove Division		**East & Mid Sussex Division**	
R. W. French	1985	I. J. McAllister	1985-1987

– and under Stagecoach

Portsmouth Division		**West Sussex Division**	
A. Barrett	1990-1991	P. Southgate	1991-1992
East Sussex Division			
A. Yates	1991-1992		

The company which called itself South Coast Motor Services 'took over the operation' of the services and equipment contributed by the three constituent companies on 1st January 1915.

South Coast Motor Services was registered on 1st April 1915.

Date of incorporation of South Coast Motor Services Ltd was entered as 31st May 1915.

Southdown Motor Services Ltd was incorporated on 2nd June 1915, a private company formed with nominal capital of £51,250 divided into £50,000 7% non-cumulative participating preference shares of £1 and 25,000 deferred shares of 1/- (5p). the following were allotted credited as fully paid up for consideration other than cash: B,H&PUO Co Ltd 10,752 and 8,000; L&SCH Co Ltd 10,830 and 4,000. Total rolling stock 42 vehicles.

October 1915: British Automobile Traction Co Ltd buy 689 £1 preference shares. William Wreathall represents BET interests on Southdown board.

March 1916: Mortgage of freeholds to secure bank account; Capital & Counties Bank Ltd.

November 1916: Thomas Tilling Ltd take 8,000 £1 non-cumulative participating preference shares in SMS.

February 1917: Thomas Wolsey, representing Thomas Tilling group joined the board and SMS became a public company.

April 1919: Mortgage transferred to Lloyds Bank.

June 1920: Both preference and deferred shares converted to ordinary.

February 1925: Bank overdraft incurred to purchase Southsea Tourist Co Ltd – 30 vehicles, properties and liabilities in Portsmouth.

March 1926: Divided only 12° per cent (against 15) because vehicle were not sufficiently written down in past and Finance Act increased road fund tax. Company overdraft was £47,350.

March 1927. Overdraft eliminated.

1928: Tilling & British Automobile Traction Co Ltd formed under the chairmanship of Southdown's chairman, Sidney Garcke. SMS operating 372 vehicles.

December 1929: Agreement of Southern Railway to purchase 33.3 per cent of shares at £3 5s 0d (£3.25p) per £1 share – 'a good deal for shareholders who sell' Stock Exchange Gazette.

September 1930: Capital increased to £276,250 by creation of 75,000 new ordinary £1 shares. £75,000, part of reserve fund capitalised and distributed to ordinary shareholders in the proportion of one new share for every three held.

November 1930: Capital increased to £426,250 by creating 150,000 £1 ordinary shares.

December 1934: Agreement between SMS and Southern Railway company on the interchangeability of return tickets, etc followed earlier (February) agreement upon use of railway station yards by SMS.

March 1936: 25,000 ordinary 1/- (5p) shares written up to £1 by capitalising £23,750 of undivided profits to bring capital to £450,000. This was then raised to £750,000 by capitalising £128,000 of the reserve, £15,000 of the investment depreciation revenue and £157,000 of the rolling stock depreciation reserve. These sums were used to create 300,000 new ordinary £1 shares allotted as a bonus to existing holders on the basis of two new to three old.

June 1936: SMS anniversary. Silver rose bowls for Mackenzie and Cannon. Travelling clocks for Mrs Eva Drake Mackenzie and Mrs Muriel Grotjen Cannon.

July 1936: Capital raised to £450,000, then to £750,000.

April 1937: SMS running 103 stage-carriage services. 690 buses.

June 1938: SMS employ nearly 2,500 members of staff.

June 1939: For first time revenue exceeds £1 million. SMS now operating over 700 'cars' – the sixth largest bus company in Britain. SMS finding new levels of custom on long distance United Kingdom coach cruises because 'a series of international crises' had frightened many people off foreign travel.

November 1939: All services trimmed to meet requirements of the 'black-out'. Of the 705 vehicles owned, 313 were coaches as a result of Cannon's policies.

December 1940: SMS running non-stop 'express buses' out of Portsmouth to Horndean, Cowplain, Lovedean, etc.

January 1941: SMS lend the government £50,000 free of all interest.

April 1941: War Weapons Week; SMS cheques for £26,000 handed over by Cannon.

October 1941: Minister of War Transport authorised a maximum of 12 standing passengers in the lower saloons of double-deckers.

June 1942: Eighty-eight bus stops removed in Worthing at Minister's request to economise on fuel, etc.

September 1942: SMS withdrew its last four express coach services. London-Eastbourne, Brighton, Worthing and Bognor. Parting of the ways for Tilling & BAT – SMS in BET camp.

November 1942: Bus curfew on south coast – last SMS bus home by 9.30pm.

June 1943: Wear and tear allowance for vehicles falling short of reality. Some vehicles on producer gas on flat roads. Heavy traffic transferring to SMS because of lack of private cars.

October 1944: New utility Guy Arabs – 'easier to maintain and more hygienic' with their wooden slatted seats.

December 1944: Death of Douglas Mackenzie aged 74.

February 1946: Coaches which had been commandeered as ambulances to be returned to SMS. Of the 24 ambulances only two had been lost (at Portsmouth).

March 1946: Of the 121 company vehicles requisitioned in WWII, only ten had been handed back. SMS restore express services and provide transport for prisoners of war on road construction and agricultural work.

June 1947: Coach cruises restored. Recount: – 160 vehicles had been requisitioned in WWII.

June 1948: SMS operating 818 vehicles and running 30,000,000 miles per annum on service.

Southdown – a BET subsidiary – avoided nationalisation in 1949, when those companies which were Thomas Tilling subsidiaries became wholly acquired by the British Transport Commission. Southdown was only one-third nationalised by comparison, as a result of the state acquiring the assets of the Southern Railway Company who, of course, possessed one-third of Southdown's share capital. In concert with other BET subsidiaries, Southdown was to remain a public company for another nineteen years. By 1964, the share capital had risen to £3,600,000 and 963 buses were in operation. That era came to an end in March 1968 when the Transport Holding Company became the formal buyer. A 'memorandum of management agreement' between Brighton Hove & District and Southdown took effect on 1st January 1969. It made SMS responsible for 'the control and management of the Brighton company's services and functions ...' Southdown would 'take over' and be entitled to use, through a current account opened between the two companies, the whole of the assets and liabilities of the Brighton company ...other than the liabilities in respect of taxation and dividends, such account to remain outstanding in the books of both undertakings without attracting interest payments.' Southdown would 'collect all revenues ...' and account to the Brighton company in such form and on such basis as the Boards of the two companies may agree.' BH&D's £600,000 capital was set aside. By virtue of the complications extant as a result of the Brighton Area Transport Services agreement with the Brighton municipality, BH&D would survive, despite outward appearances to the contrary. That single fact would have a profound effect upon Southdown following the election of Margaret Thatcher's Conservative government. The rest, as they say, is history – please see Volume 1.

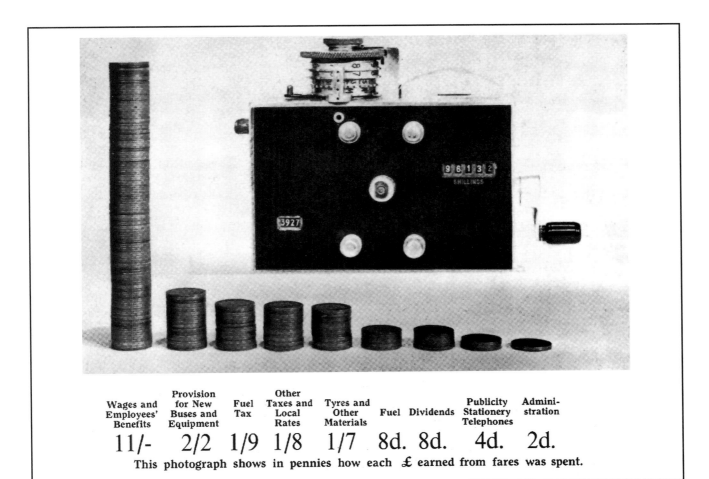

Wages and Employees' Benefits	Provision for New Buses and Equipment	Fuel Tax	Other Taxes and Local Rates	Tyres and Other Materials	Fuel	Dividends	Publicity Stationery Telephones	Admini-stration
11/-	2/2	1/9	1/8	1/7	8d.	8d.	4d.	2d.

This photograph shows in pennies how each £ earned from fares was spent.

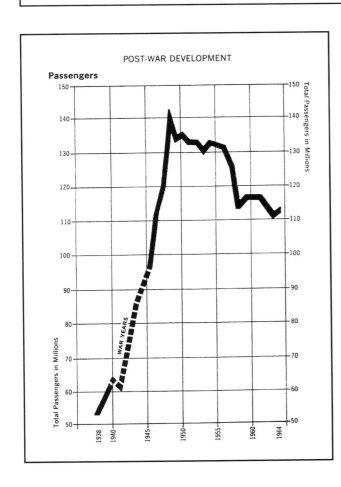

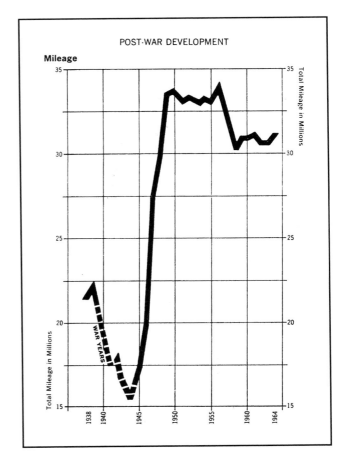

ADDENDA to Volume I

Typographical and other errors or misinterpretations and omissions occur in the best of books. The advantage of a Volume 2 is an opportunity to correct some of them. For the sake of increased accuracy, the following should be noted:

p12   Picture reversed
p12   Bottom picture: BP 317 is now thought to have been one of the pair of Clarkson steam buses. The identity of this Milnes Daimler remains unknown.
p26   The bodywork is almost certainly an ex-WMOC example
p29   Wrong caption: the L&SCH Daimler in this illustration is CD 2645 with bodywork by Brush and featuring an advanced fully-enclosed driving position. The chassis of these Daimlers were soon after requisitioned by the War Department, but the bodies were acquired by Southdown at the formation and used upon chassis of different makes such as Caledon, etc.
p32   Leyland X, DL 493 was new and purchased in 1913.
p34   The bodywork in this picture is of WMS own-build.
p36   The bulkhead remained in its original position and new bodywork was extended forward to provide the special compartment upon a longer chassis than that which originally carried the body.
p37   Bottom picture: Bodywork here is a Harrington 37-seater.
p67   Despite reference to Havant 'High Street' for several years in Southdown timetables, there is no such street in Havant. The office was in South Street.
p68   Top picture: It was the traffic commissioners not Eastbourne Corporation whose duty it was to make the decision to permit open-topped double-deckers on this route.
p75   The six Tilling-Stevens B9B chassis were acquired direct from Thames Valley by Southdown. Only the bodywork applied to them by Southdown came from Chapmans.
p82   Centre picture: Southern Gliderway Coaches Ltd should be Southern Glideway Coaches Ltd.
p88   The hovercraft service was not 'the final leg' of an advertised express service from London; it was a self-contained experiment. The point intended was that after many years of Southdown coaches having carried 'Isle of Wight' on their destination boards, here was a 'Southdown vehicle' actually going there.
p89   The inspectors at Ryde are Messrs Murphy and Martin not Arthur Ball, who remained on the mainland.
p93   On the day that this vehicle was photographed it carried *white* fleetnames and NBC 'double-N' logo.
p98   Top right: fleetname green, NBC logo red and blue.
p102   Top picture: Martin Harris was marketing office at the time; Christine Watts was coaching manager.
p103   Escort Country Rider should be Escort County Rider.
p107   The Estate Divided: delete *Vicarage* and insert *The Lane, Park Street*: in the list of garages acquired by Brighton & Hove.
p108   First word: 'past' should be 'part'.
p109   Below: picture reversed.
p116   The increased mini-bus frequencies at Haywards Heath were run 'commercially'.
p121   Caption: 'desparately' should be 'desperately'.
p123   The addition at the end of this caption is an editorial error. Mackenzie was always referred to as *Douglas* Mackenzie.
p126   Below: 'Southdown-style' should be 'Southampton-style'.

'Up in the attic', the signwriting sub-department. 'Queue here' signs, fleetname transparencies for the rear of coaches, bus-station bay letters and blinds or a straight-forward advertisement for tours and private parties – all part of the work of a skilled graphic artist.

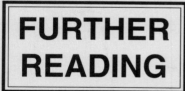

FURTHER READING

Anon The ABC of SOUTHDOWN Buses & Coaches Ian Allan Ltd 1950
Anon The Southdown Story 1915-1965 Southdown Motor Services Ltd 1965
Hibbs, John The History of British Bus Services David & Charles 1969
Morris, Colin History of Hants & Dorset Motor Services Ltd David & Charles 1973
'Bell Street' East Surrey – the East Surrey Traction Co Ltd H. J. Publications 1974
Morris, Colin History of British Bus Services: South East England TPC 1980
Lambert, Alan Hants & Sussex Lambert 1983
Morris, Colin Southdown Vol. 1: The History Venture Publications 1994

– and a large number of ongoing publications by The Southdown Enthusiasts Club. SAE, 43 Stone Cross Road, Crowborough, East Sussex, TN6 3DB

Index

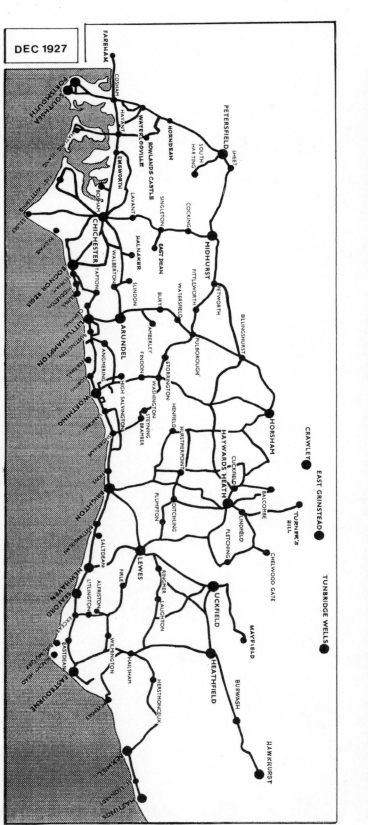

DEC 1927

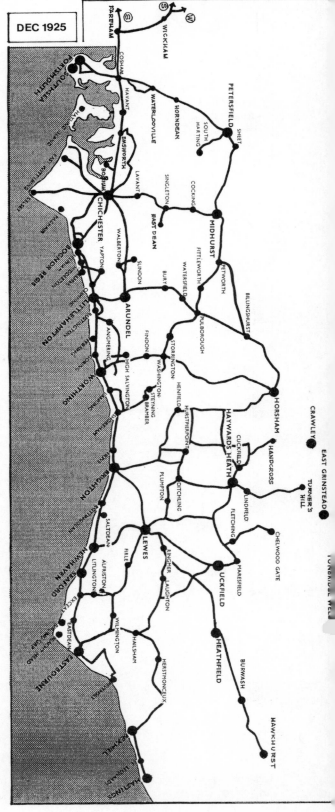

DEC 1925